IMAGES
of America

SURRY COUNTY

ON THE COVER: After the 1895 courthouse at Surry was destroyed by fire, the county built a two-story, Neoclassical-style brick building distinguished by a two-story Ionic portico and a large cupola on the roof. People are celebrating the opening of the new courthouse in 1909. (Courtesy of Gordon "Bo" Bohannan.)

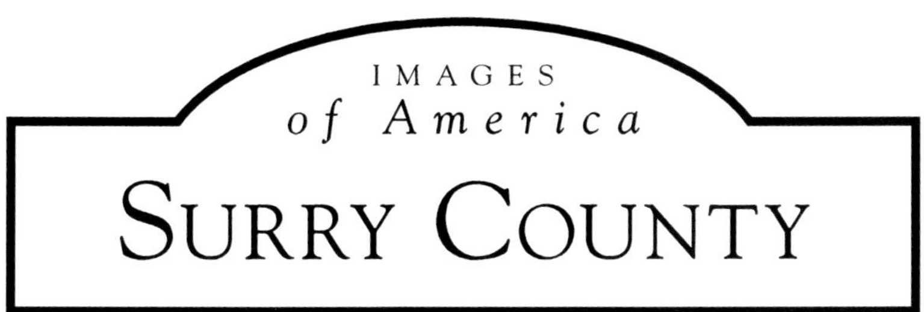

Deborah Harrison Dawson on behalf of
Surry County, Virginia, Historical Society & Museums, Inc.

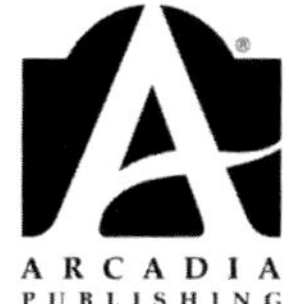

ISBN 978-0-7385-9219-0

Published by Arcadia Publishing
Charleston, South Carolina

Printed in the United States of America

Library of Congress Control Number: 2011936150

For all general information, please contact Arcadia Publishing:
Telephone 843-853-2070
Fax 843-853-0044
E-mail sales@arcadiapublishing.com
For customer service and orders:
Toll-Free 1-888-313-2665

Visit us on the Internet at www.arcadiapublishing.com

To Mom and in memory of Dad, who gave lots of love, a sense of self, and history lessons around the 5:30 dinner table

Contents

ACKNOWLEDGMENTS

Many thanks to the history buffs who came out for Saturday scanning sessions or offered their collections: Mary Alma Savedge, Gordon "Bo" Bohannan, Claude Reeson, Celia Emory Parson, Norma Roach, Bill Richardson, Faye Grandison, William Fox, Mary Grace Padgett, Troilen G. Seward, Donna Slade, James M. Harrison, Jean Stewart, Bess Richardson, and Surry County Public Schools.

Unless otherwise noted, all images appear courtesy of Surry County, Virginia, Historical Society & Museums, Inc.

Special thanks are extended to the Dendron Historical Society, Robert L. Bartlett, Beth Roach, Mary E.C. Drew, Catherine J. Dawson, Giron Wooden Sr., Katherine Johnson Fox, Edwin O'Neal, Jonathan Judkins, Judy Jones, the historical society's board of directors, and everyone who offered encouragement as we worked on the book project.

We have made all possible attempts to identify residents in photographs; however, some names may be incomplete or missing. If the reader can help with corrections to future reprints, we welcome your comments.

INTRODUCTION

For more than 350 years, Surry has depended on an agriculture economy and remained a rural community. This work entitled *Surry County* is a photographic record of a rural people in their own historic environment sharing life events, working, laboring together in local industry, developing institutional traditions, and creating memories that are transmitted throughout the county today, centuries since its birth among Virginia's first counties.

Surry was cut off from James City County and formed in 1652. Early Virginia histories suggest numerous counties were formed from Surry: Sussex, Brunswick, Lunenburg, Halifax, Bedford, Charlotte, Mecklenburg, Pittsylvania, Henry, Campbell, Franklin, Patrick, part of Greensville, and a part of Appomattox. It is located on the James River in southeastern Virginia 10 miles south of Williamsburg, 50 miles southeast of Richmond, and 50 miles northwest of Norfolk. Tourists find that Surry is an interesting side trip when they visit the Virginia Historic Triangle—Williamsburg, Jamestown, and Yorktown. A free vehicle ferry gives tourists and county residents direct access to Jamestown and Williamsburg. Surry was probably named by early colonists in honor of the English county of Surrey and in recognition of its location; Surry in Virginia lies across the James River from Jamestown, just as Surrey lies across the River Thames from London.

The images capture life in Surry's three incorporated towns of Claremont, Dendron, and Surry and its unincorporated communities of Cabin Point, Scotland, Spring Grove, Carsley, Elberon, and Bacon's Castle. The population has been as low as 5,585 in 1870 and as high as 9,305 in 1920. Businesses developed around the meat processing industry, lumber harvesting, and farming. The lumber industry helped to support the highest population in 1920 when the Surry Lumber Company and the Surry, Sussex & Southampton Railway were the major employers. Throughout the county were farming communities that usually supported small schools, country stores, and several churches.

In 1998, Surry County Historical Society & Museums, Inc., was founded with the goal of preserving Surry's history, making resources available for local and family research, and providing educational programming that would encourage a greater interest in local history. As the association grew, so did the many donations of materials. Making these materials available to a wider audience became an important goal.

Among the many donated collections are materials from a former writer for the *Richmond News Leader*, former local educators, and family histories. As the list of donations grows and materials are organized, the society will have additional opportunities to publish and share history with a larger audience.

One

Early History and Historic Buildings

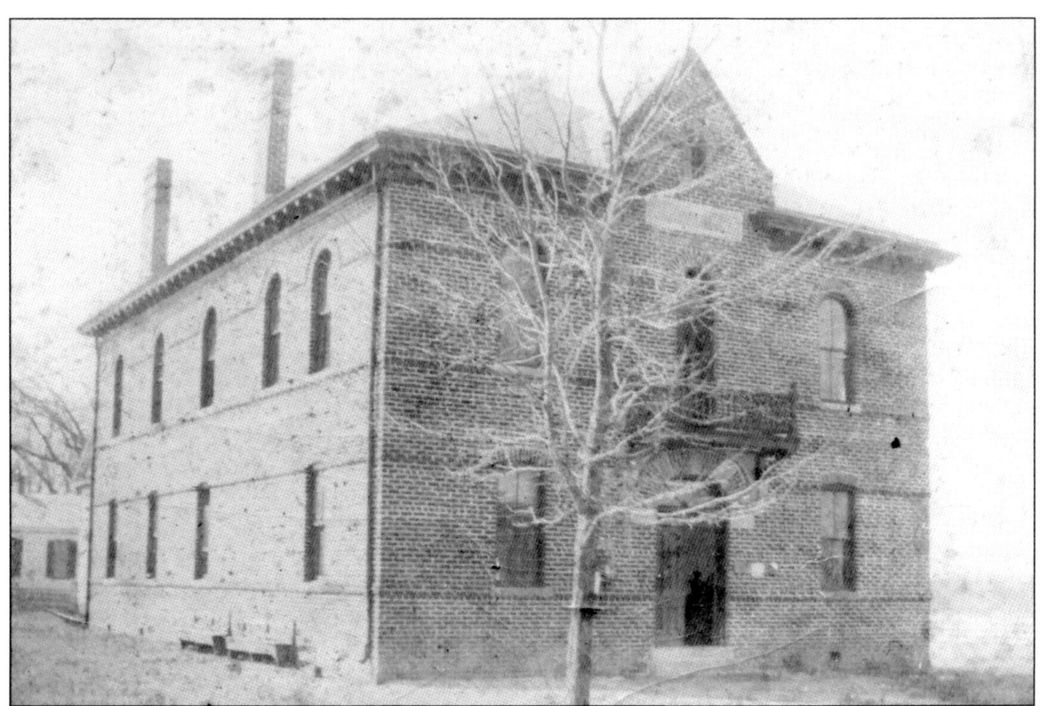

Pictured is the 1895 courthouse located in the town of Surry, know as McIntosh's Crossroads during that time. The land for the courthouse was given to the county by Robert McIntosh, who owned a tavern and inn directly across from the building site. This was the second and larger courthouse building in the town after the county seat was moved from Wareneck-Troopers in 1797. The 1797 courthouse became too small to handle the growing county's business, making it necessary to build the larger structure. (Courtesy of Gordon "Bo" Bohannan.)

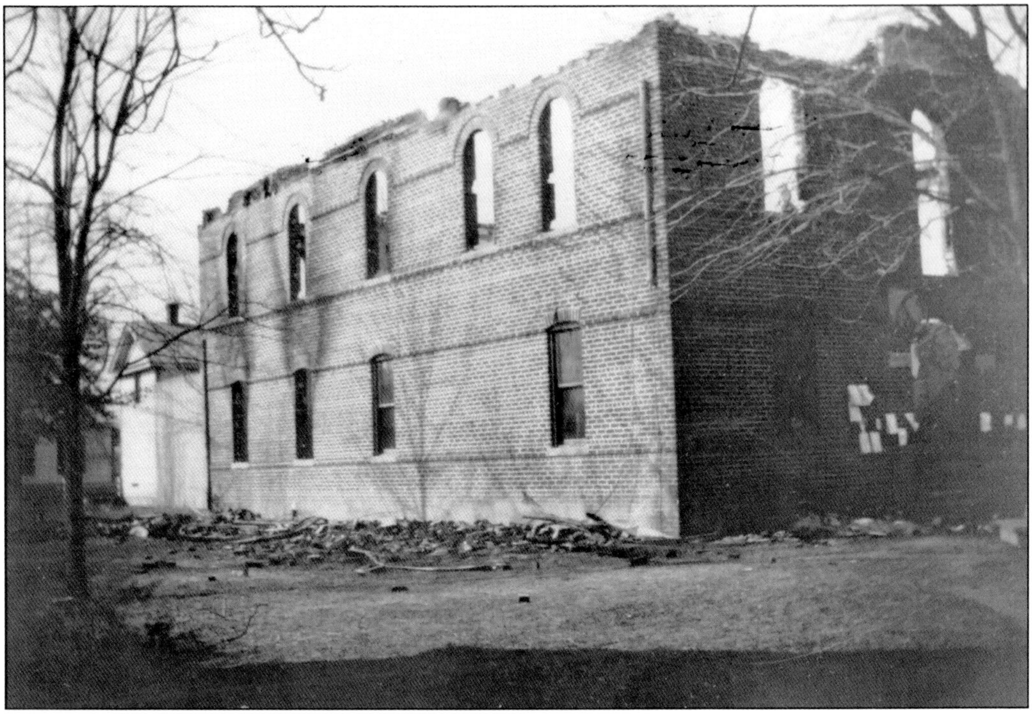

The 1895 courthouse was destroyed by fire on December 6, 1906. On the same site, the county built the third courthouse, which was completed in 1907. (Courtesy of Gordon "Bo" Bohannan.)

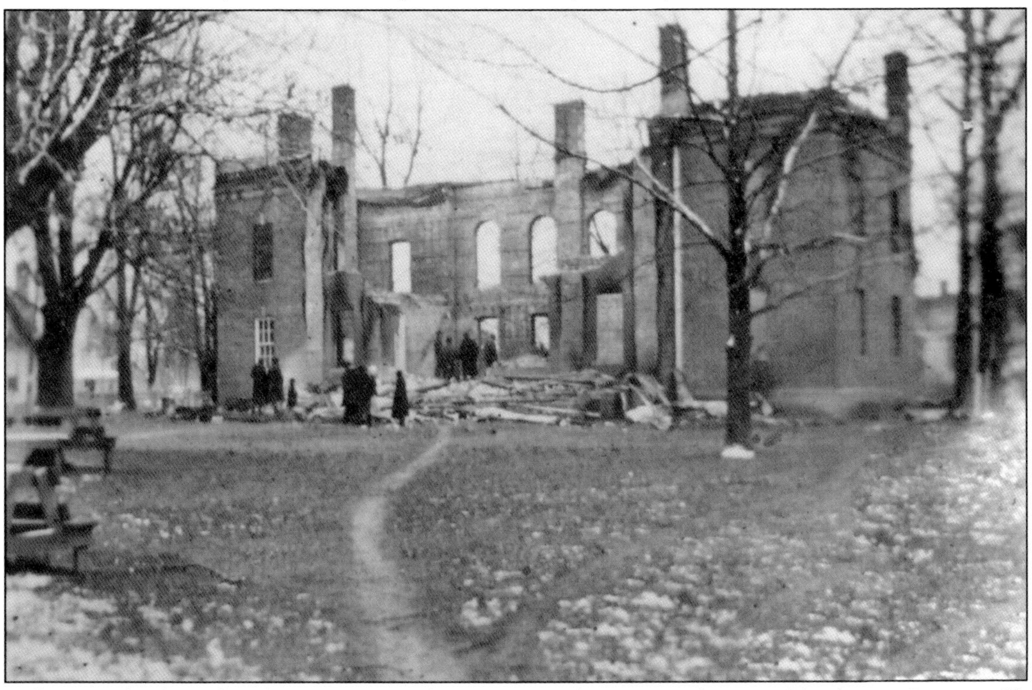

Following the fate of earlier structures, the 1907 courthouse was destroyed by fire on January 17, 1922. The county immediately started construction on a new building that was completed in 1923 and included a fireproof vault to store and preserve old records.

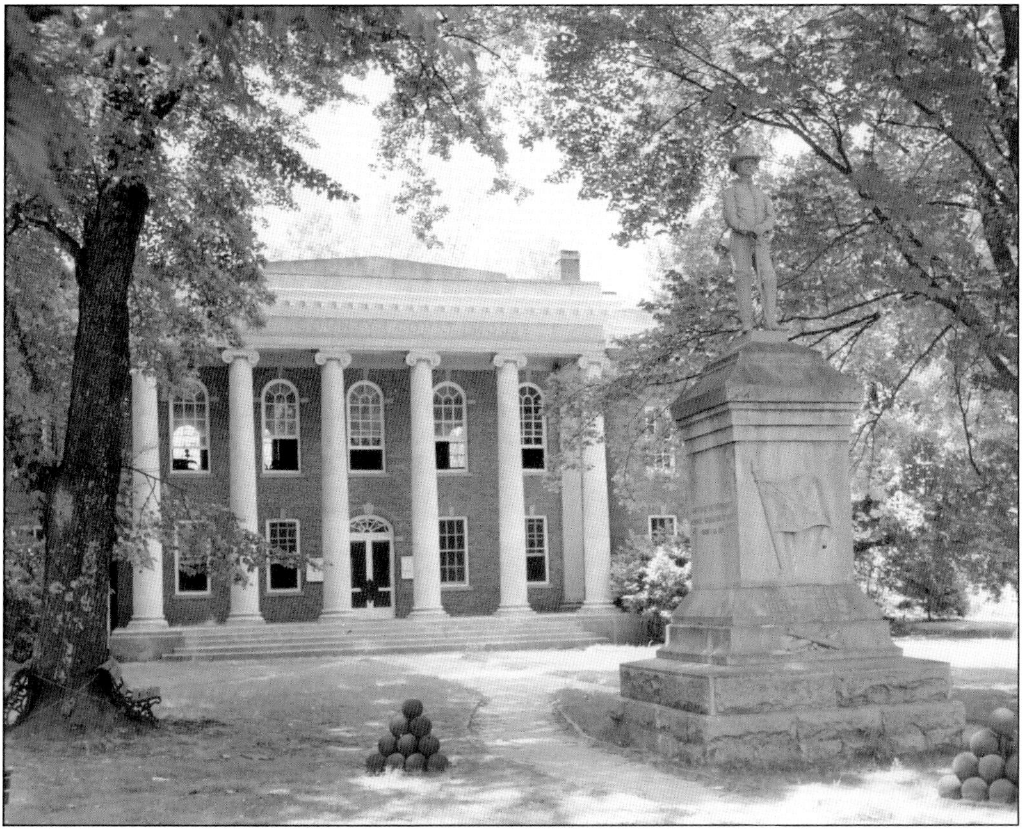

The 1923 courthouse at Surry still stands today with the Confederate Monument and cannon balls in the courthouse square. A major renovation and expansion was completed in 2008. The new facility houses the circuit court, the circuit court clerk's offices, court records, and judges' chambers. The courthouse complex is listed in the national and state historic registers.

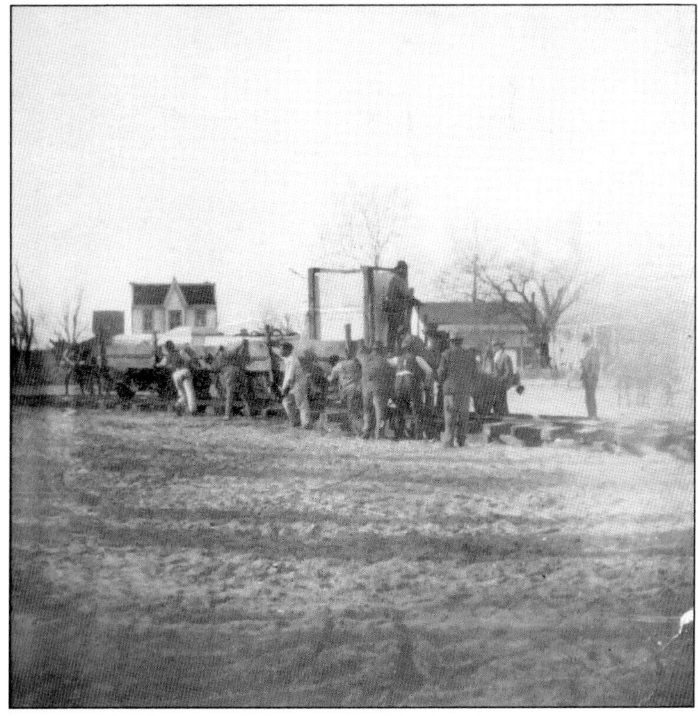

In July 1910, workers transport the granite for the Confederate Monument from the nearby railway station to the courthouse square.

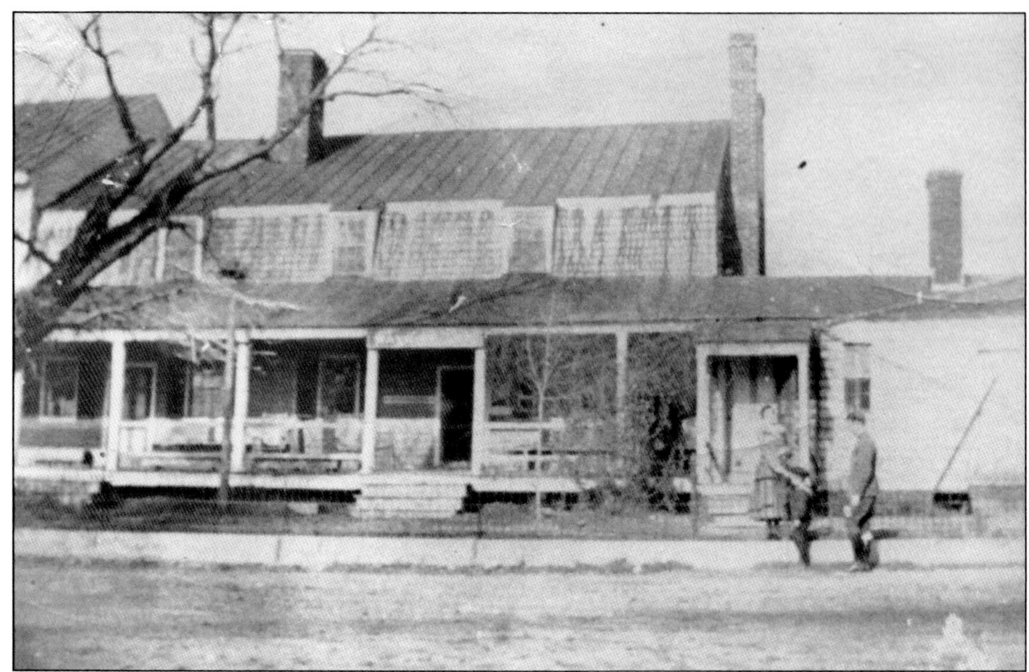

Records show that the McIntosh Tavern and Inn existed as early as 1782, suggesting it had been built before the American Revolution. Robert McIntosh, who donated land for the courthouse at Surry, owned and operated the "Old Tavern" until about 1814. It was a well-known establishment and the location of much activity. From 1869 to 1920, it was owned by the Land family. Like many wood structures of that time, it was destroyed by fire on June 16, 1925.

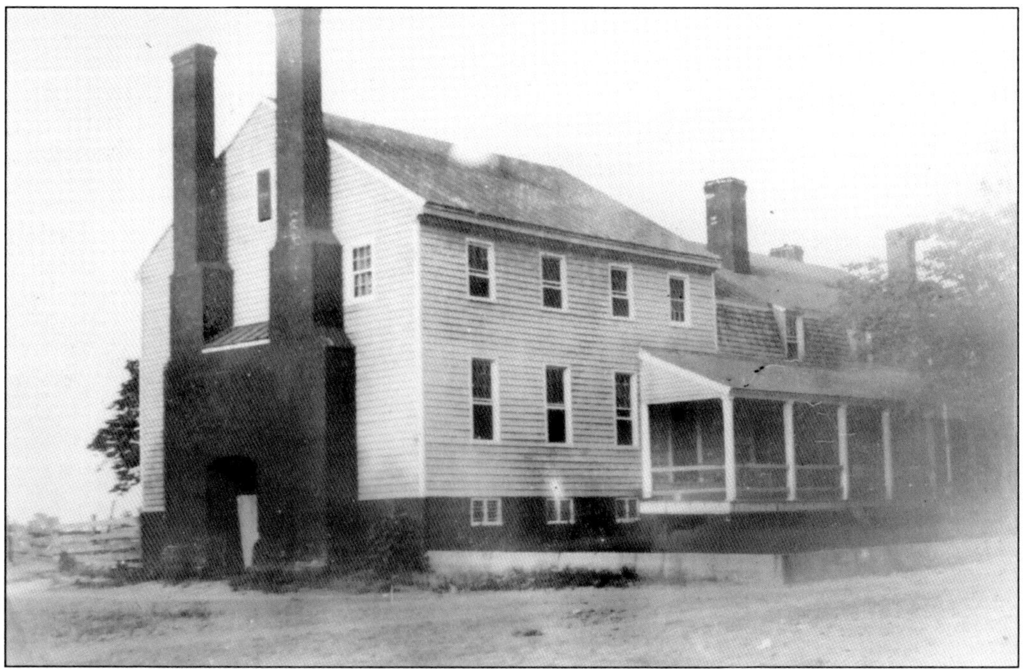

Pictured is a northwest view of McIntosh Tavern, also known as the Old Tavern and the Old Hotel.

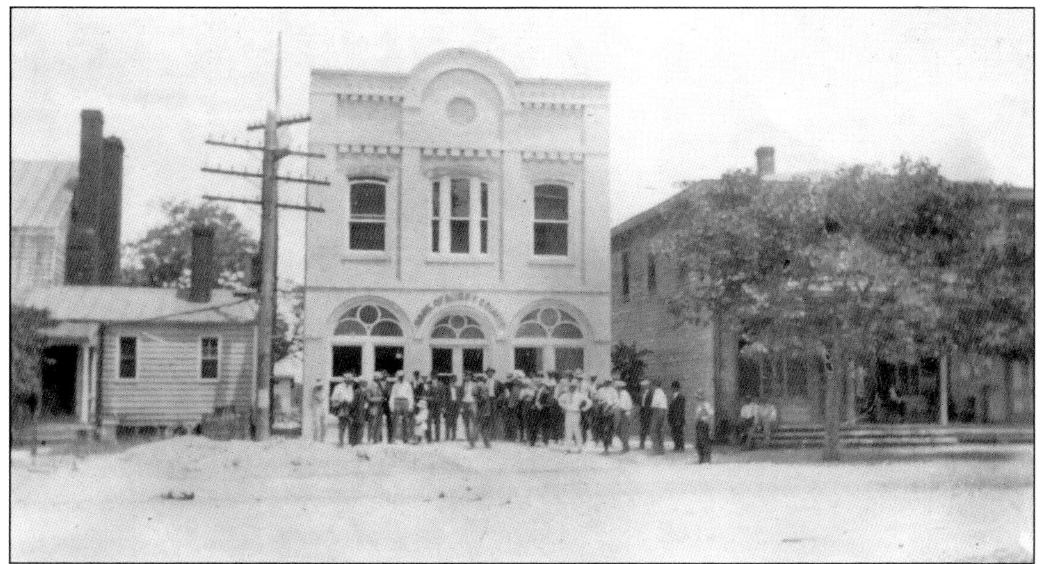

The Bank of Surry County, Inc., was a prominent establishment on Main Street in the town of Surry. It was organized on March 3, 1914, by a group of businessmen and farmers. The bank is flanked by the W.E. Land Store on the right and the McIntosh Tavern on the left. Today, the former bank building houses the Surry Town Hall and real estate offices. (Courtesy of Mary Alma Savedge.)

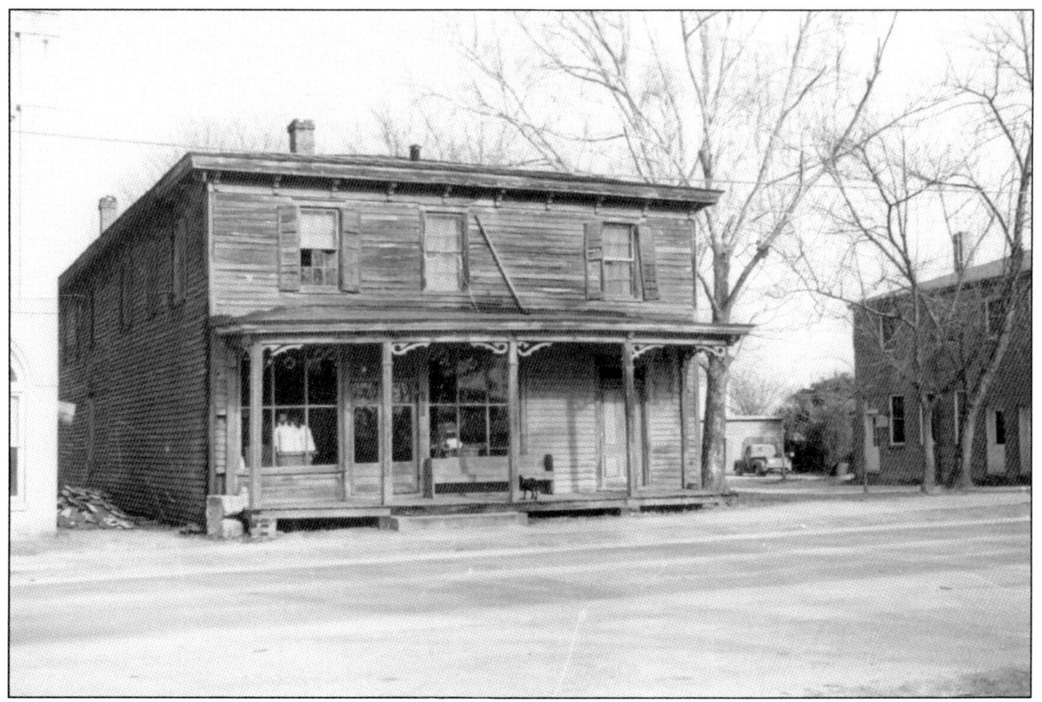

In the 1960s, the W.E. Land General Merchandise building was still standing but not operating. It was eventually torn down.

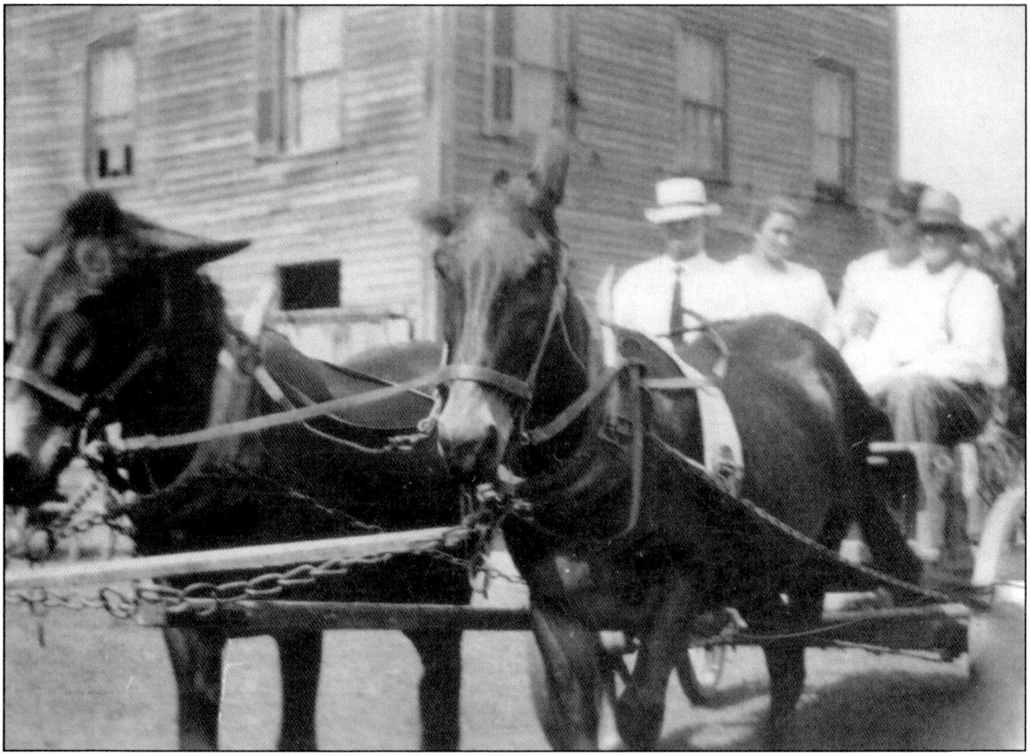

The Haff family of Spring Grove, a village west of the town of Surry, is pictured around 1921 with the Spring Grove Hotel in the background. (Courtesy of Claude Reeson.)

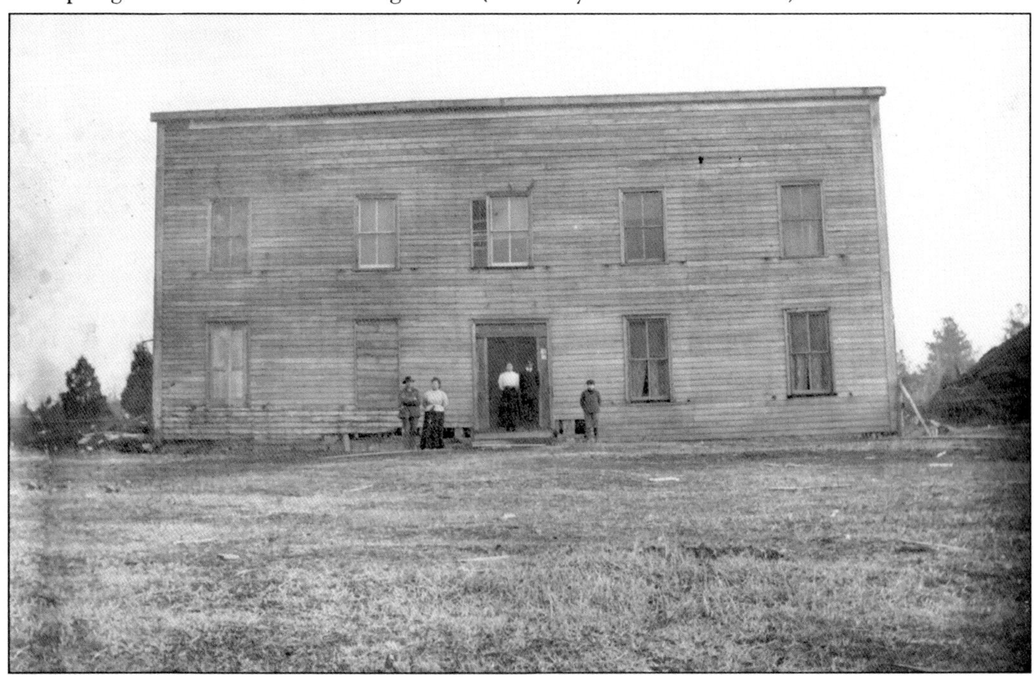

The Spring Grove Hotel owned by the Haff family is featured on a 1921 postcard. Spring Grove was a busy area with stores and a railway depot. (Courtesy of Claude Reeson.)

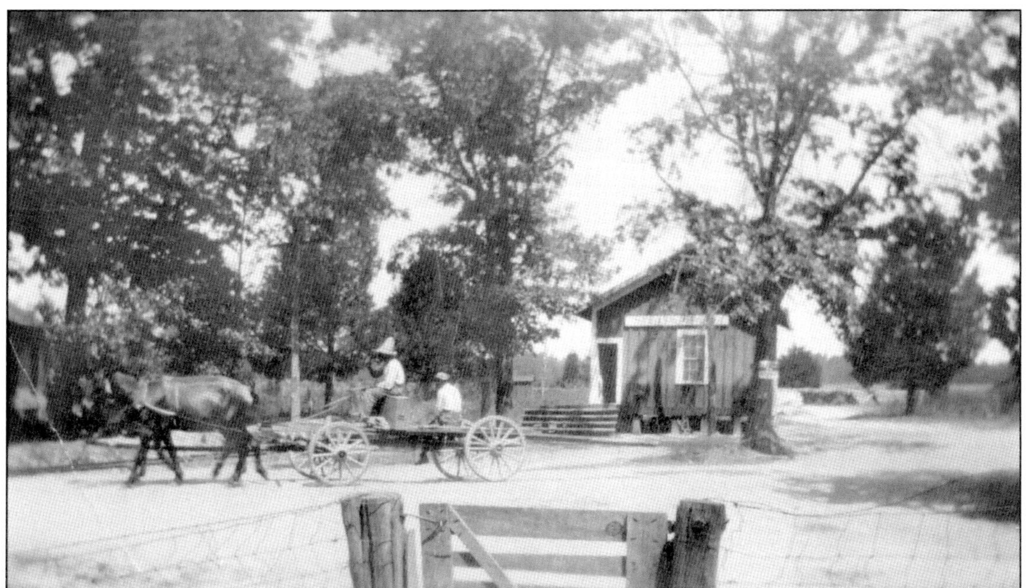

In the early 1930s, unidentified travelers were photographed passing the Spring Grove railway depot. The Atlantic and Danville Railway Company (A&D) was built in 1883 and was a narrow three-foot-gauge railway, as opposed to the wider, four foot, eight-and-one-half-inch railway standard set in the two decades following the Civil War. The narrower railway was cheaper to build, equip, and maintain. It had stations in the counties of Greenville, Sussex, and Surry. The Surry depots were located at Savedge, Spring Grove, Claremont, and Claremont Wharf. (Courtesy of Claude Reeson.)

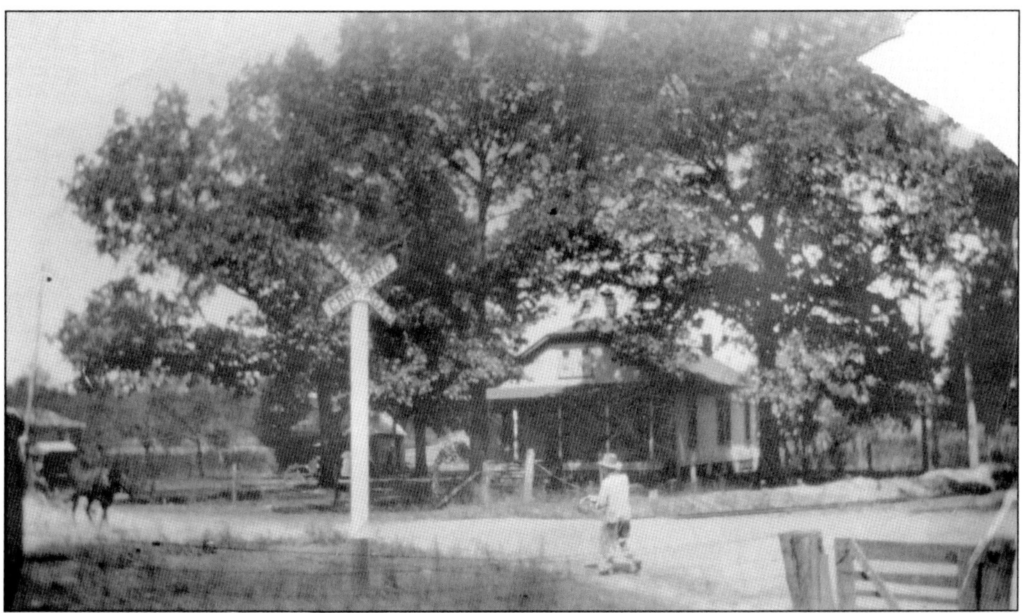

Pap (in the buggy) and Edwin Reeson are pictured at Spring Grove around 1921. (Courtesy of Claude Reeson.)

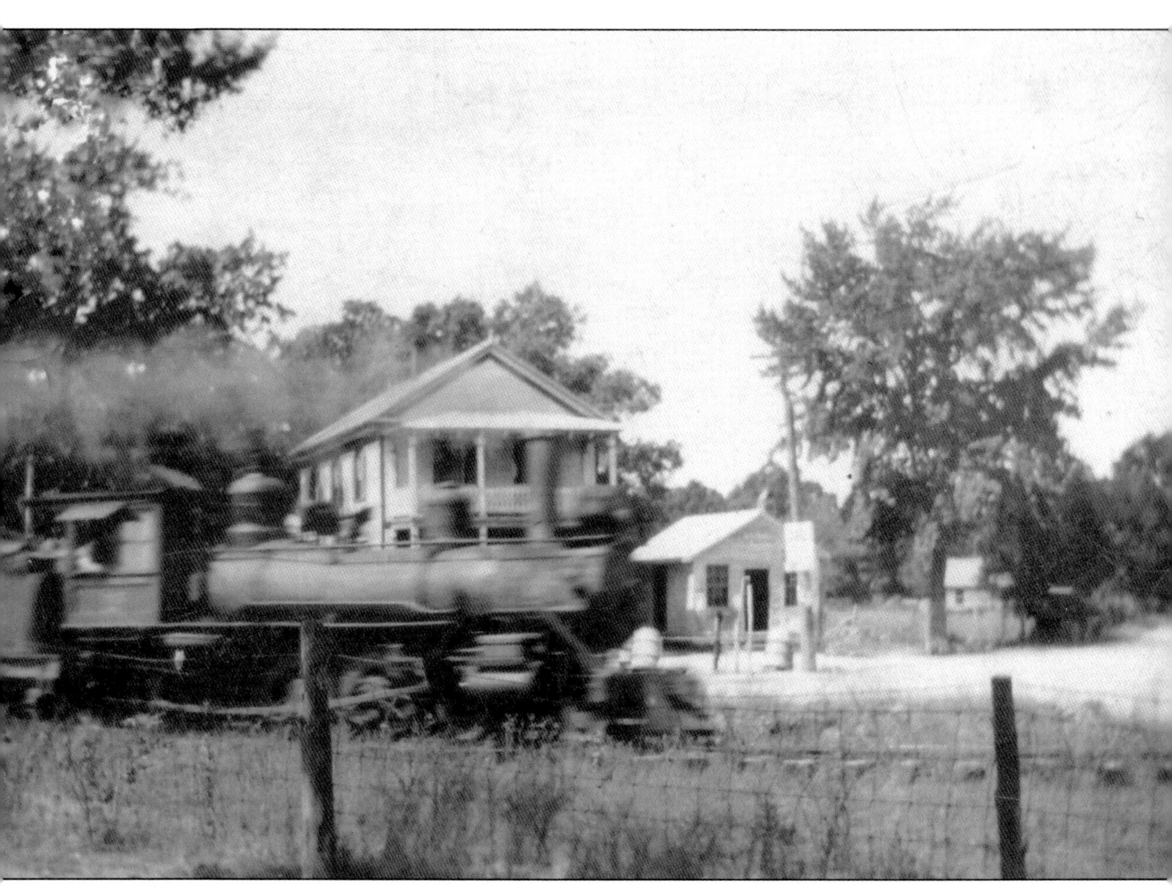

Southern engine No. 3 speeds through Spring Grove heading to Claremont from Waverly in this 1921 photograph. (Courtesy of Claude Reeson.)

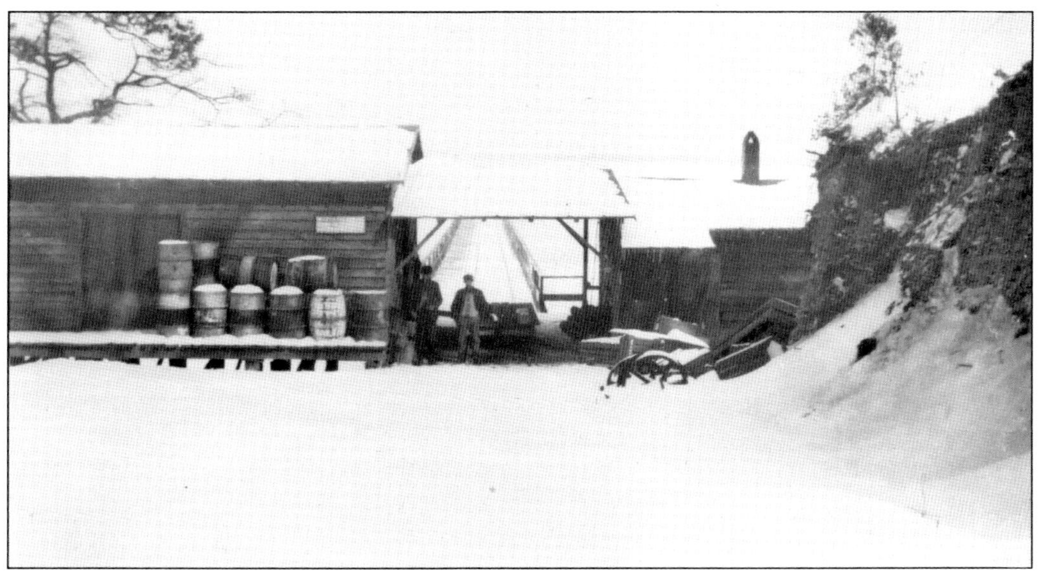

Cobham Wharf on the James River was a busy place in the 1920s. Pictured here is a warehouse that stored shipments from river and railway traffic. (Courtesy of Mary Alma Savedge.)

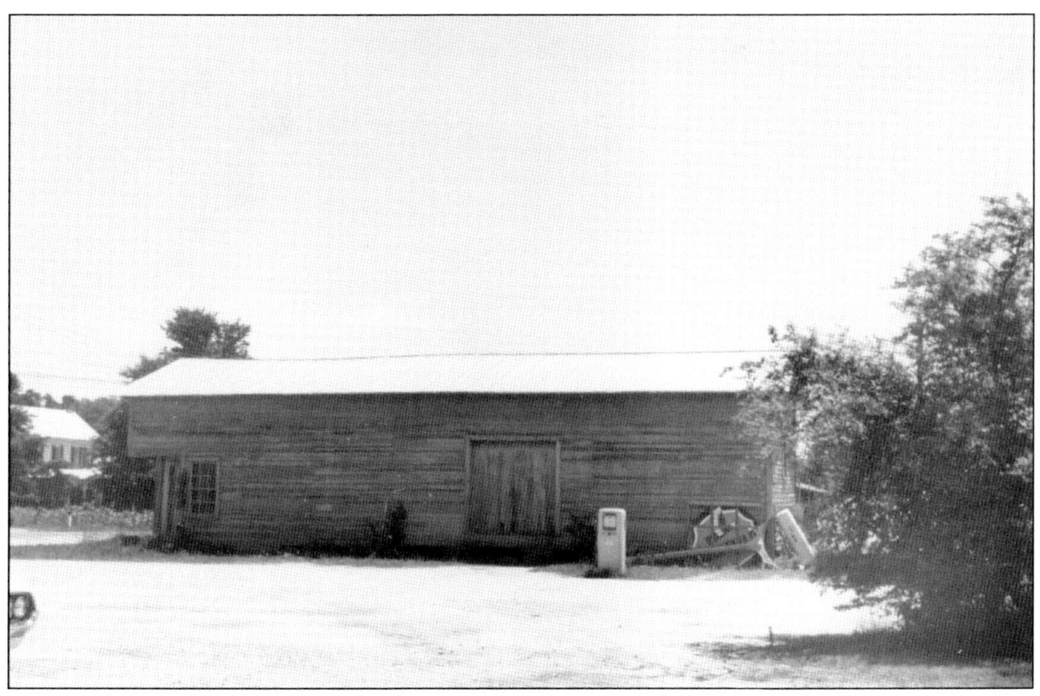

Pictured here is the Surry depot of the Surry, Sussex & Southampton Railway.

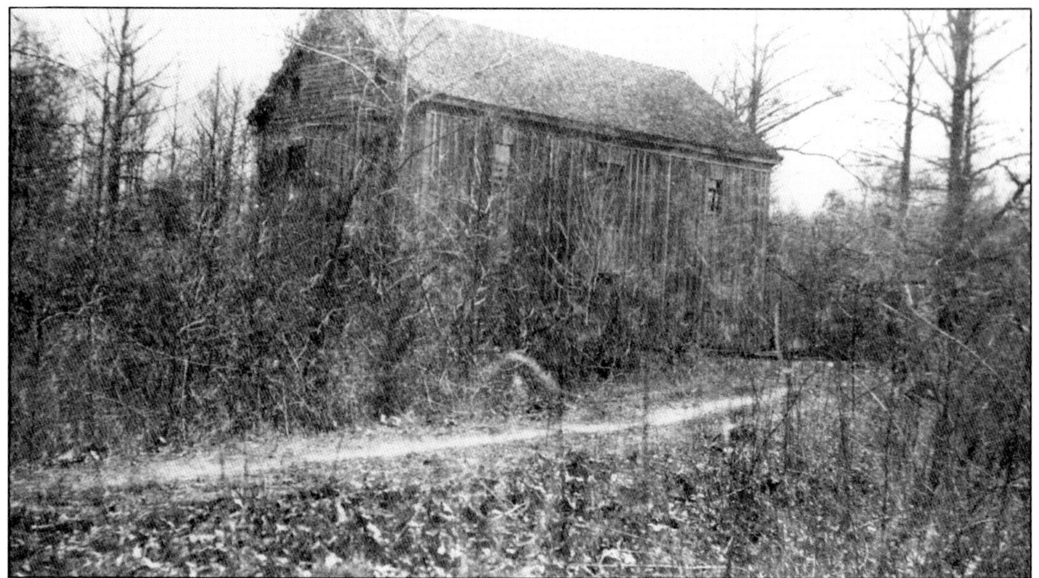

Known as the "Mill at the head of the Gray's Creek," Gill's Mill was purchased by G.S. Gill in the 1850s from the estate of William Clements. Milling was an important business in Surry as early as 1652 when the county was formed. Surry was ideal for milling because of its many streams. (Courtesy of Gordon "Bo" Bohannan.)

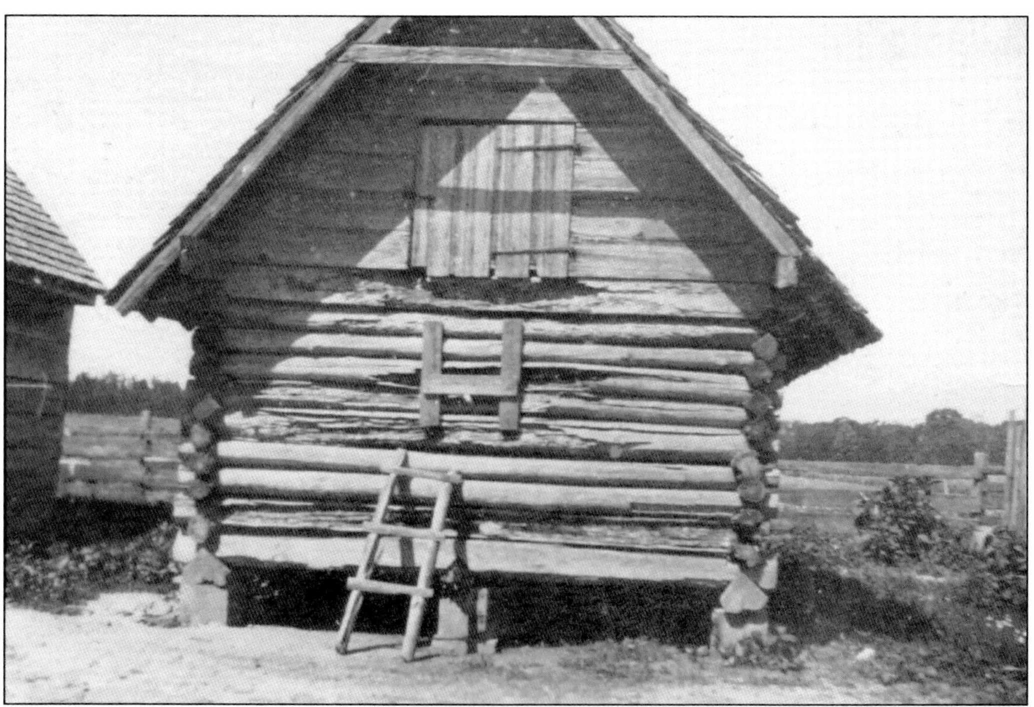

This corncrib was built before the Civil War and was located on Broomfield Farm, which was owned by the Hanscom family. The placement of the door at the top was designed to keep out animals. (Courtesy of Mary Grace Padgett.)

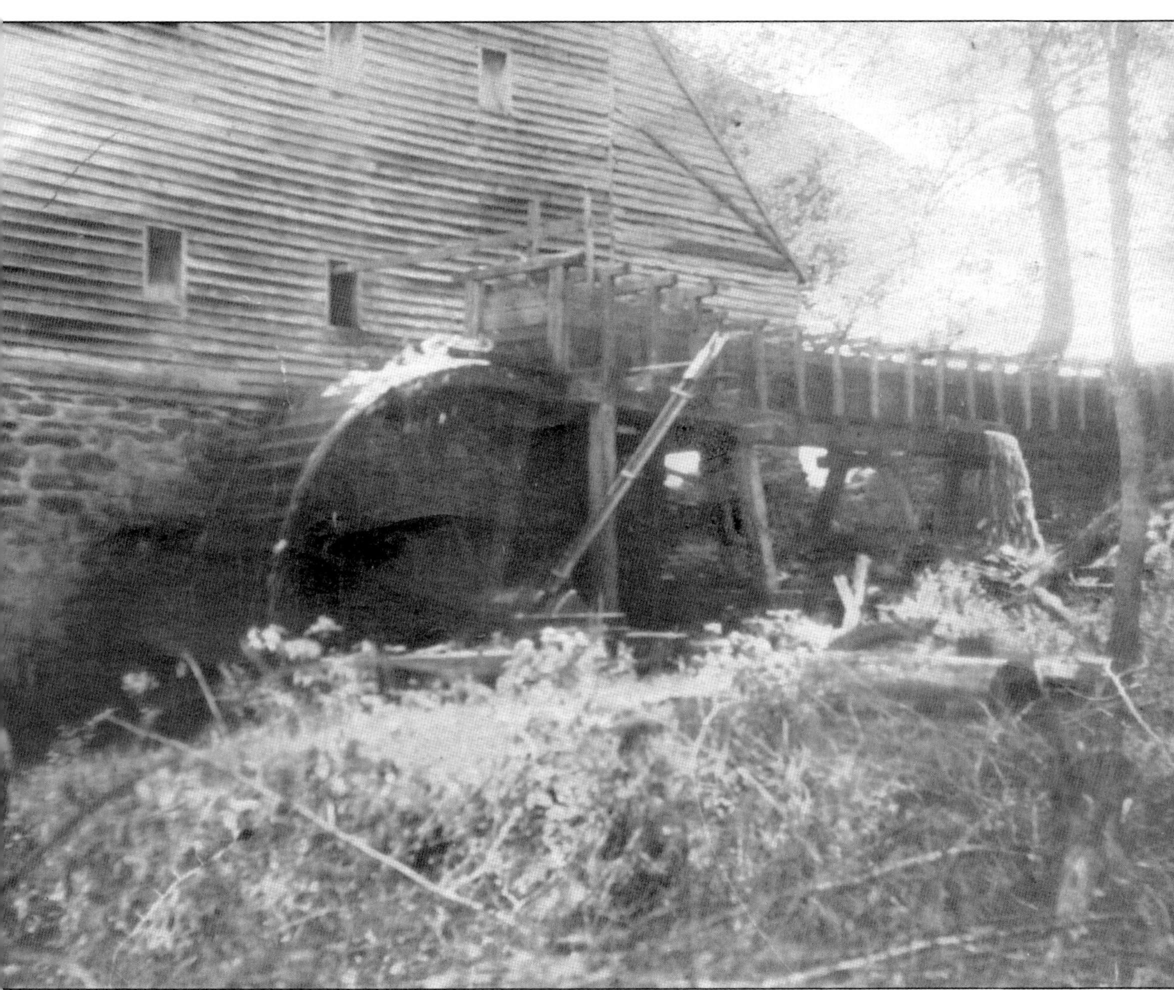

Pictured here is an unidentified mill in one of the early Surry County communities. Surry has a number of streams and creeks where waterpower mills operated to provide residents with freshly ground flour and cornmeal in the 19th and early 20th centuries. Families would take wheat or corn to the mill and wait patiently until it was ground and ready for use. The mills were the focal point of communities and a place to learn the latest news and trade goods.

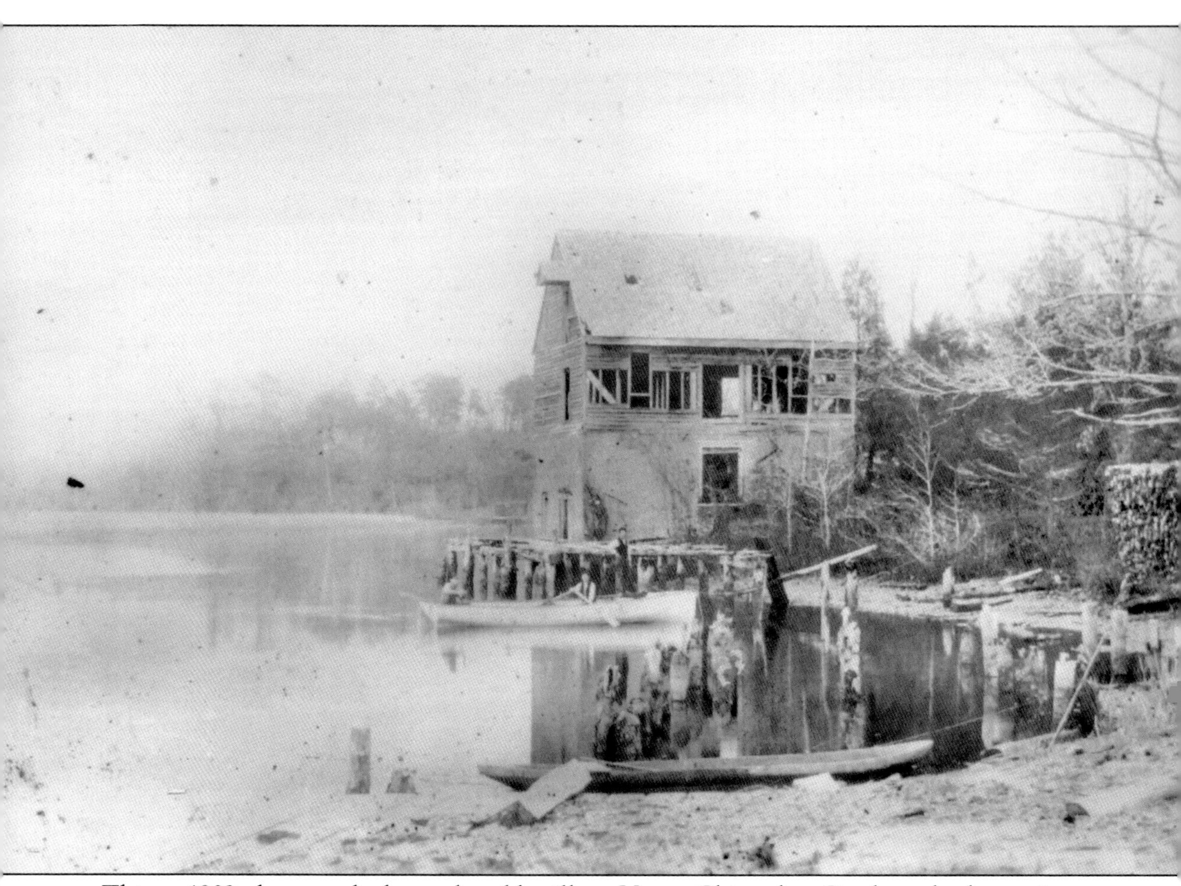

This c. 1902 photograph shows the old mill on Upper Chippokes Creek at the low point near Cabin Point.

The Surry County Picnics began in 1931 when the county could no longer afford to sponsor an annual agricultural fair. The picnics were a way for residents to showcase their various crafts and come together for recreation. The first picnic featured four exhibit classes, special events, and school athletic contests. (Courtesy of Claude Reeson.)

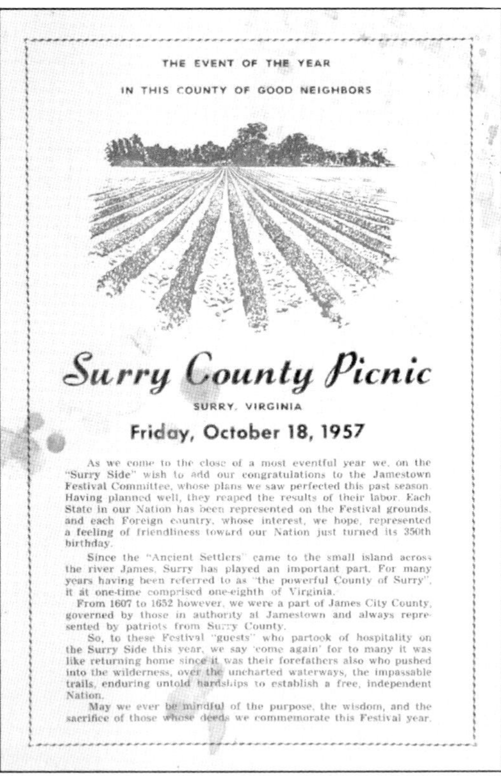

THE EVENT OF THE YEAR

IN THIS COUNTY OF GOOD NEIGHBORS

Surry County Picnic

SURRY, VIRGINIA

Friday, October 18, 1957

As we come to the close of a most eventful year we, on the "Surry Side" wish to add our congratulations to the Jamestown Festival Committee, whose plans we saw perfected this past season. Having planned well, they reaped the results of their labor. Each State in our Nation has been represented on the Festival grounds, and each Foreign country, whose interest, we hope, represented a feeling of friendliness toward our Nation just turned its 350th birthday.

Since the "Ancient Settlers" came to the small island across the river James, Surry has played an important part. For many years having been referred to as "the powerful County of Surry", it at one-time comprised one-eighth of Virginia.

From 1607 to 1652 however, we were a part of James City County, governed by those in authority at Jamestown and always represented by patriots from Surry County.

So, to these Festival "guests" who partook of hospitality on the Surry Side this year, we say 'come again' for to many it was like returning home since it was their forefathers also who pushed into the wilderness, over the uncharted waterways, the impassable trails, enduring untold hardships to establish a free, independent Nation.

May we ever be mindful of the purpose, the wisdom, and the sacrifice of those whose deeds we commemorate this Festival year.

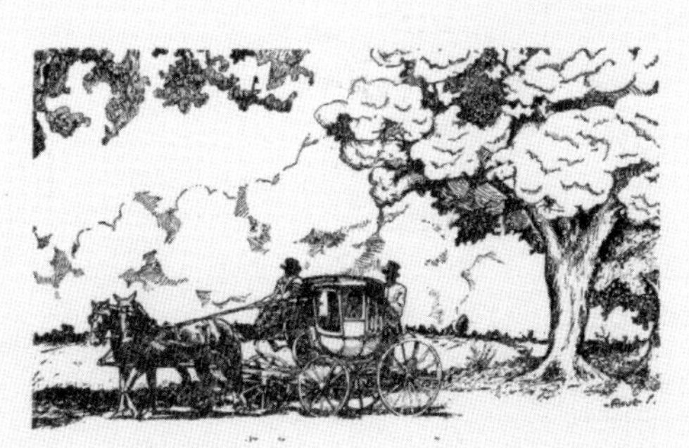

Old Virginia

Tilting Tournament

SURRY, VA.

- 1939 -

In the 1930s, Surry hosted a tilting tournament during which residents in costumes participated in various popular sports of medieval Europe. According to *Encyclopedia Britanica*, "tilting, or riding at the rings is a form of jousting in which the horseman rides at full gallop and inserts his lance through small metal rings." (Courtesy of Donna Slade.)

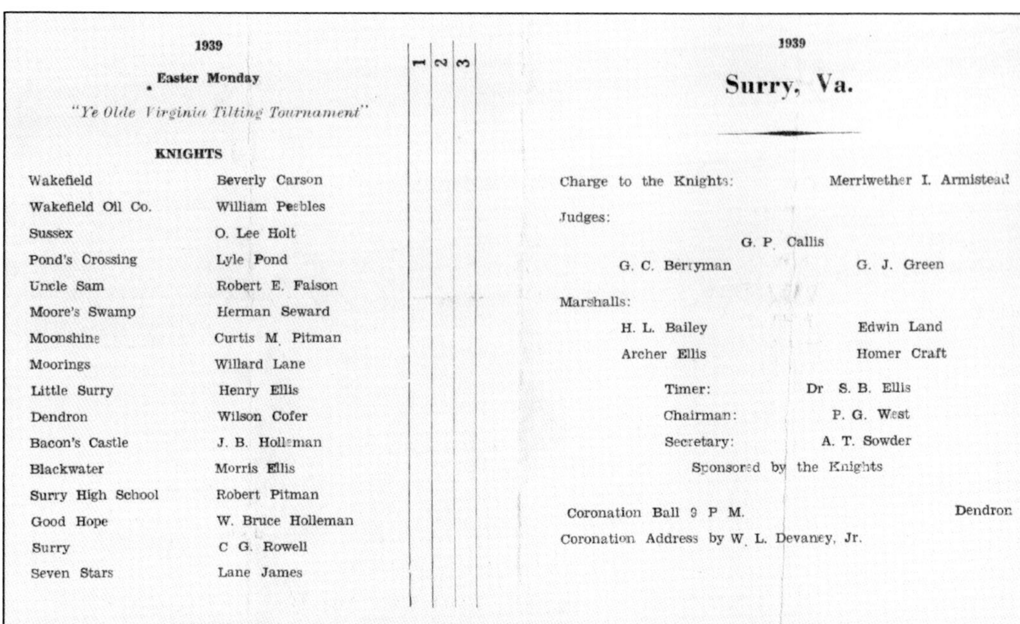

1939

Easter Monday

"Ye Olde Virginia Tilting Tournament"

KNIGHTS

Wakefield	Beverly Carson
Wakefield Oil Co.	William Peebles
Sussex	O. Lee Holt
Pond's Crossing	Lyle Pond
Uncle Sam	Robert E. Faison
Moore's Swamp	Herman Seward
Moonshine	Curtis M. Pitman
Moorings	Willard Lane
Little Surry	Henry Ellis
Dendron	Wilson Cofer
Bacon's Castle	J. B. Holleman
Blackwater	Morris Ellis
Surry High School	Robert Pitman
Good Hope	W. Bruce Holleman
Surry	C G. Rowell
Seven Stars	Lane James

1 2 3

1939

Surry, Va.

Charge to the Knights: Merriwether I. Armistead

Judges:

G. P. Callis

G. C. Berryman G. J. Green

Marshalls:

H. L. Bailey Edwin Land

Archer Ellis Homer Craft

Timer: Dr S. B. Ellis

Chairman: P. G. West

Secretary: A. T. Sowder

Sponsored by the Knights

Coronation Ball 9 P M. Dendron

Coronation Address by W. L. Devaney, Jr.

The program from the 1939 tilting tournament suggests that the event took place in the spring and on Easter Monday. Following the tournament and lasting into the evening, residents enjoyed a coronation ball. (Courtesy of Donna Slade.)

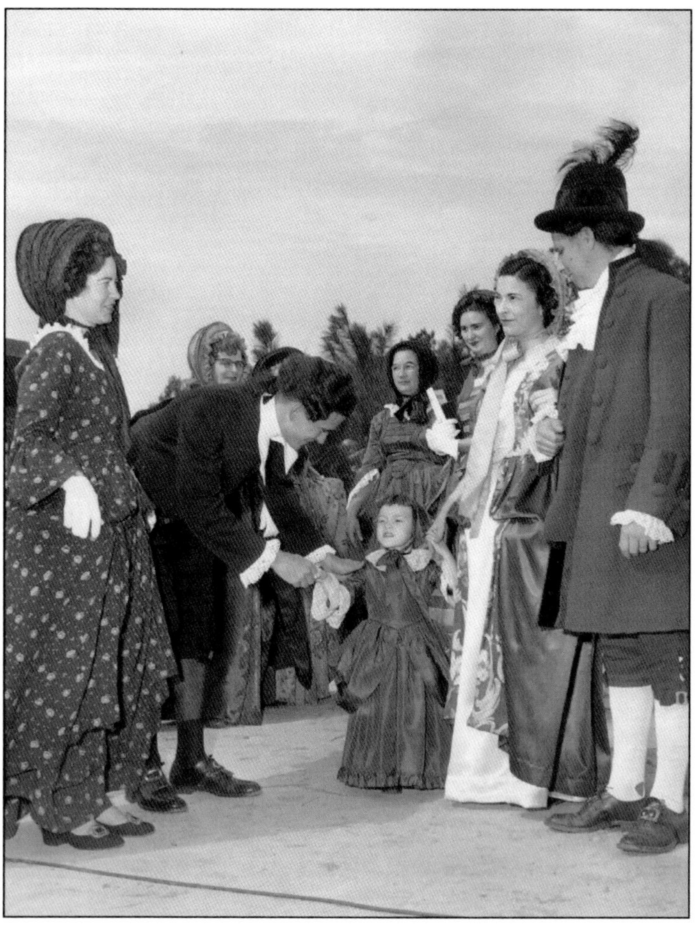

In 1952, the county celebrated its tri-centennial, which featured drama presentations of notable events in the county's history. The dramatic program entitled *Surry Through Three Centuries* included episodes that began in 1607 and ended with events after World War II. The Surry residents dressed as early English settlers include Elizabeth Gwaltney Clark, Vernell Huber, Judith Rae Price (child), and Armistead Slade (holding child's hand.)

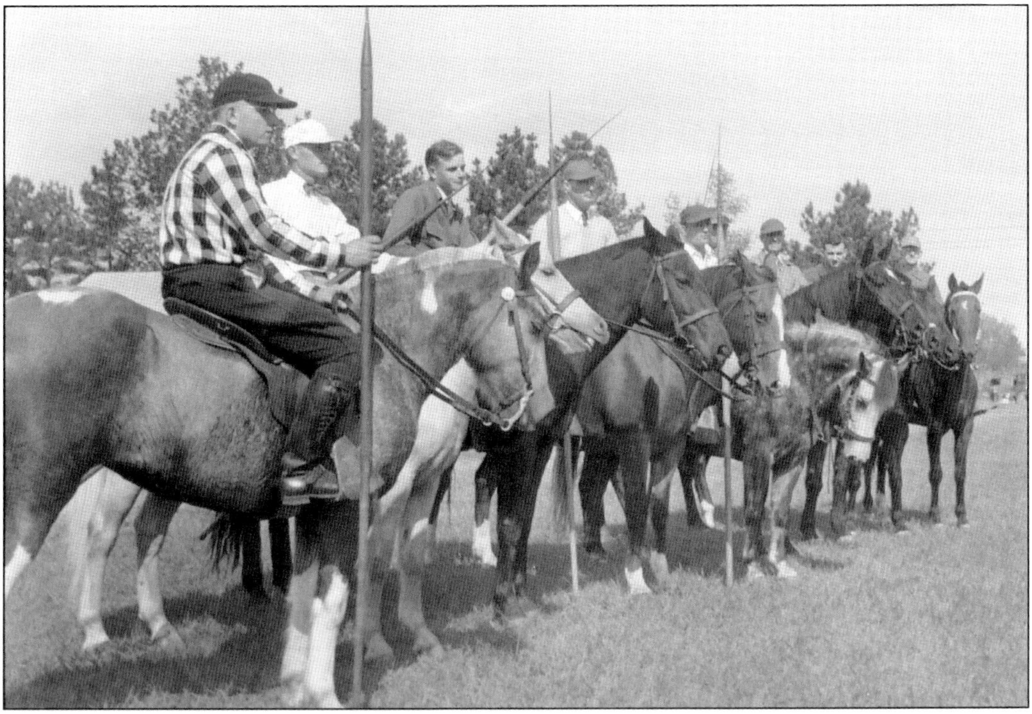

At the 1952 tri-centennial celebration, horsemen line up for the tilting tournament.

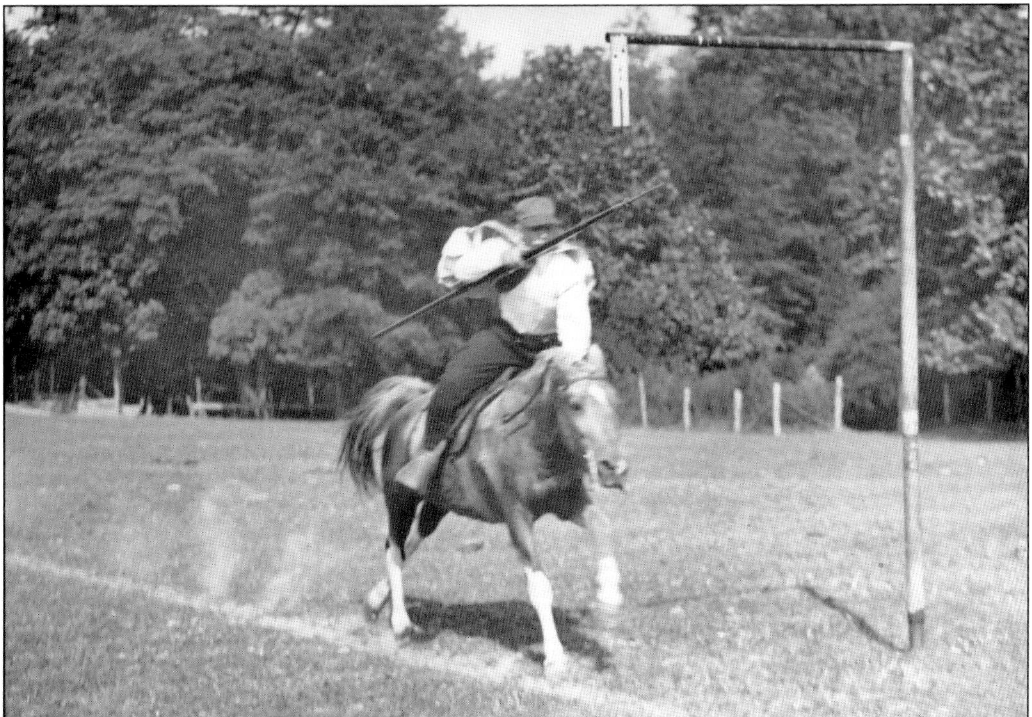

The unidentified rider is moving at full gallop, trying to win the 1952 tilting tournament held during the tri-centennial celebration. Will M. Gwaltney Jr. was declared the tournament winner.

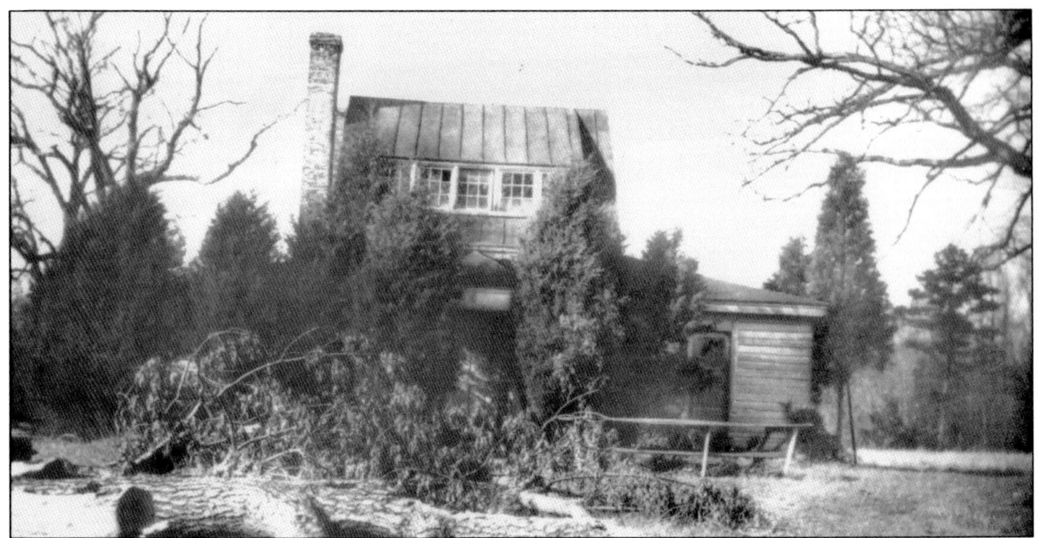

The house called Floods at Pipsico Plantation was built in the late 18th century. Constructed in several stages, it featured a continuous dormer, or clerestory bank of windows. The name suggests that it was possibly part of the Flood/Fludd family plantation located nearby. But according to the Virginia Historic Landmarks Commission, the house was built too late to have any connection to the family, and it was situated on land owned by the Brownes. (Courtesy of Gordon "Bo" Bohannan.)

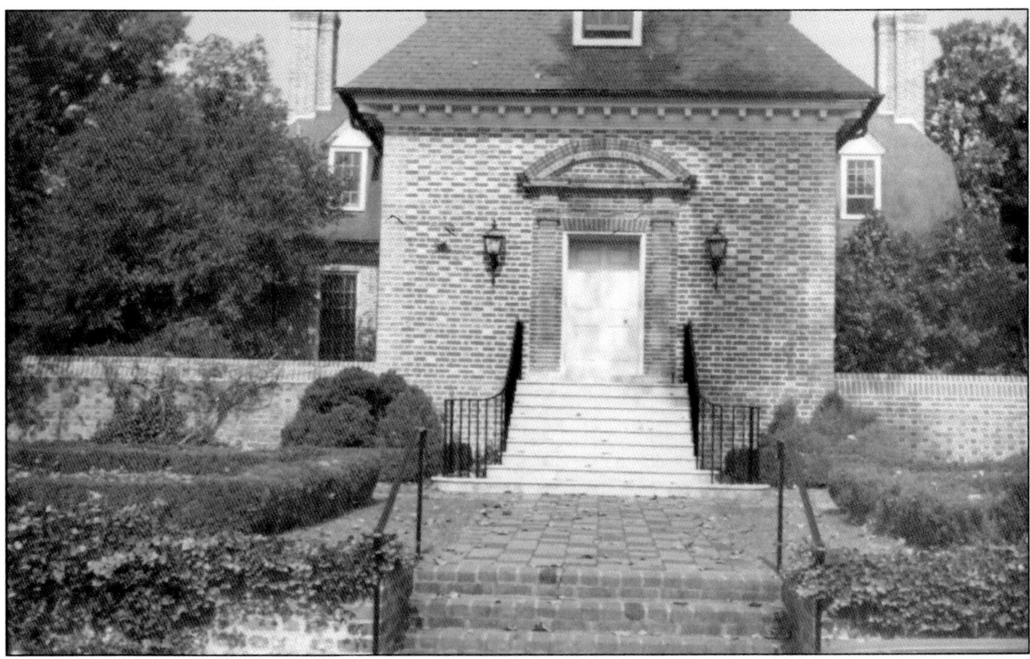

The above photograph features a road view of the main house at Claremont Manor. Owned by the Allen family from 1656 until 1882, Claremont Manor is one of the county's best documented plantations. Ownership changed hands many times over the years, and in 1964, it was given to the Felician Sisters, OSF, who established an elementary school on the site. Around 1976, the school closed and the property was again sold, except for acreage immediately surrounding the school. (Courtesy of Gordon "Bo" Bohannan.)

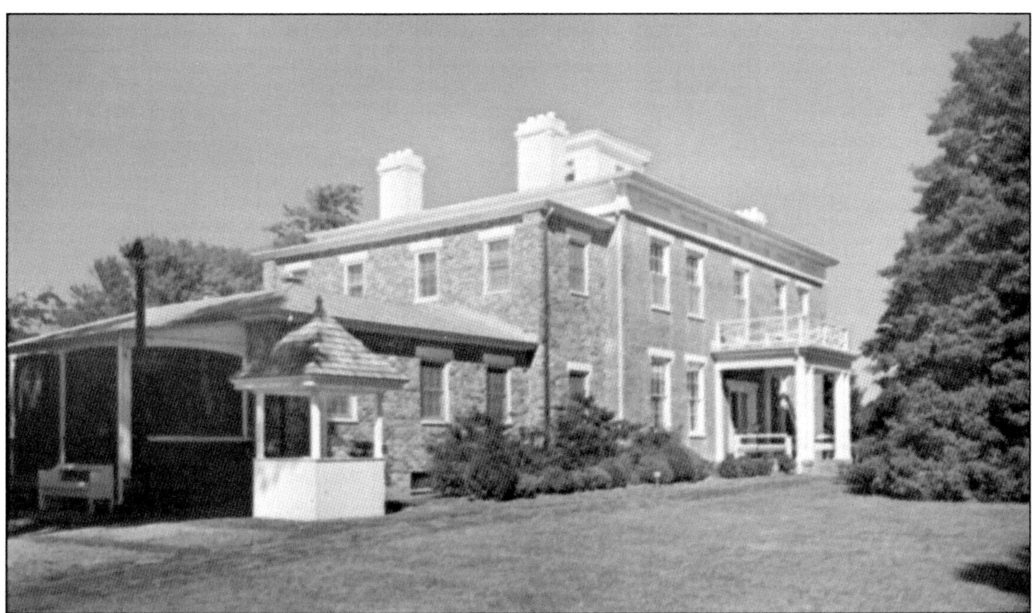

The postcard image above shows the Stewart Mansion, built in the 1800s at Chippokes Plantation. Situated directly across the James River from Jamestown, the property was an original part of the first permanent English settlement and has been a continuous farm since the early 1600s. In 1969, the last owner, Evelyn Bleakley Stewart, bequeathed the plantation of 1,400 acres to the Commonwealth of Virginia in memory of her husband. The property is currently known as Chippokes Plantation State Park and has rental cabins, camping sites, museums, nature trails, a swimming pool, and conference facilities. (Above, courtesy of Gordon "Bo" Bohannan.)

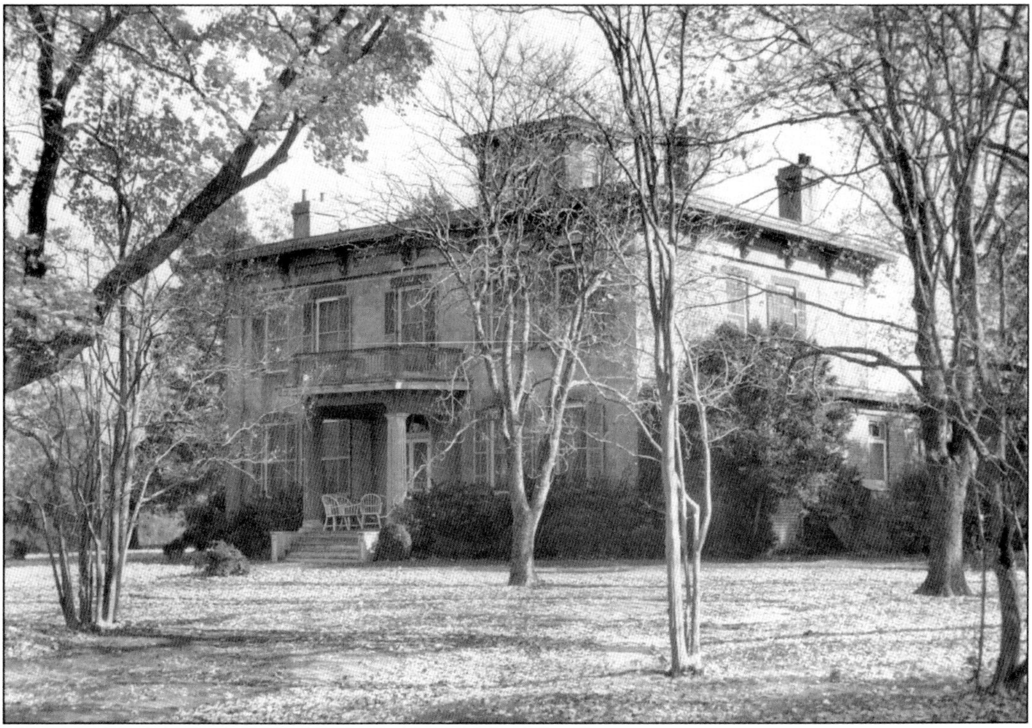

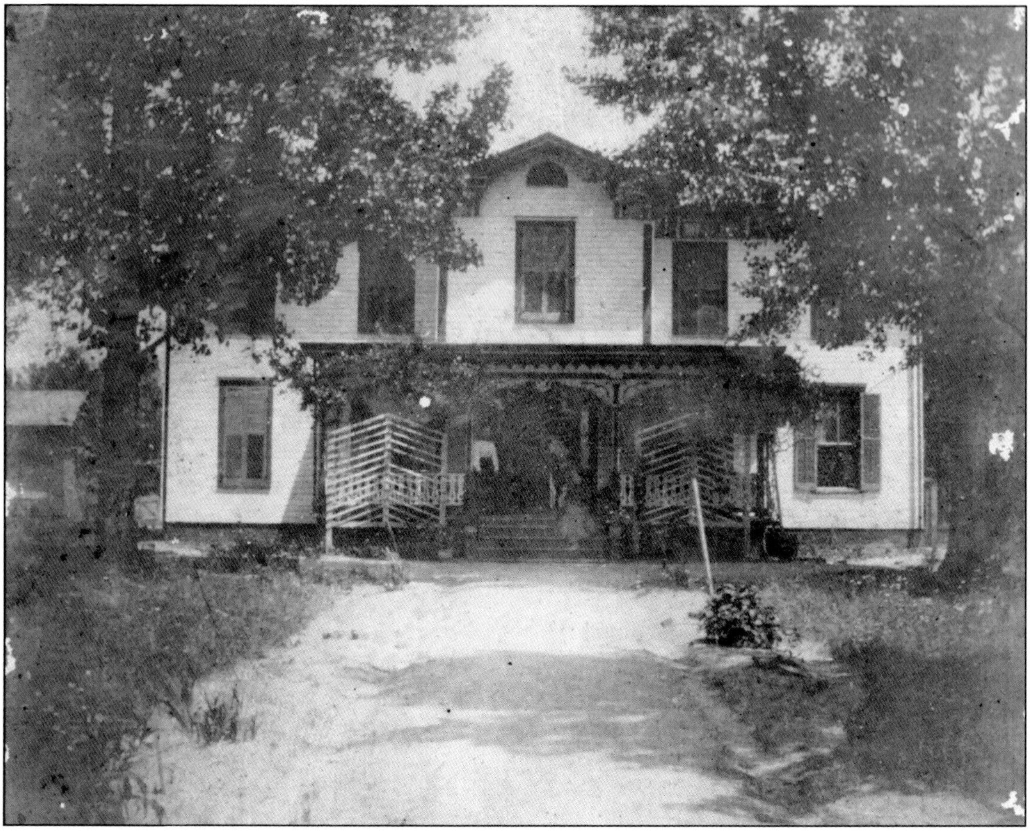

Known as the Clark family home, this property is located in the town of Surry. (Courtesy of Gordon "Bo" Bohannan.)

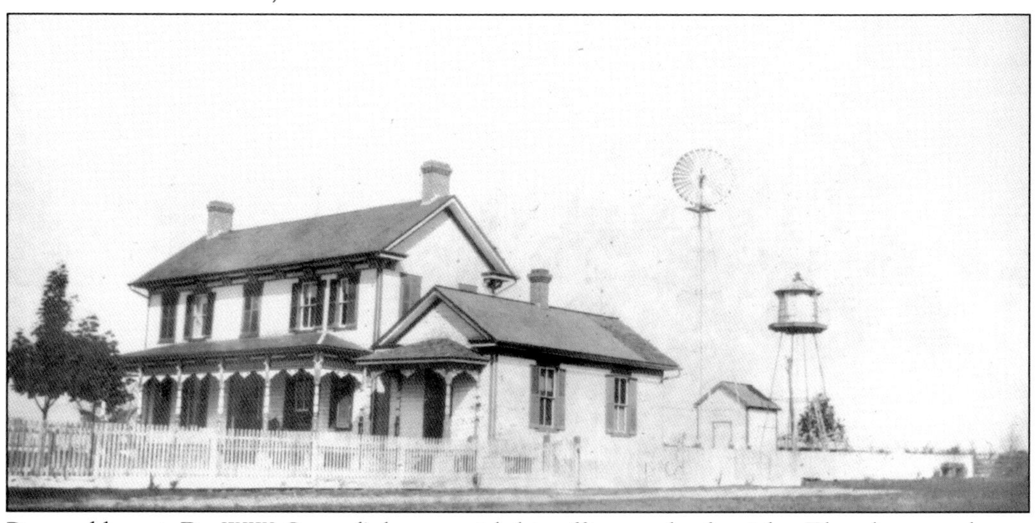

Pictured here is Dr. W.W. Seward's house, with his office on the far right. The photograph was taken in the early 1900s. Dr. Seward was active in the Confederate Memorial Association of Surry and served as chairman of the Virginia World War I Medical Advisory Board Region No. 12, which included Surry and Sussex Counties. In recent years, the home has been a private residence and then a bed-and-breakfast. (Courtesy of Mary Alma Savedge.)

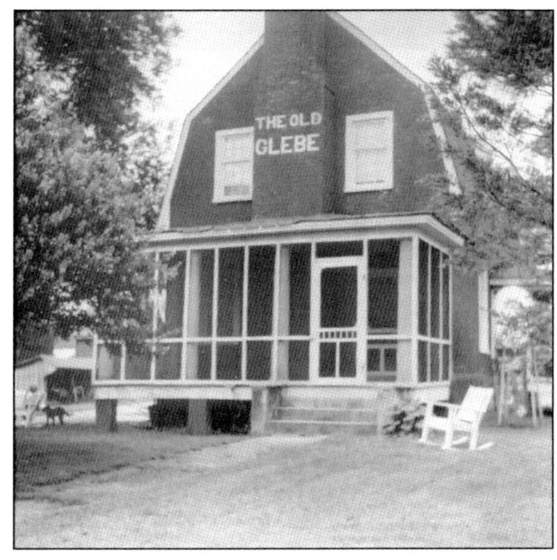

The Old Glebe House is located on Route 10 west of the town of Surry and was originally built as a home for ministers of Southwark Parish. The exact construction date is not known; however, an act was passed by the general assembly in March 1661 requiring that "glebes" be provided with living facilities for parish ministers. The early-1960s photograph below shows the side porch of the house.

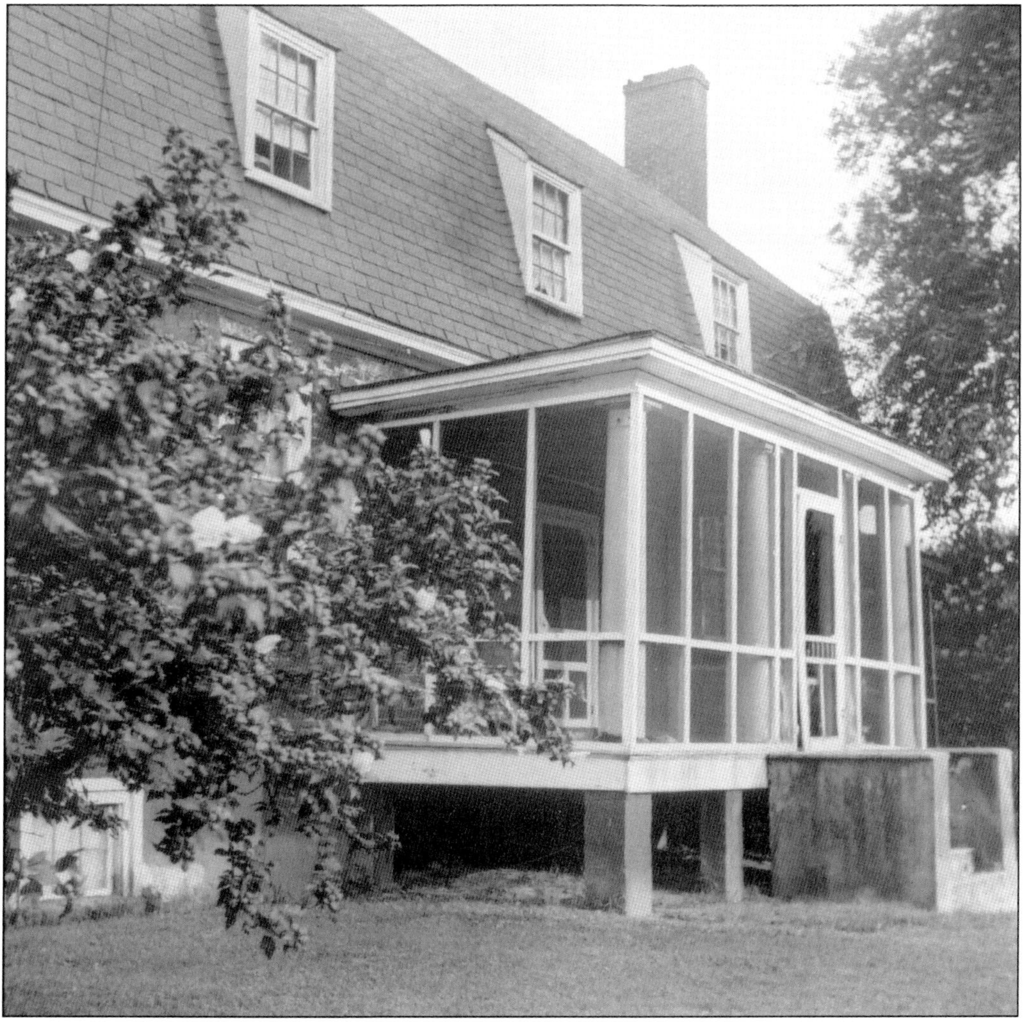

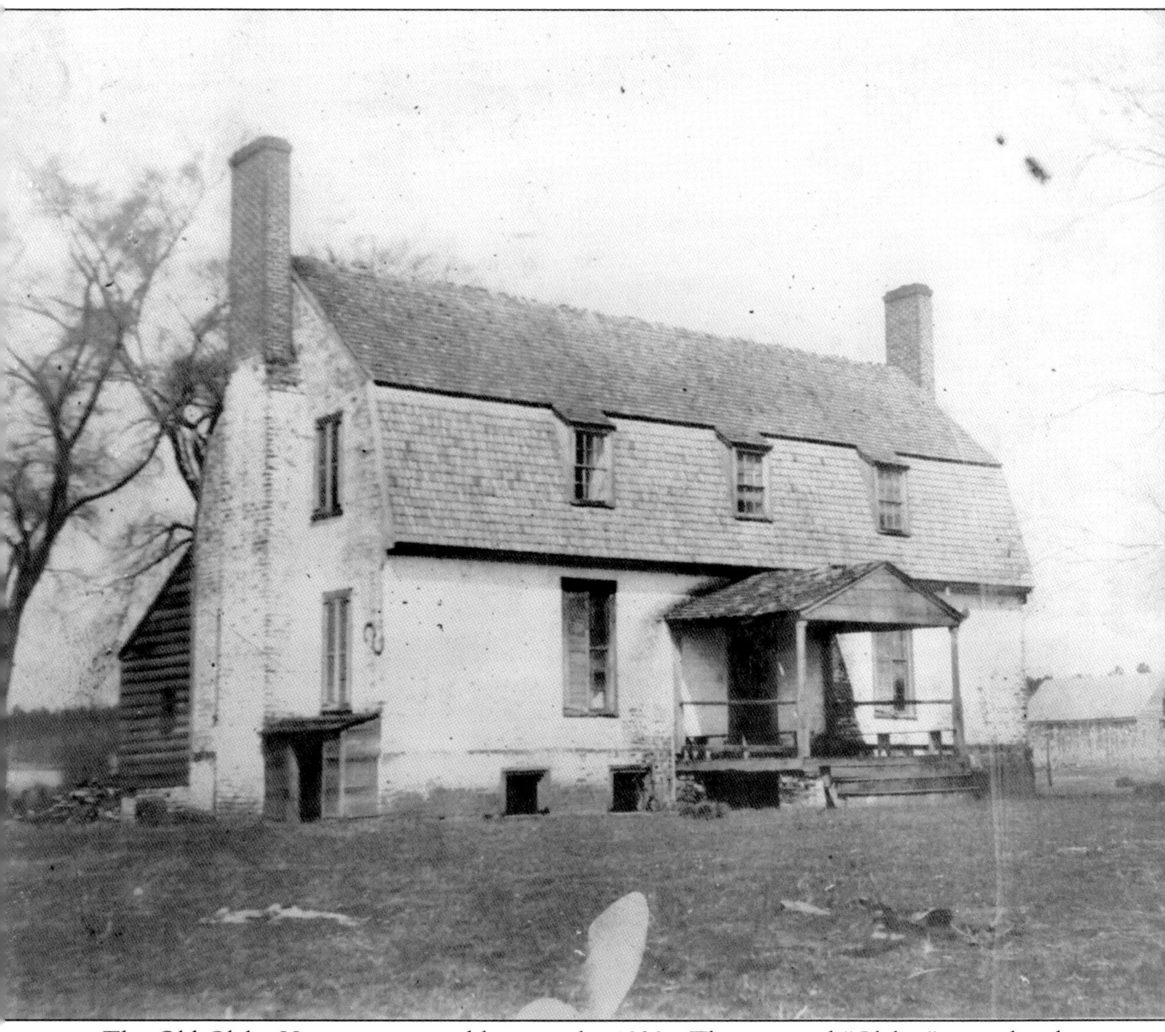

The Old Glebe House is pictured here in the 1930s. The required "Glebes" served as living quarters for parish ministers, and each parish was also responsible for building a kitchen, barn, stable, dairy, meat house, and corn house. In the early 1950s, the Old Glebe was the home of Mr. and Mrs. E.M. Bryant.

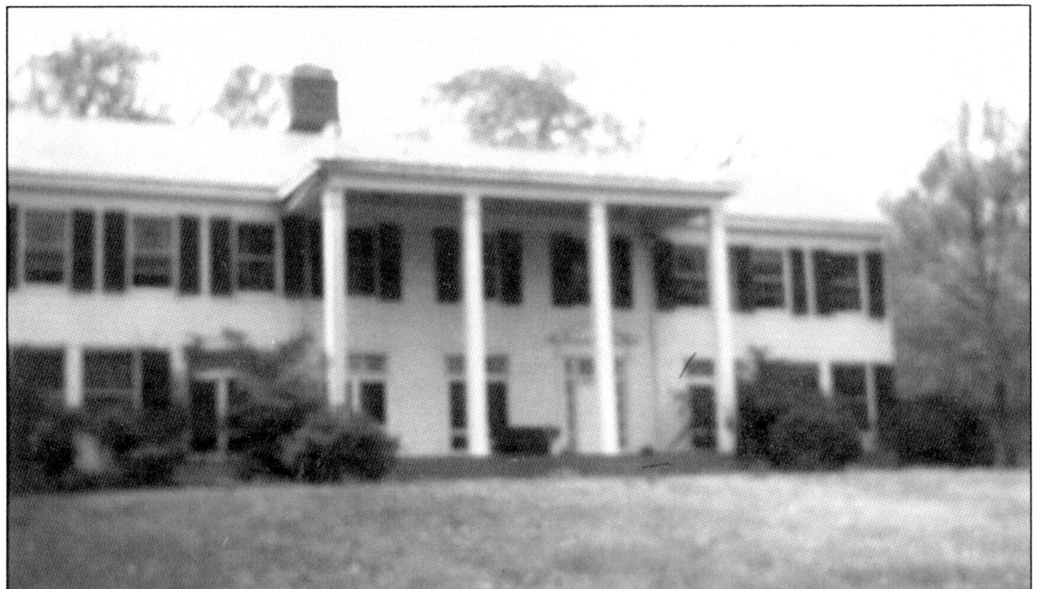

As early as 1628, William Perry established rights to Perry's Point, which later became Swann's Point. The name changed in 1635 when Col. Thomas Swann, a burgess and member of the Council of Sir William Berkeley, became owner of the property. Records show that in the late 1600s and into the 1700s, a ferry on the property went to Jamestown. In the 1950s and after, the property served as the summer home for Sen. Garland Gray and his wife, Agnes Taylor Gray. (Courtesy of Gordon "Bo" Bohannan.)

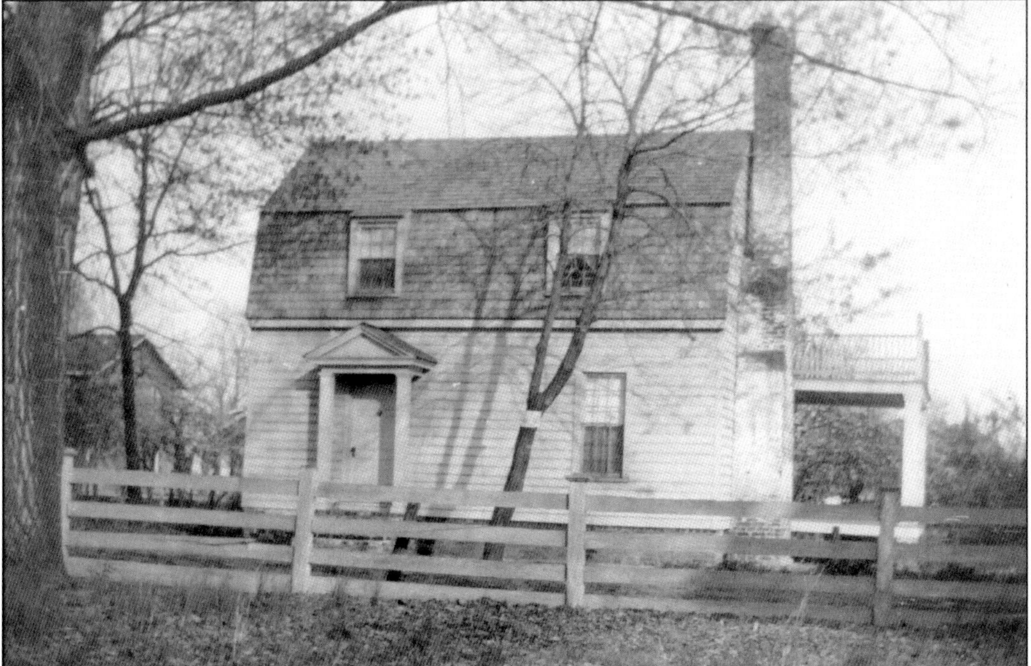

The Old Dutch Roof House, located east of the Surry courthouse, is one of the oldest known houses located in the town of Surry. According to A.W. Bohannan in *Old Surry*, the location suggests that the house was built prior to 1796 and dates to the time of the American Revolution.

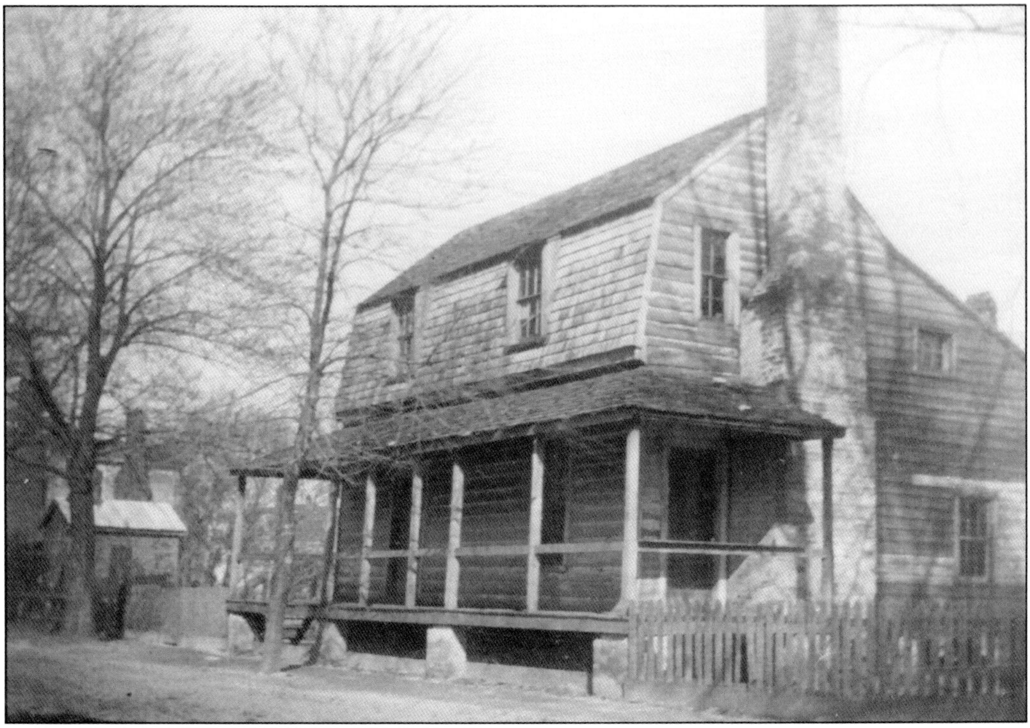

Known as one of the oldest houses in Surry, the Old Dutch Roof House is shown as it looked during the Revolutionary War and before major restoration was done.

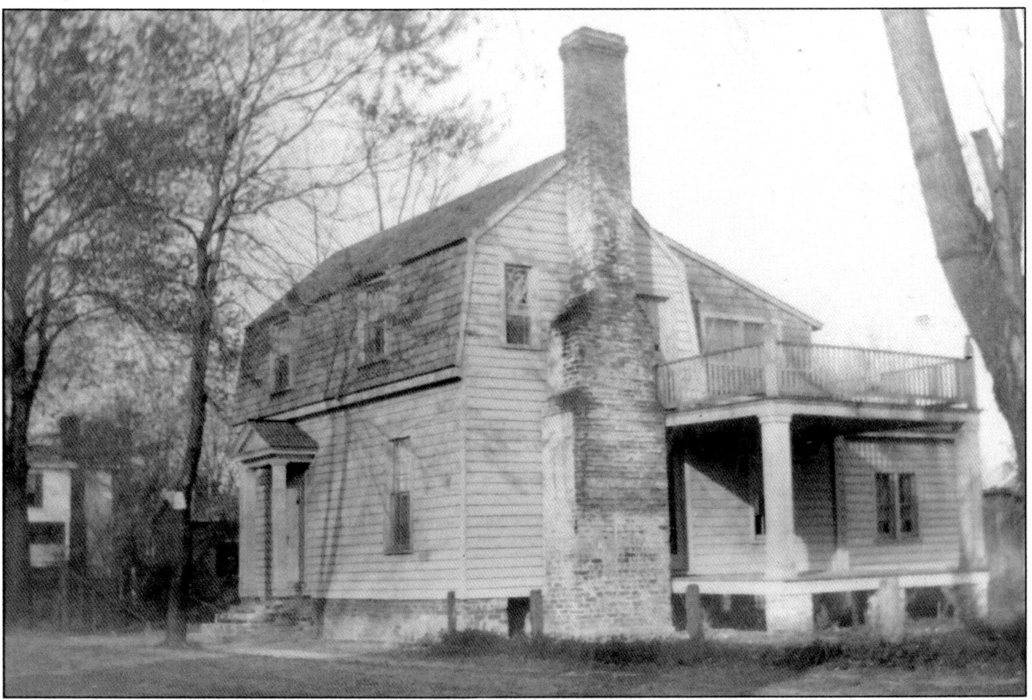

This 1923 photograph was taken by A.W. Bohannan after restoration of the Old Dutch Roof House.

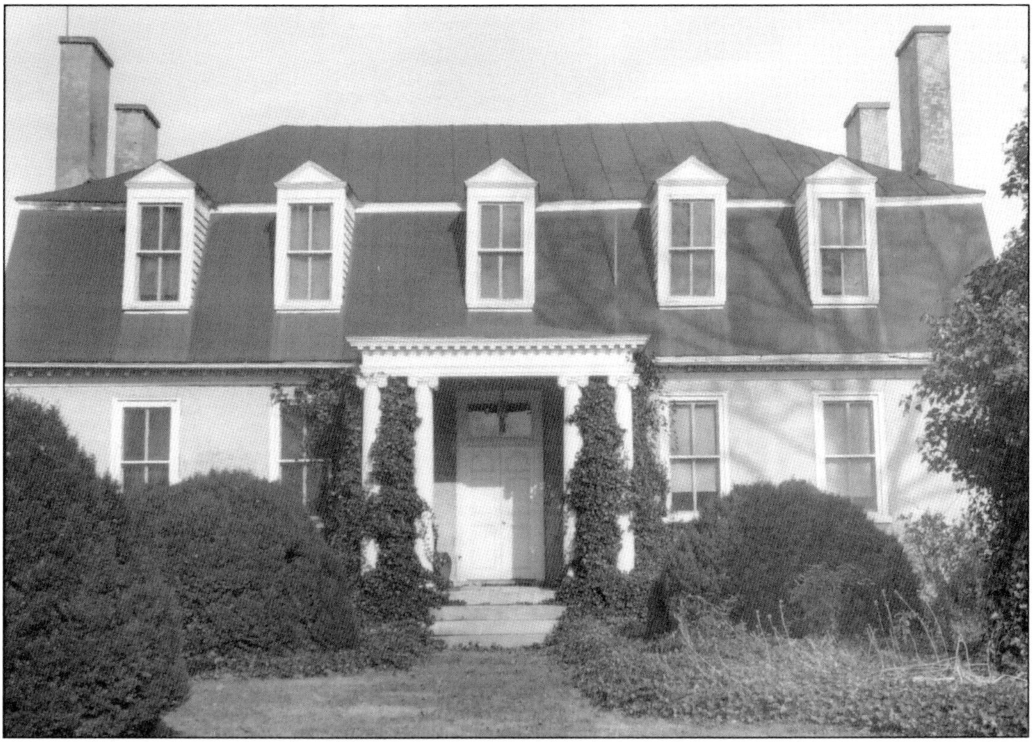

The Four Mile Tree Plantation House was built by the Browne family sometime in the 1700s. It is the successor to Burrow's Hill and Pace's Paines, the earliest plantations in Virginia. In 1619, the property received its name from a tree that was four miles from the western boundary of Jamestown. A grave site that contains the oldest legible tombstone in Virginia is one of the most prominent features of the plantation. In 1970, Gov. Linwood Holton nominated the Four Mile Tree Plantation House for inclusion in the National Register of Historic Places, and it is listed in the Virginia Landmarks Register.

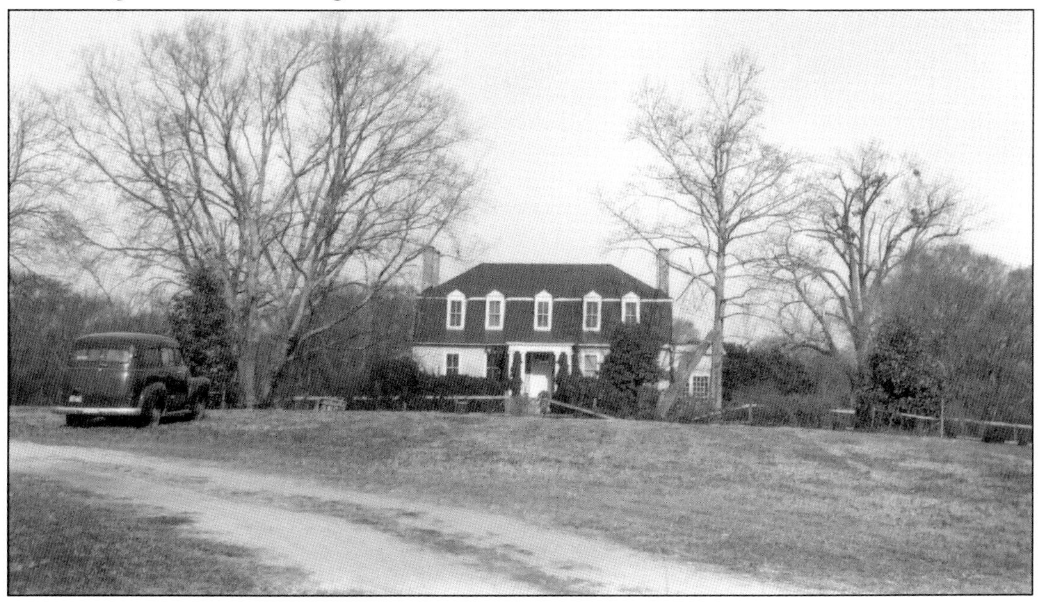

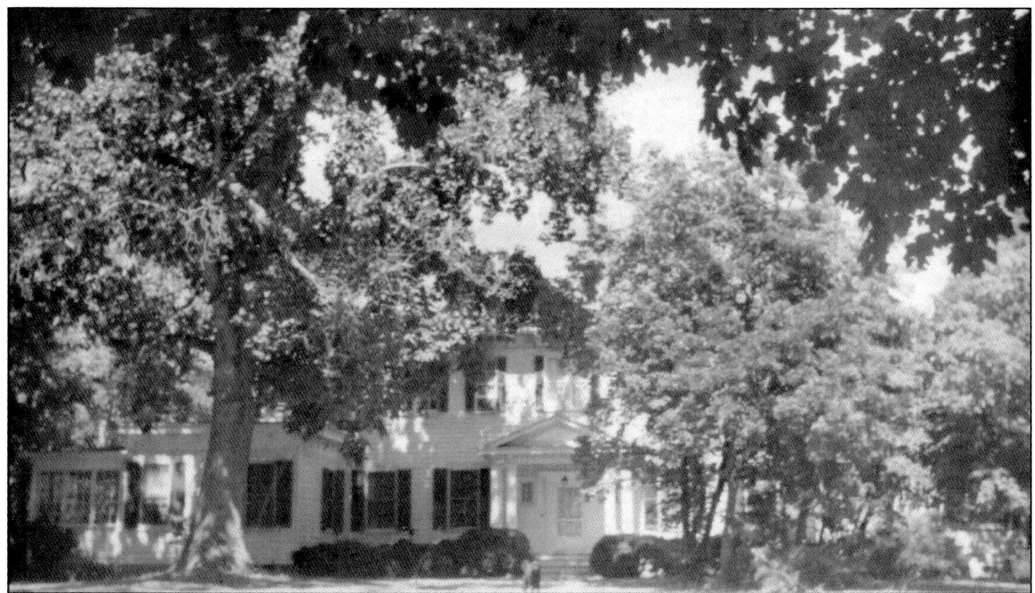

The Eastover property was once part of Pipsico Plantation and dates back to 1657. The manor house pictured here features a beautiful unobstructed view of the James River for about two miles. For most of the 20th century, the property was owned and farmed by Albert Ochsner. In 1972, the Peninsula Baptist Association purchased the property and developed it as a retreat center. Today, it includes a chapel, bed-and-breakfast, dormitory, and hotel with pool and meeting facilities. (Courtesy of Gordon "Bo" Bohannan.)

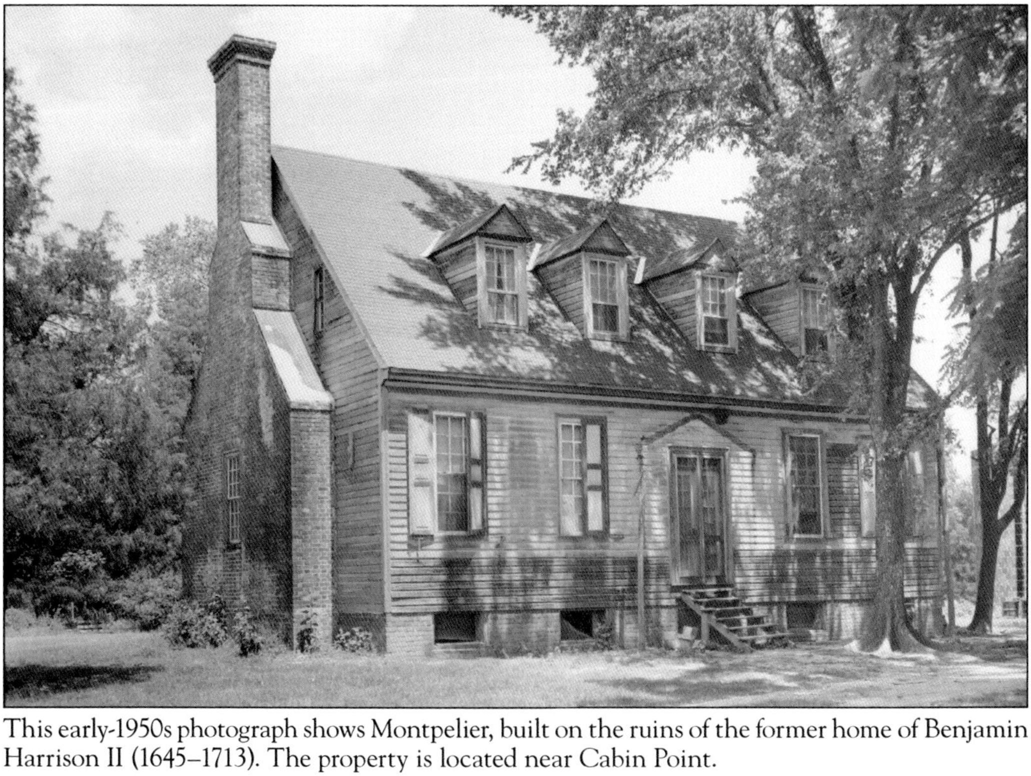

This early-1950s photograph shows Montpelier, built on the ruins of the former home of Benjamin Harrison II (1645–1713). The property is located near Cabin Point.

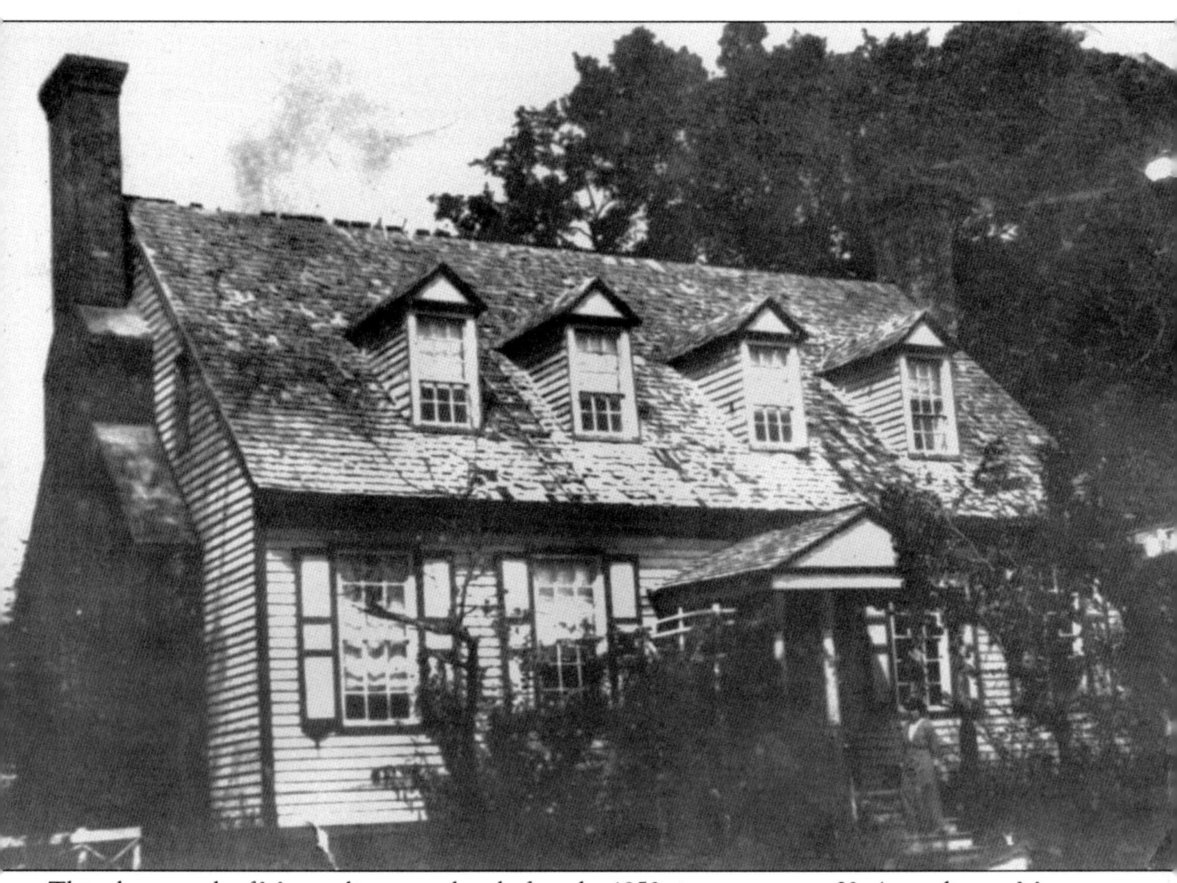

This photograph of Montpelier was taken before the 1950s image on page 32. According to Mary A. Stephenson in *Old Homes in Surry and Sussex*, the two brick chimneys, which measure 20 feet at their bases, are a unique feature of this house.

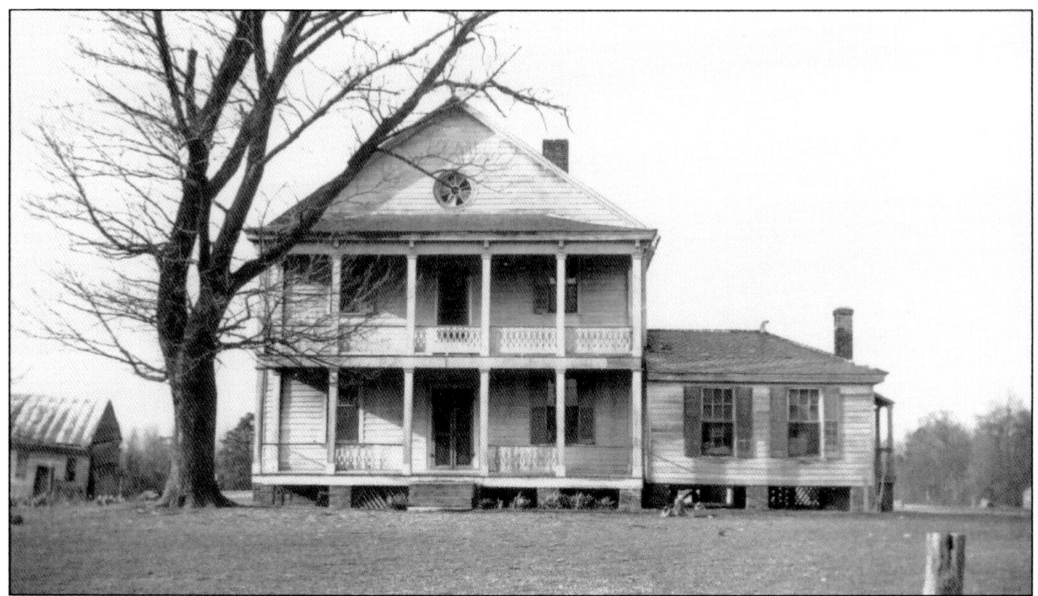

The Grayland Farm was located off Route 626 and owned by the Crenshaw, Gill, and Gwaltney families. The Gill family was associated with Gill Mill near Wareneck. The name *Gray* was probably for the Gray family that patented land in the vicinity before 1640. (Courtesy of Gordon "Bo" Bohannan.)

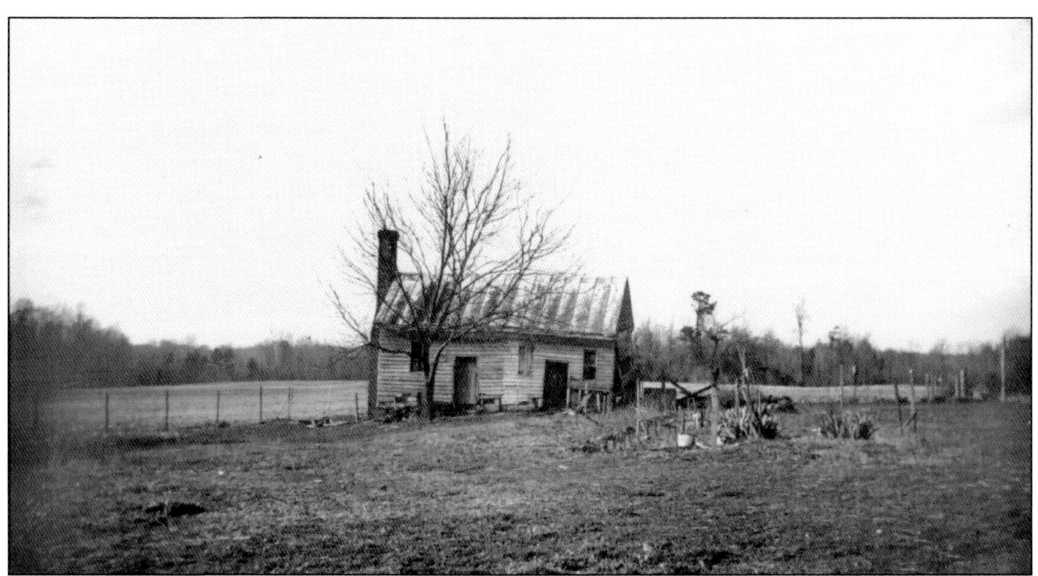

Pictured here is the kitchen building at Grayland Farm. (Courtesy of Gordon "Bo" Bohannan.)

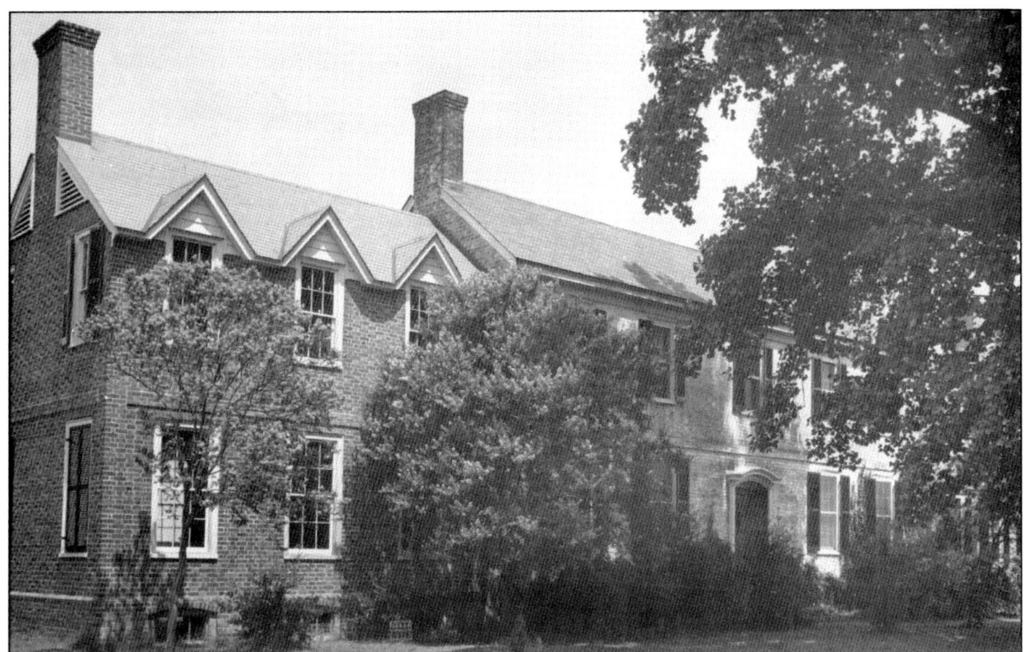

The Mount Pleasant Plantation history can be documented as early as 1620 when about 600 acres on the property were granted to Richard Pace and became know as Pace's Paines. The house pictured here was built during the 18th century and owned by the Cocke family. The Franz von Schilling family completed an extension to the house in the 1950s.

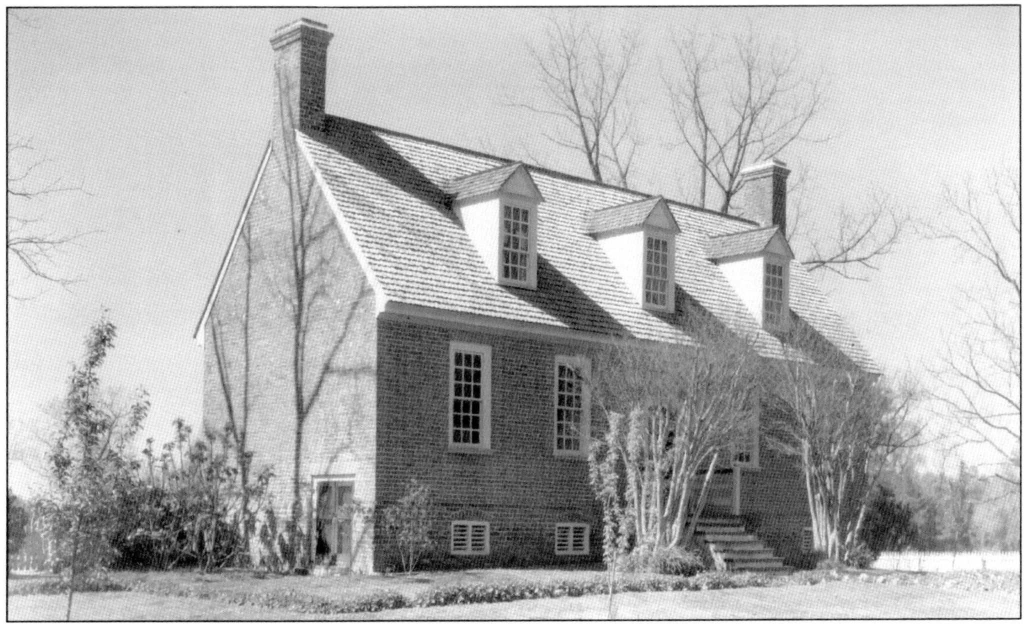

The Rolfe-Warren House on Smith's Fort Plantation was erected in 1652 and is said to be the oldest brick dwelling in Virginia. Early in its history, the property was owned by Thomas Rolfe, son of Pocahontas, and later by Thomas Warren. The Association for the Preservation of Virginia Antiquities (APVA) acquired the property in 1933 and has completed a full restoration. (In 2009, the APVA shortened its name to Preservation Virginia.)

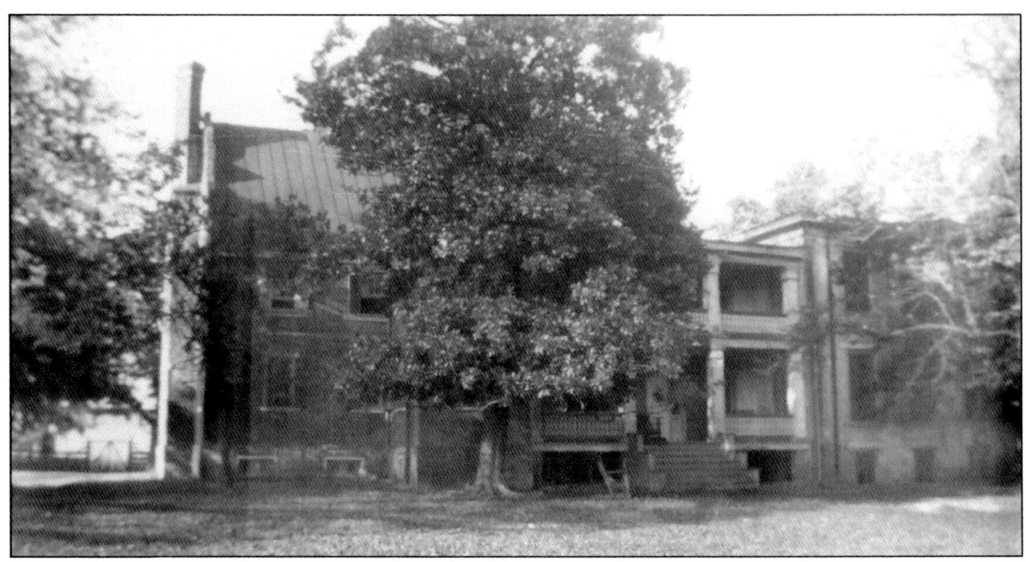

Bacon's Castle was built by the Allen family during the 17th century. It has been said that Bacon's Castle is the county's most historically significant property because of its architecture and its role in Bacon's Rebellion. The house has two rare features—the two chimneys on either side of the house and the Jacobean cornice found on the ends of the roof. During Nathaniel Bacon's rebellion against Gov. William Berkeley in 1676, Bacon's followers seized and fortified the property against the English from late summer to the end of December 1676. Today, the property is open to the public and owned by Preservation Virginia.

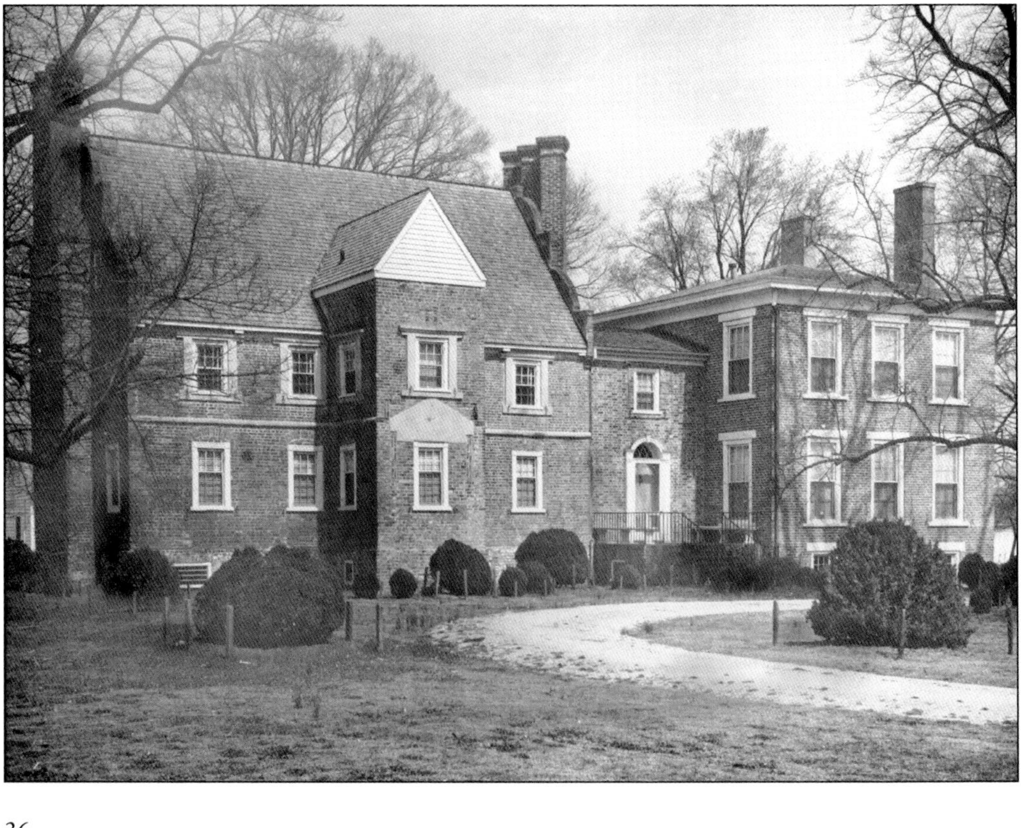

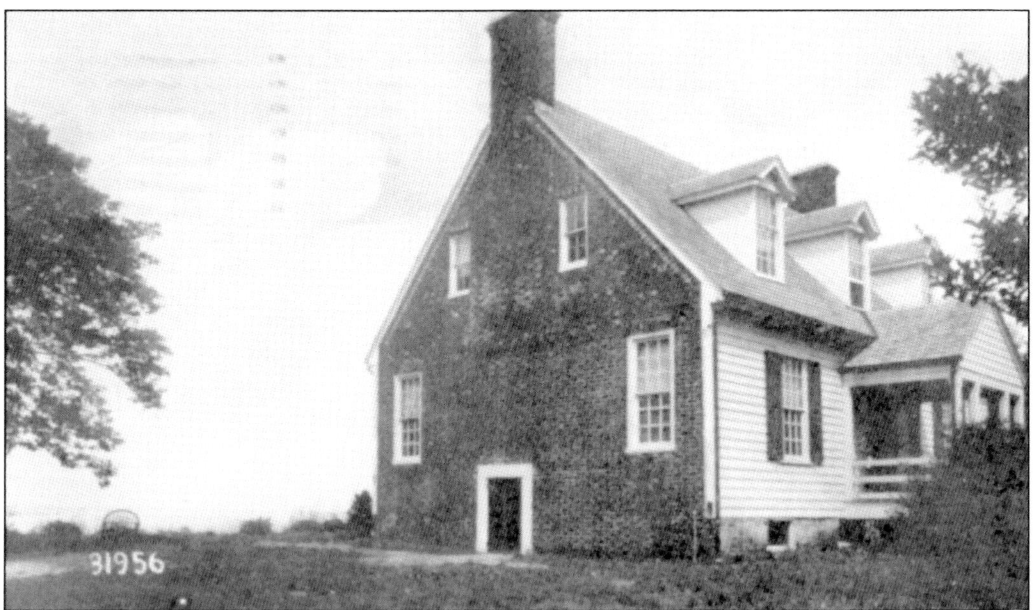

The Pleasant Point estate was patented by William Edwards in 1657. The house sits on a high hill and offers scenic views of the James River for about 15 miles. The location is directly across the river from the lower portion of Jamestown Island. During the Civil War, a Confederate signal station was located on the property.

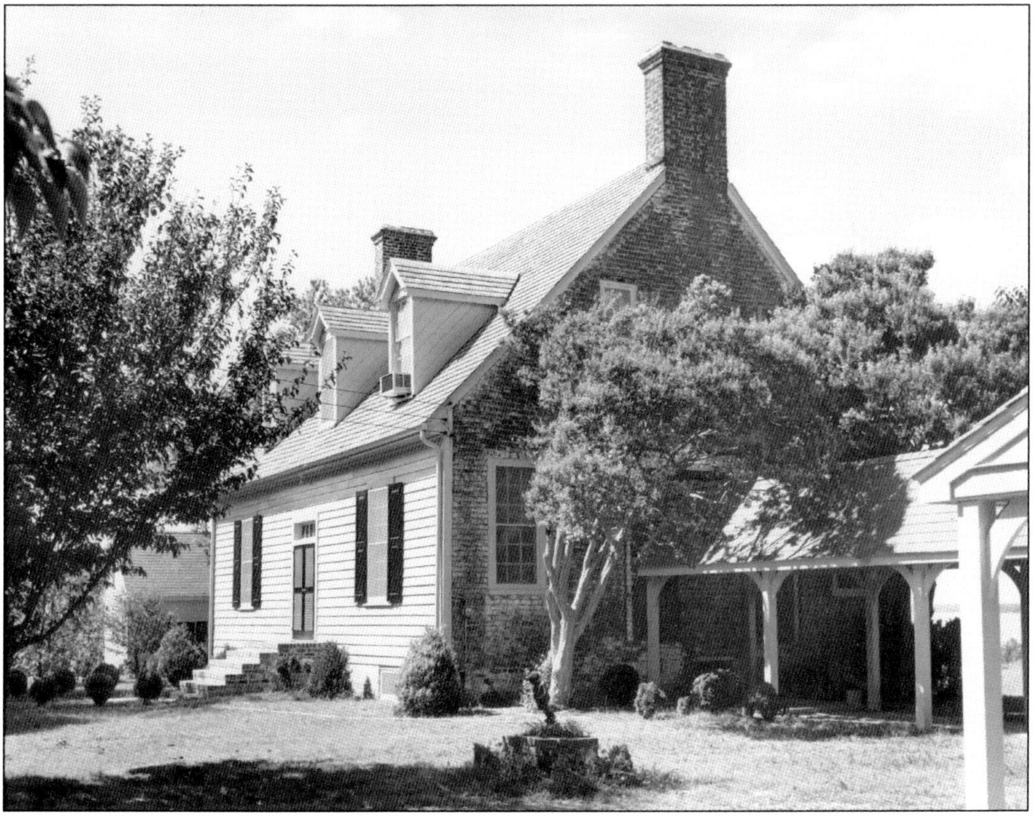

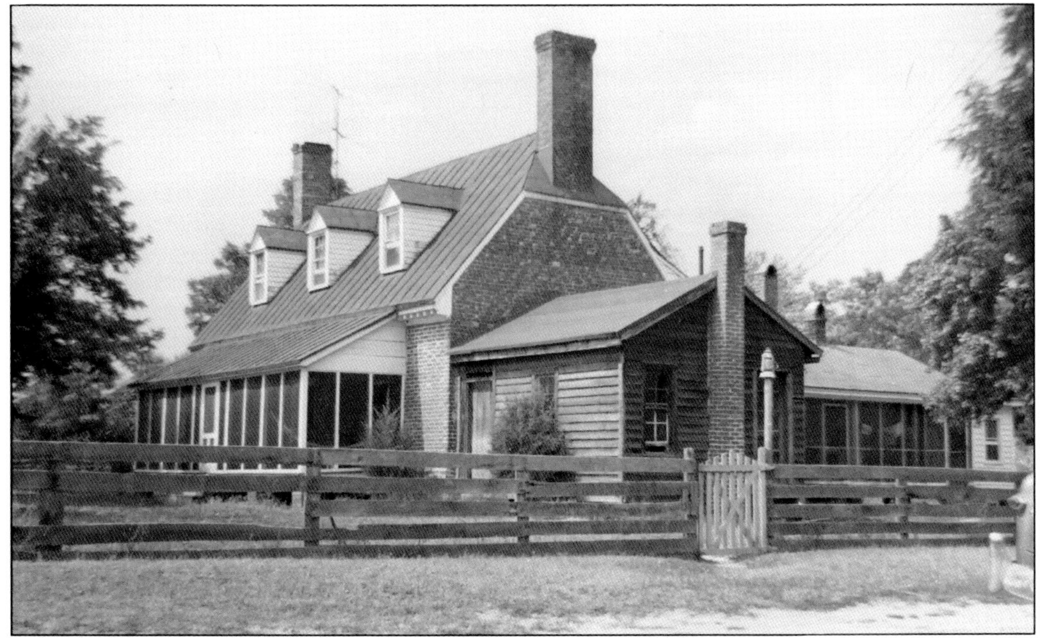

The Melville Plantation House is located off Route 636. It has been owned by the Binns, Faulcon, and Savedge families.

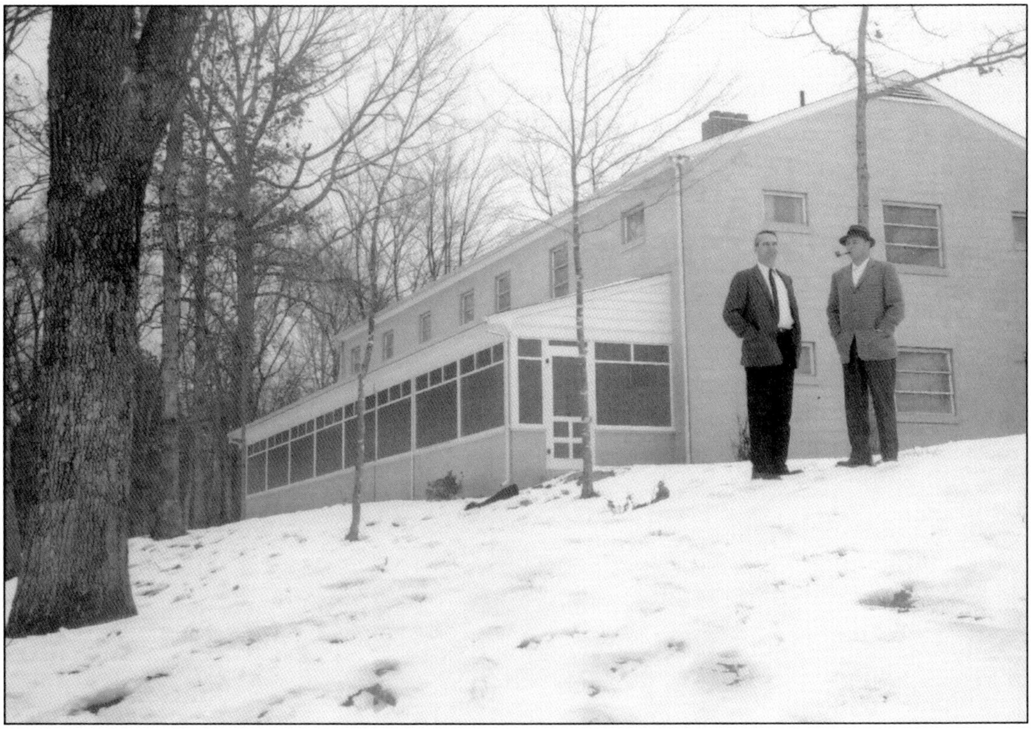

Before the Brown and Williamson Tobacco Company closed operations in Petersburg, management personnel owned a retreat and training facility in Surry. The structure was built on Gray's Creek, and according to a March 17, 1960, article in the *Richmond News Leader* by Courtney Ward, the informal rural setting was perfect for management seminars.

Two

Farming and Businesses

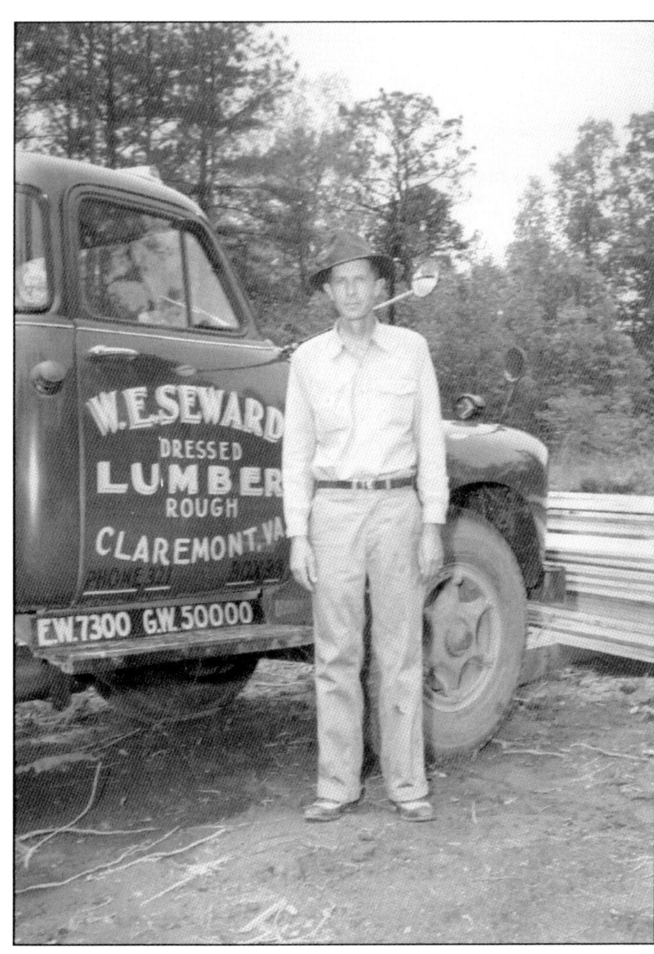

William E. Seward is pictured with his 1954 Chevy truck. He founded Seward Lumber Company in the 1930s. The company has been a major employer in the Spring Grove/ Claremont area since it began operations. (Courtesy of Troilen G. Seward.)

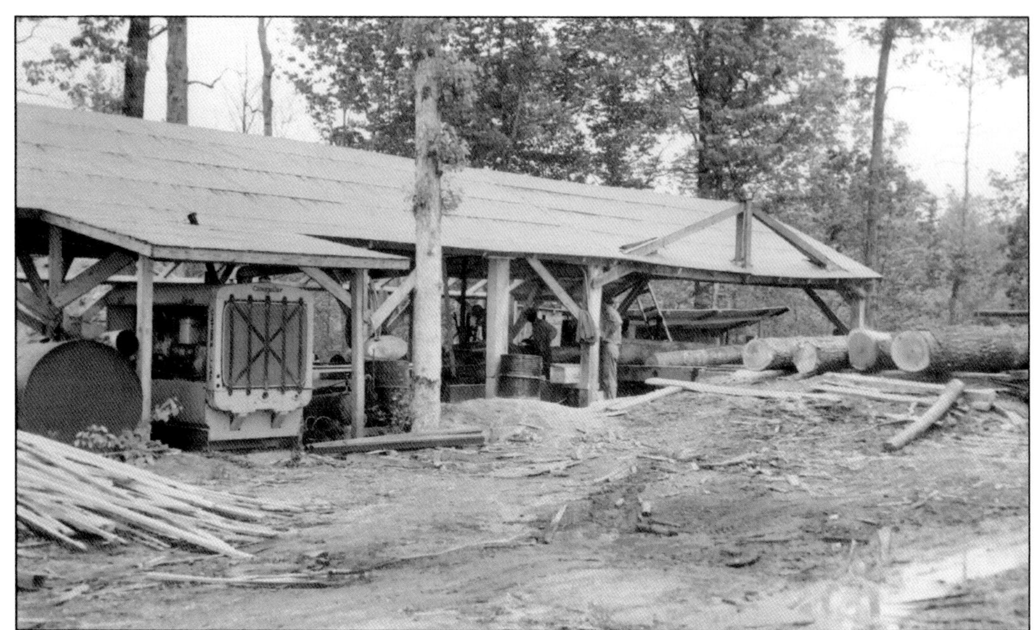

This photograph was taken in May 1953 when the Seward Lumber Company began using the newly developed Caterpillar D13000 Power Unit in its milling operations. The new equipment saved up to 40 percent. Mill workers were able to process between 15,000 and 20,000 feet of hardwood each day. On the far right, logs are pictured entering the cutting station. (Courtesy of Troilen G. Seward.)

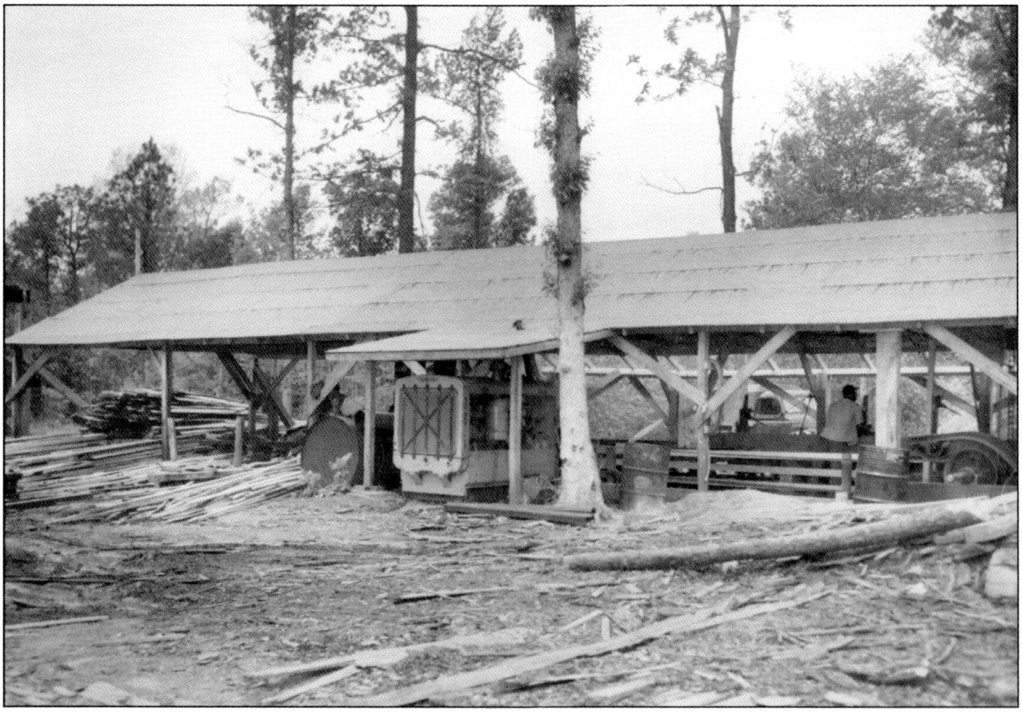

On the far left of this image, the finished product emerges from the conveyor belt. (Courtesy of Troilen G. Seward.)

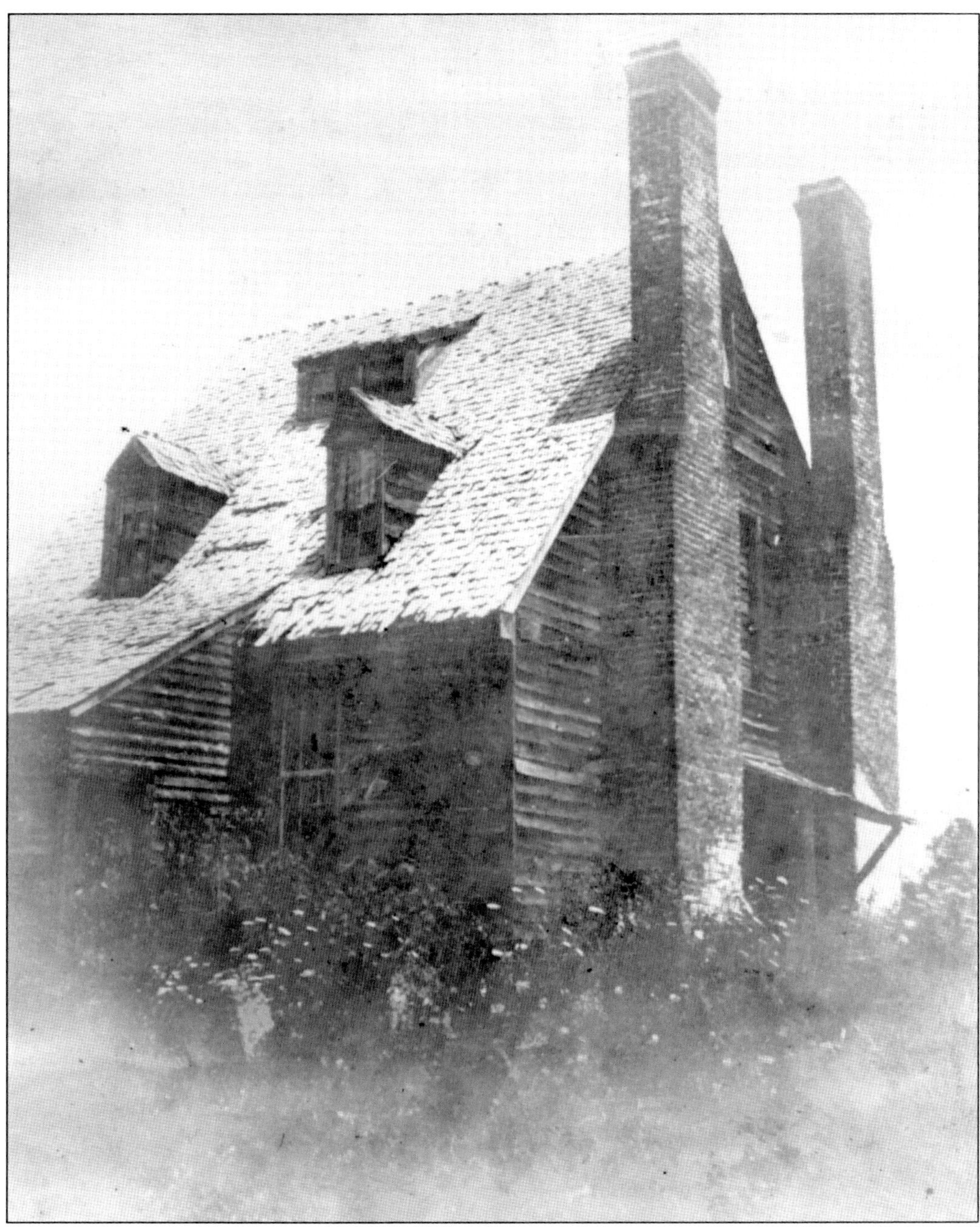

Parker's Tavern at Cabin Point was owned by John James Parker. It was located on Old Stage Road and served as an overnight resting place for stagecoach travelers, the drivers, and horses on the journey from Suffolk to Petersburg.

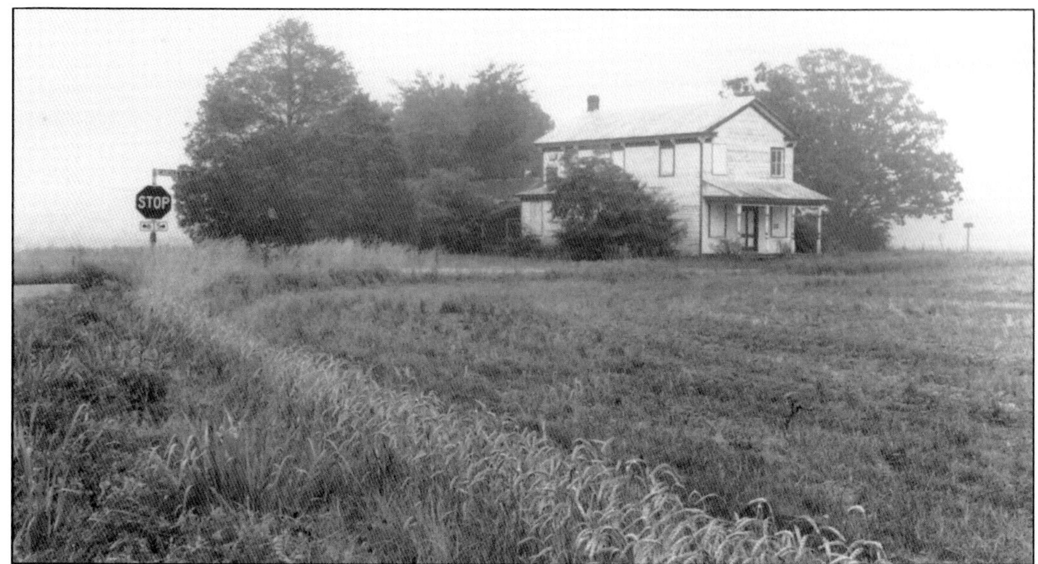

Shown in a morning mist and before major renovations were completed, the abandoned Rogers' Store at Carsley was donated to the historical society in 1999 by Becky Rogers and her son John. The Rogers' Store was a prominent local establishment from the time it opened in 1827 until it closed in 1952. It is located at the intersection of Routes 615 and 612. During its 130 years, it acted as an early post office, pharmacy, repair shop, publishing company, lumber company, chemical company, and telephone company. The store was the center of the community. It is now listed in the National Register of Historic Places.

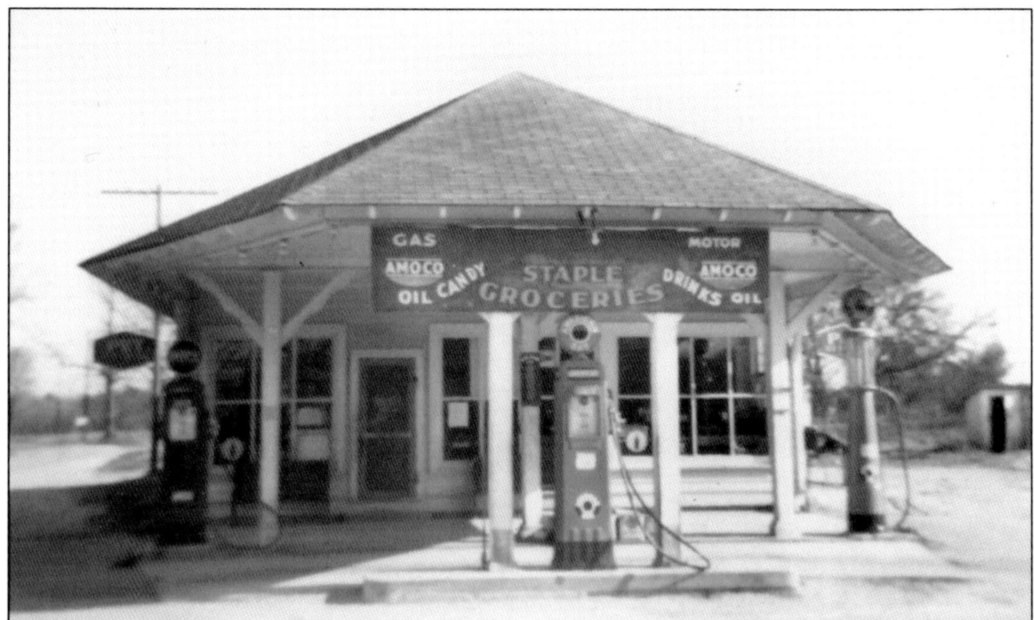

In the 1940s, there was enough traffic and movement in Spring Grove to support at least two "convenience" stores. Pictured here is a service station/general merchandise store operated by the Haff family. Later in the 1950s and 1960s, it was known as Cofers Store. Residents could get the general merchandise they needed, local game offered for sale from hunters and fishermen, and all the latest news.

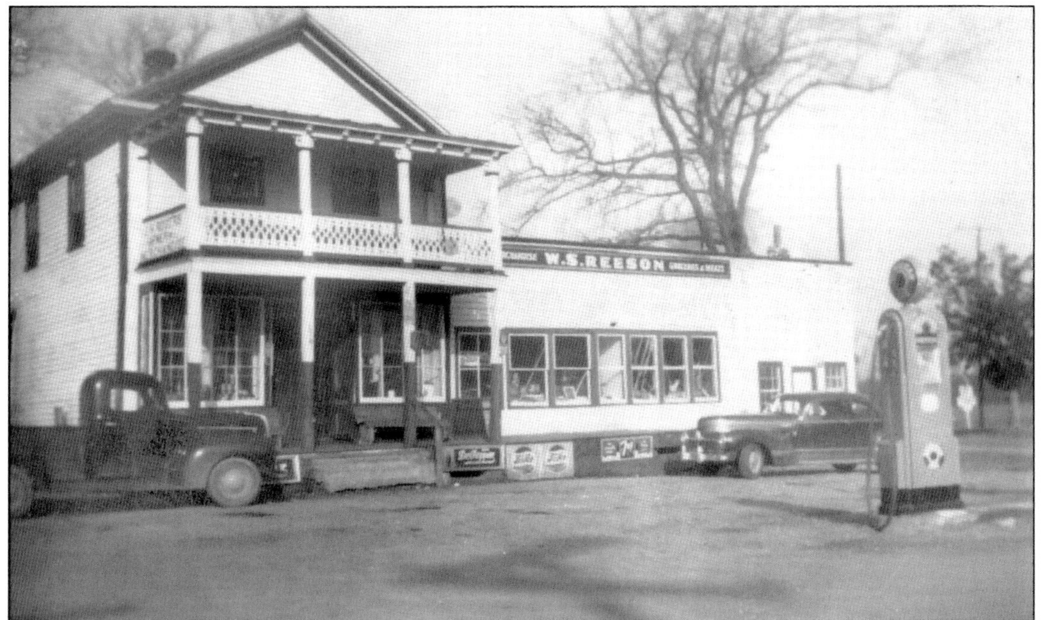

In March 1948, this photograph was taken of the W.S. Reeson general merchandise store (also know as the Spring Grove Store) at Spring Grove. The earliest known owner was the Baugh family, and the village was known as Baugh's Store. The name was later changed to Spring Grove because of the many natural, freely flowing springs in the area. In the 1970s, H.H. Hardenberg built and operated a water-bottling plant at Spring Grove.

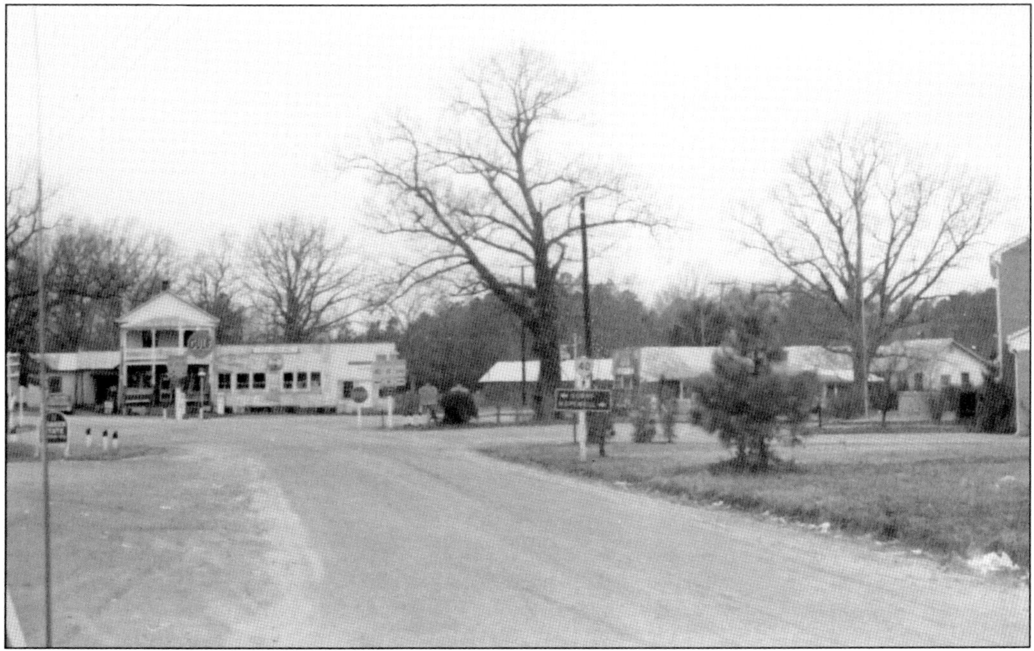

By December 1966, the Spring Grove Store was being operated by Frank and Cassie Fields. It was originally owned by the Baugh family. This image shows a north view on the road coming from Claremont. The store had living quarters on the second floor and behind the facility. It was torn down in the late 1960s. (Courtesy of Gordon "Bo" Bohannan.)

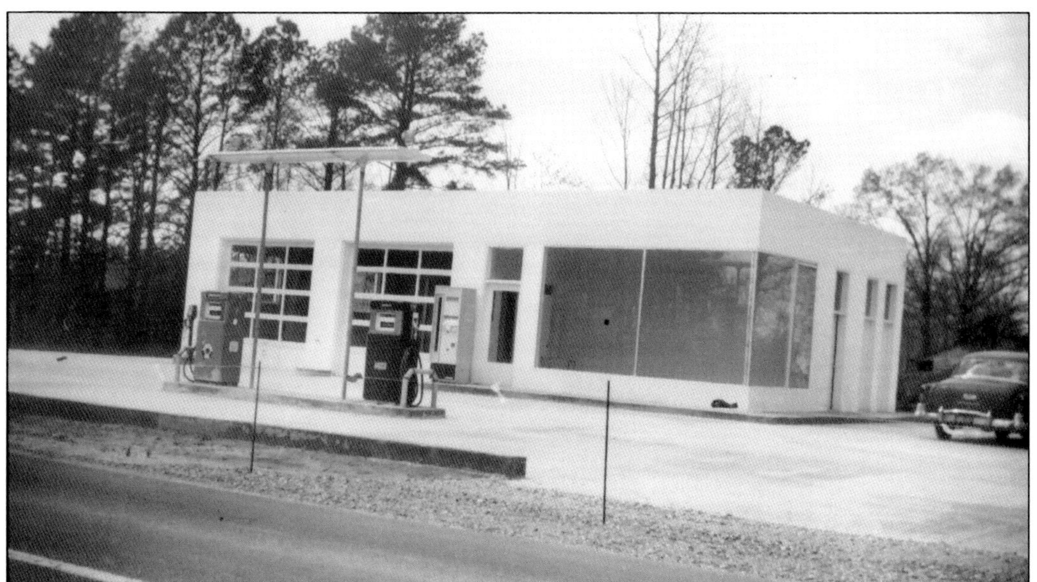

The local Amoco service station in the town of Surry was built by John A. "Jack" Savedge in the late 1950s. It changed ownership throughout the years and eventually closed in the early 1980s. (Courtesy of Mary Alma Savedge.)

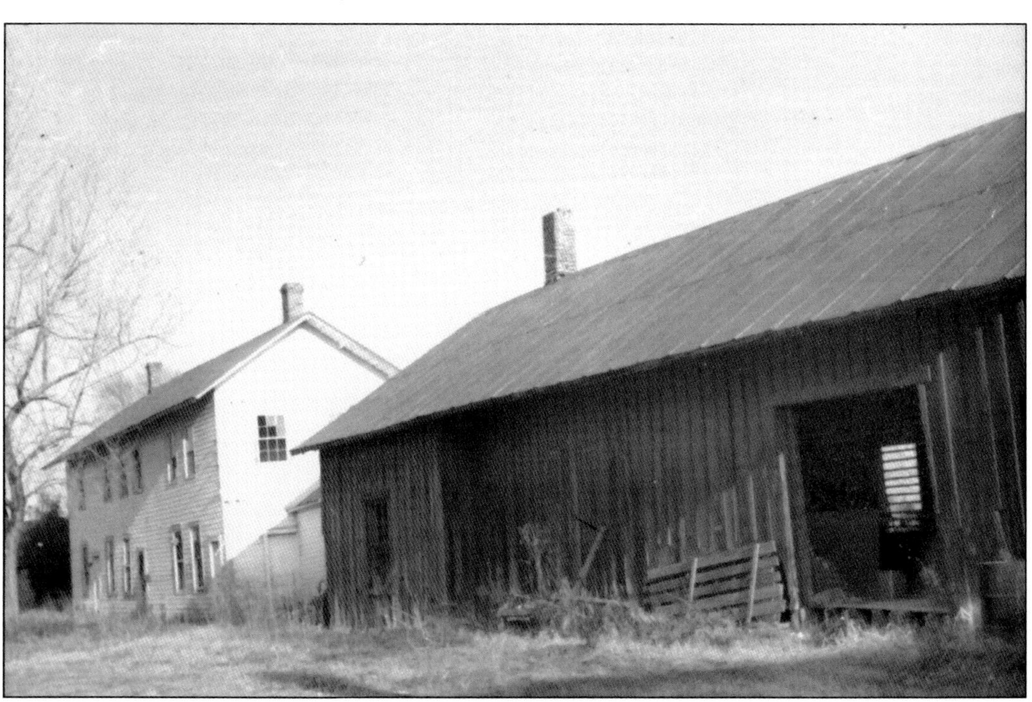

Located in the town of Dendron, the Surry Lumber Company was charted around January 1886 by R.T. Waters & Son of Baltimore, Maryland. Dendron became a company town and grew along with the lumber company. In 1906, the population had grown to 1,513, and the town had 298 dwellings, two hotels, 18 stores, and five churches. The company ceased operation on October 27, 1927. The building on the left is the Surry Lumber Company office, and next to it is the railway depot at Dendron. This photograph was taken in 1966, and both buildings were later torn down.

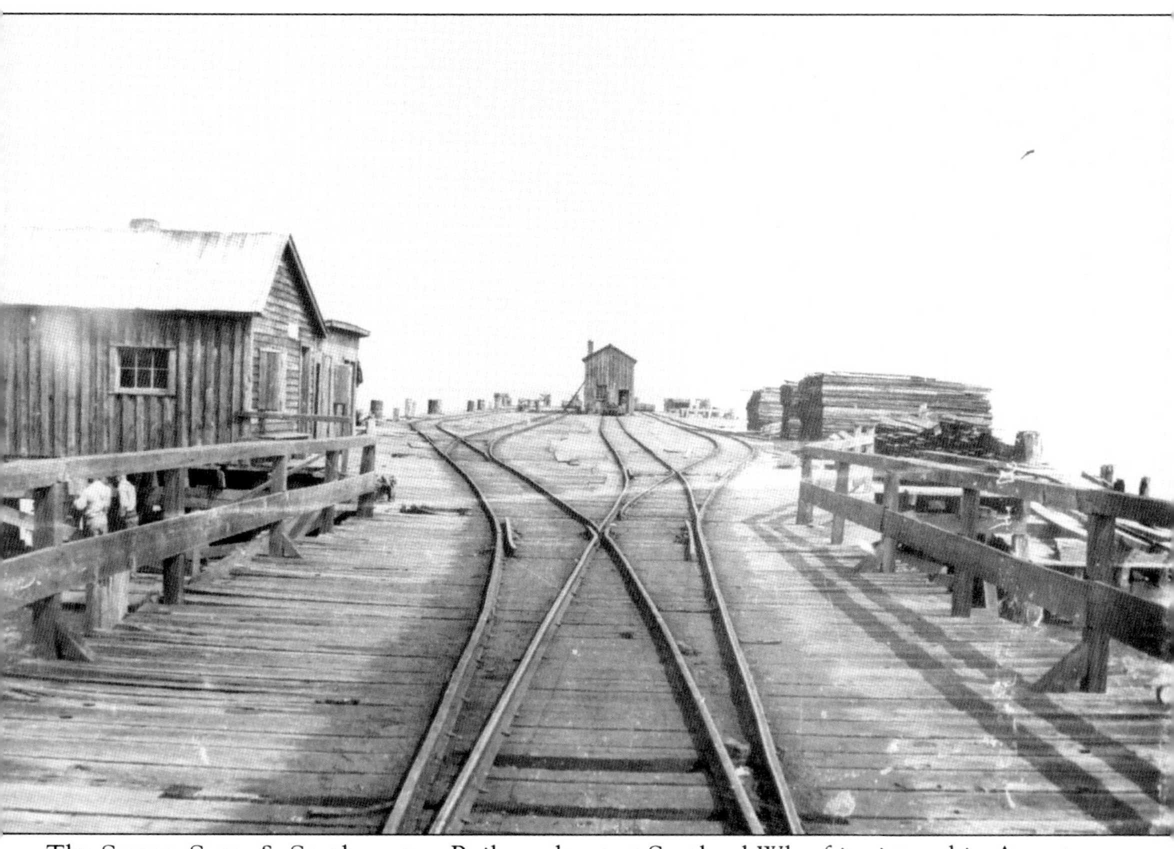

The Sussex, Surry & Southampton Railway depot at Scotland Wharf is pictured in August 1959.

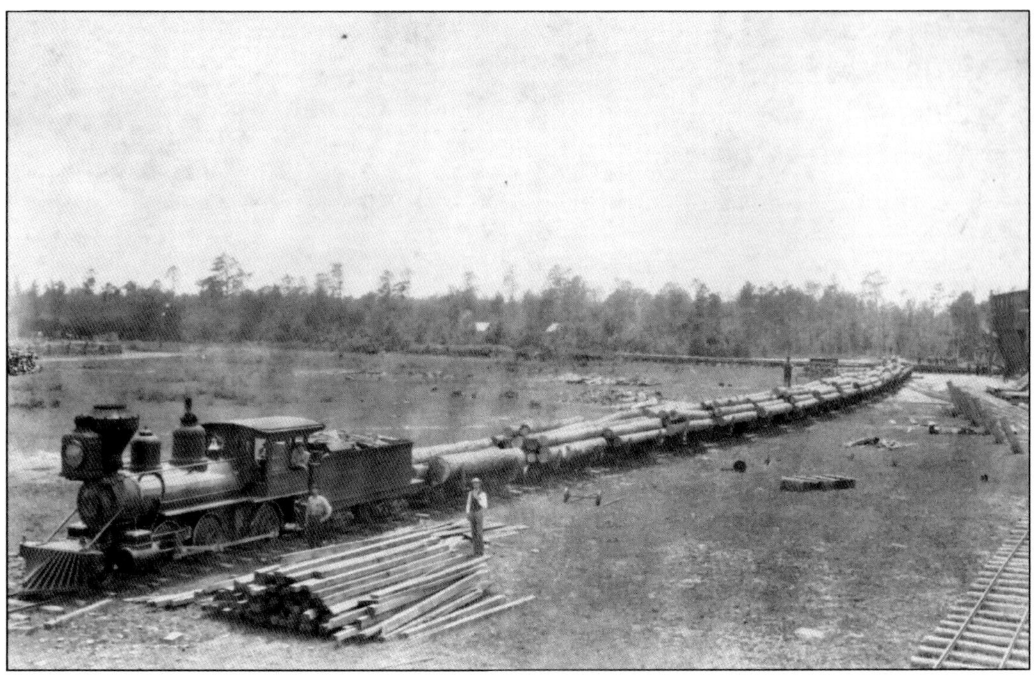

This panoramic view shows the Surry, Sussex & Southampton Railway that was operated by the Surry Lumber Company. The log train appears to be bringing a load of wood into the mill yard. (Courtesy of the Dendron Historical Society.)

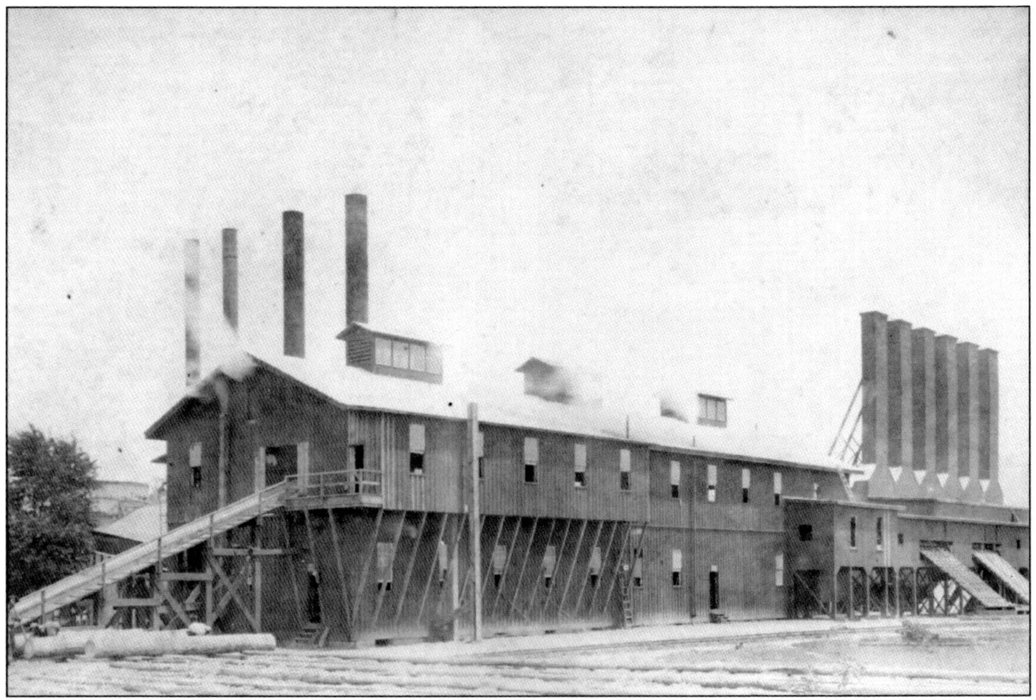

Featured here is the Surry Lumber Company's B Mill in about 1921. Logs were moved to the second floor where they were sawed into lumber and then transported to the dry kilns. (Courtesy of the Dendron Historical Society.)

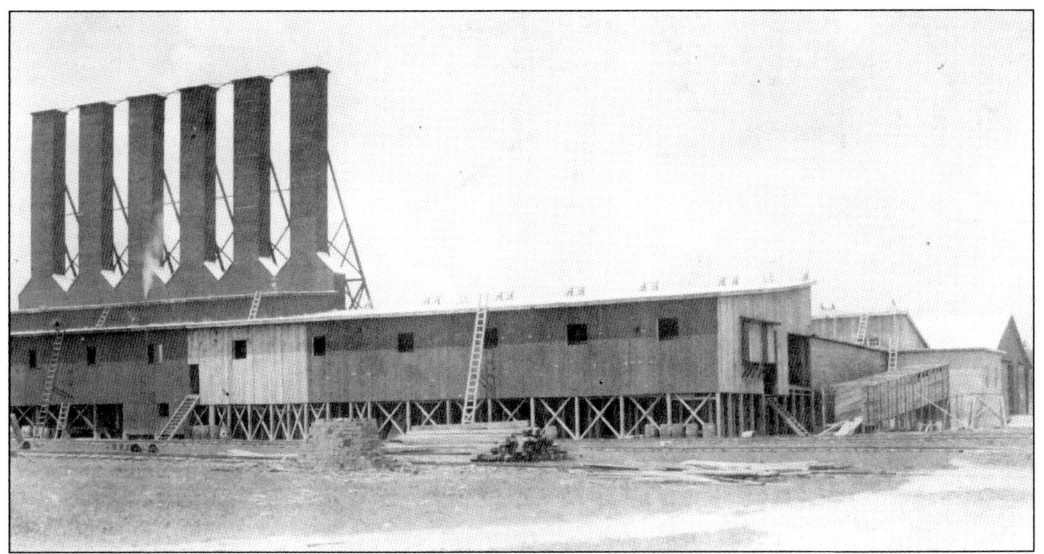

This is one of the mills operated by the Surry Lumber Company. They had three sawmills and two finishing mills. All that remains today are parts of the brick foundations and building supports. (Courtesy of the Dendron Historical Society.)

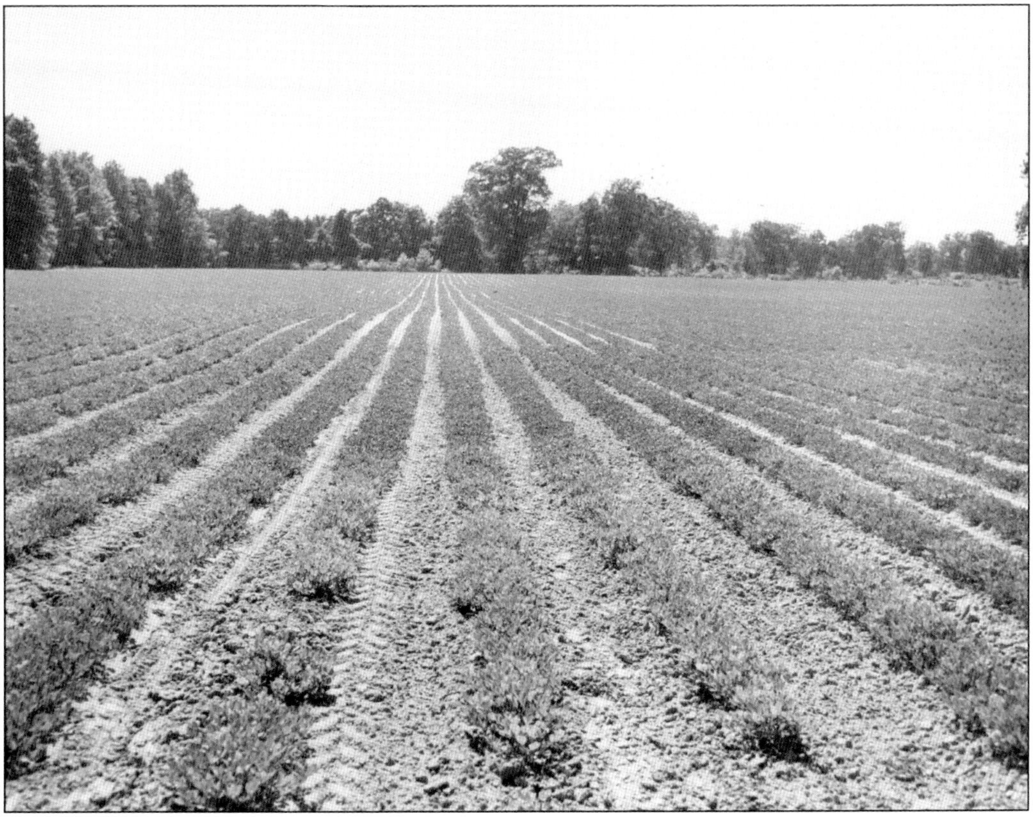

Pictured here is a field of peanuts, one of the important crops grown in Surry since the 1600s. The peanut grows on a plant that flowers above the ground and matures underground. Once matured, the peanuts are uprooted and dried.

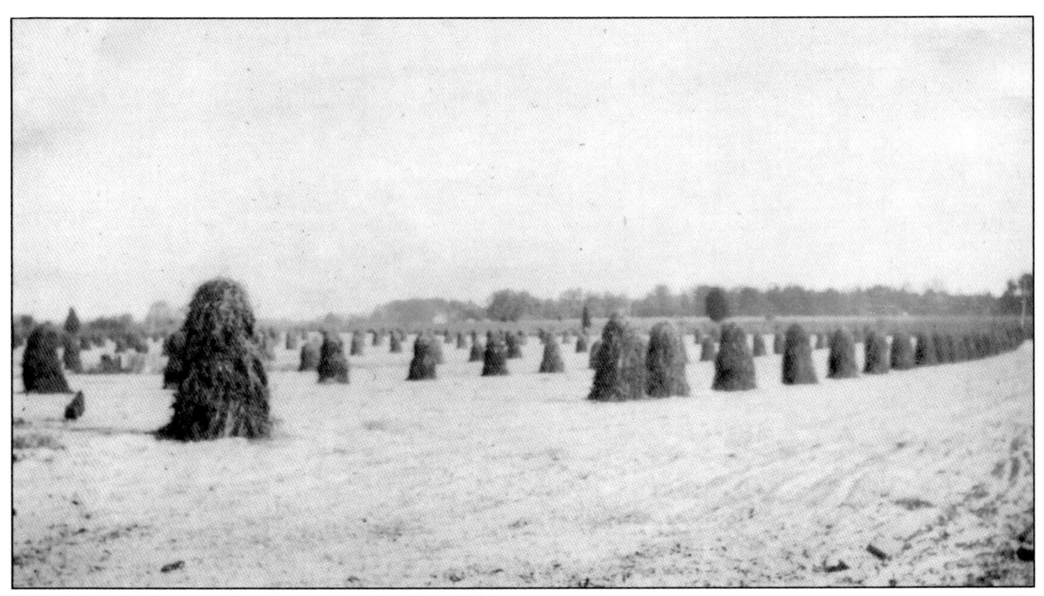

Peanut shocks were used to field-dry freshly dug peanuts before field-drying equipment was widely used. The shocks provided good air circulation for drying. (Courtesy of Mary Alma Savedge.)

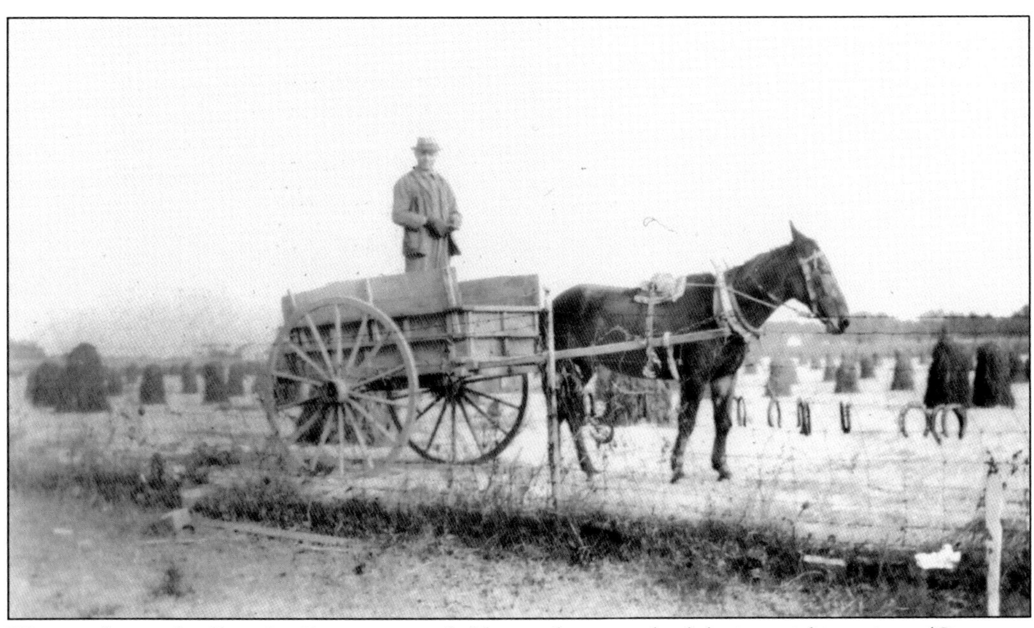

This worker at the Savedge Farm peanut field was photographed during picking time. (Courtesy of Mary Alma Savedge.)

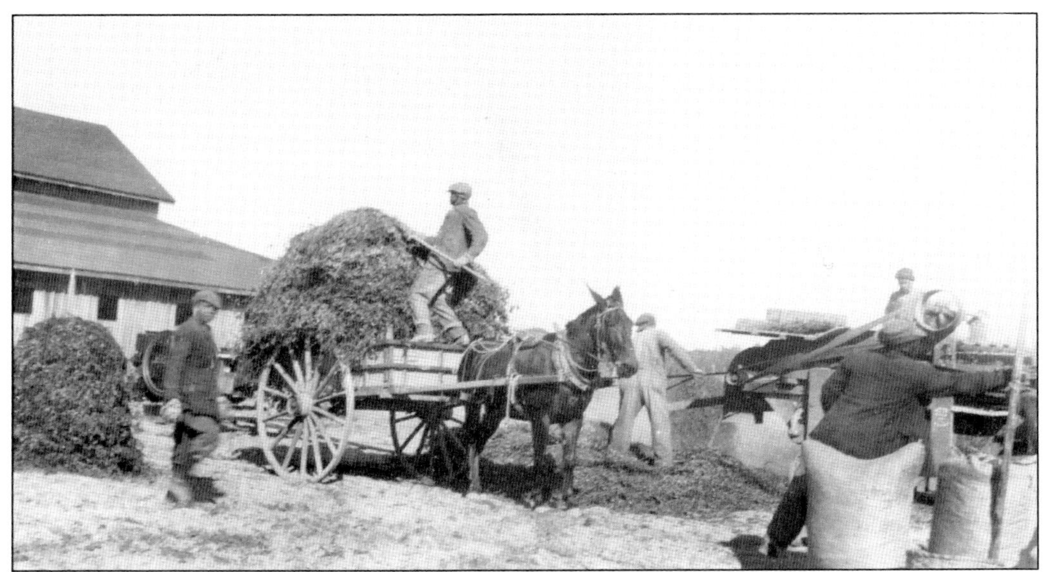

Workers on the Savedge Farm are loading a cart with peanut vines and moving them to the peanut-picking machine. This was hard, dirty work, and workers sometimes would be injured using the machinery. (Courtesy of Mary Alma Savedge.)

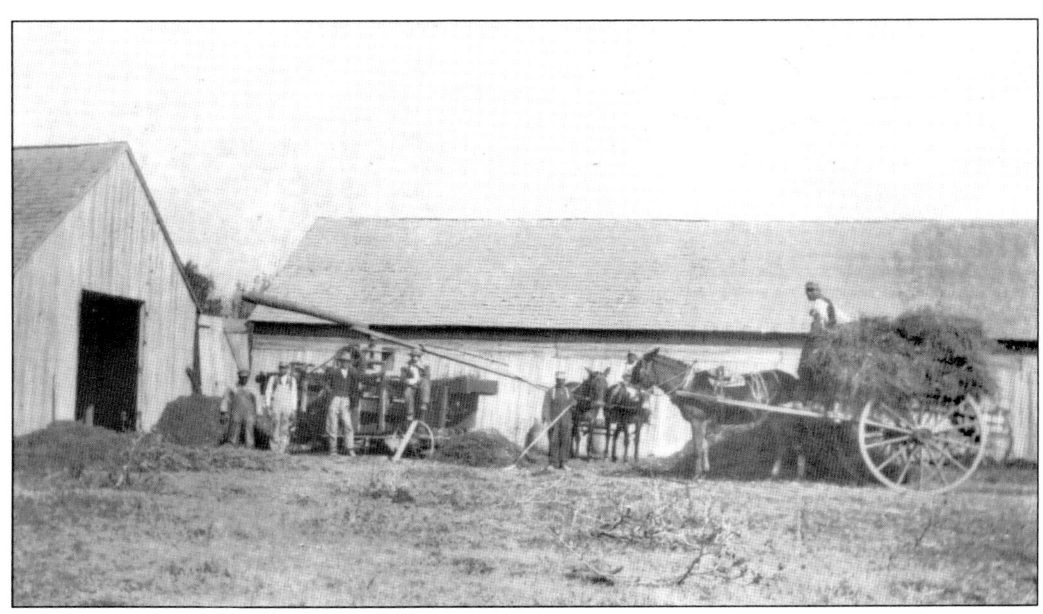

Here, workers stop for a photograph before unloading peanut vines. The vines were often used as a food source and bedding for farm animals. (Courtesy of Mary Alma Savedge.)

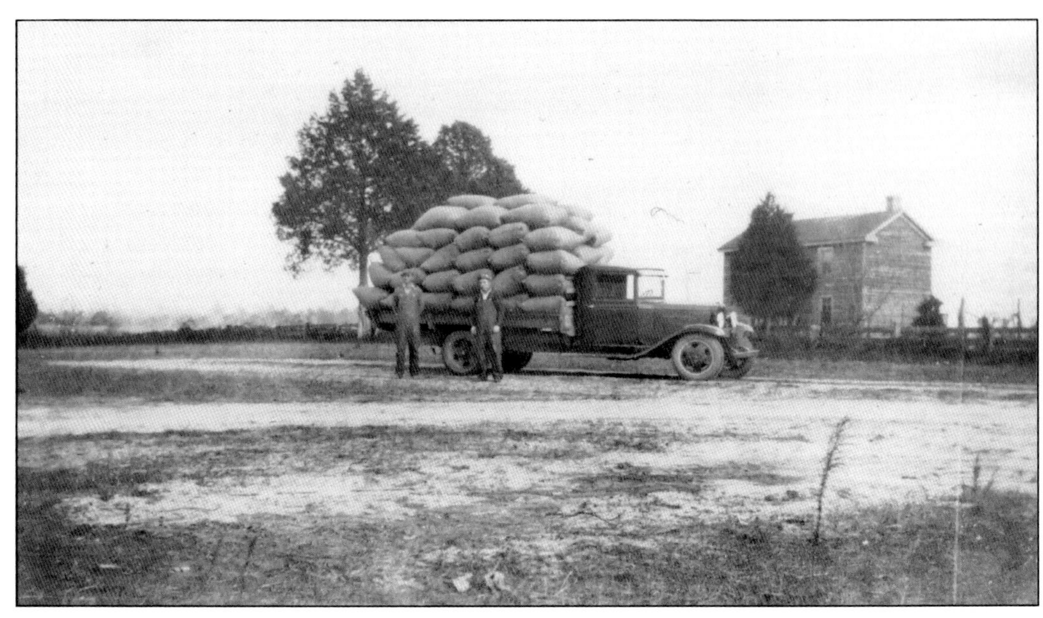

Jack Savedge and Jimmie Rowell stop for the camera before taking the freshly bagged peanuts to be sold. (Both, courtesy of Mary Alma Savedge.)

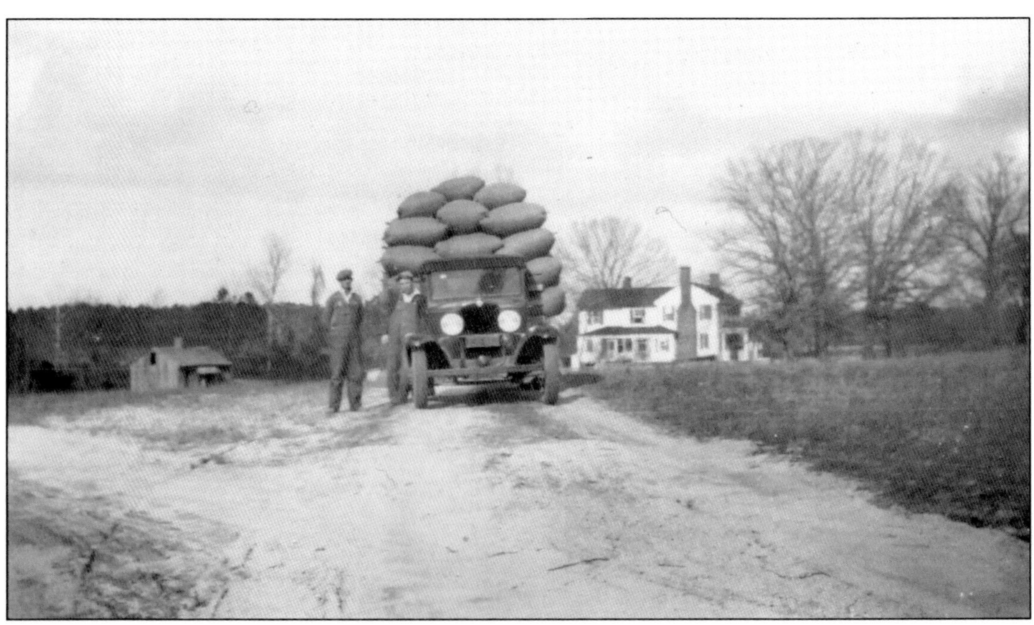

In the early 1930s, the Virginia Carolina Chemical Corporation was the fourth largest producer of fertilizer in the United States. (Courtesy of Mary Grace Padgett.)

TIME PRICES: Time prices are determined by adding 10% flat to the CASH SALE PRICE as follows:

As of May 1—On shipments made prior thereto and after the preceding December 1

As of July 1—On shipments made between the preceding April 30 and July 1

As of October 1—On shipments made between the preceding June 30 and October 1

As of December 1—On shipments made between the preceding Sept. 30 and Dec. 1.

Plus interest at 6% per annum beginning with the date the time price becomes effective.

FREIGHT DIFFERENTIALS: Where the lowest trucking rate as figured below from the nearest port to the city or town nearest to or in which buyer's farm is located is less than $3.75 per ton, deduct from the price per ton the difference between $3.75 and the truck rate so figured.

DELIVERY: At our option, deliveries will be made by rail or truck. If delivery is made by truck from our factories we will pay hauling expense on the following basis:

.75 per ton for a distance up to 15 miles
1.00 per ton between 15 and 25 miles
1.50 per ton between 25 and 40 miles
1c per ton per mile for additional mileage.

Use shortest highway mileage from our factory to destination. If hauled by or for our agent, mileage will be figured from our factory to agent's place of business.

When delivery is taken by consumer from a factory not located at a port, boat landing, rail siding, or agent's warehouse, deduct 75c per ton.

When delivery is made to consumer's premises from a railhead, boatlanding or warehouse, as distinguished from delivery direct from factory, and the transportation cost (in no case to exceed the lowest published tariff rates or the trucker's maximum trucking rate) to the consumer's premises from the railroad station nearest thereto exceeds 75c per ton, such excess may be added to the consumer's delivered price.

BAGS: When bags other than those shown on the reverse side of this price list are used, add to the consumer's 100-lb. paper bag cash prices the following:

For 100-lb. Burlap Bags add $1.80 per ton
For 100-lb. Cotton Bags add 2.80 per ton
For 125-lb. Burlap Bags add 1.50 per ton
For 125-lb. Cotton Bags add 2.50 per ton

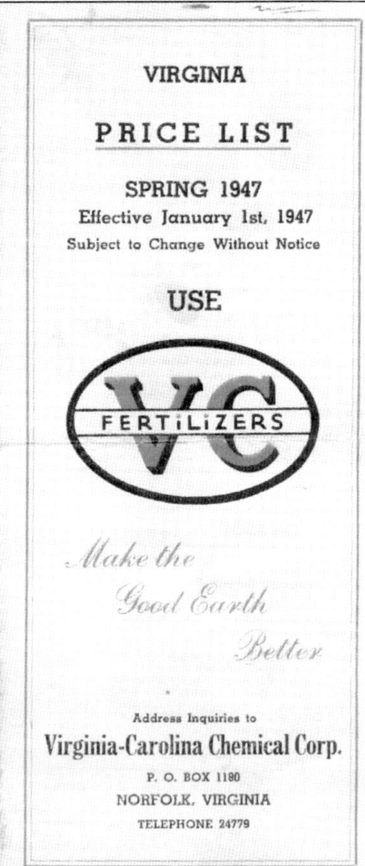

VIRGINIA

PRICE LIST

SPRING 1947

Effective January 1st, 1947

Subject to Change Without Notice

USE

VC FERTILIZERS

Make the Good Earth Better

Address Inquiries to

Virginia-Carolina Chemical Corp.

P. O. BOX 1180

NORFOLK, VIRGINIA

TELEPHONE 24779

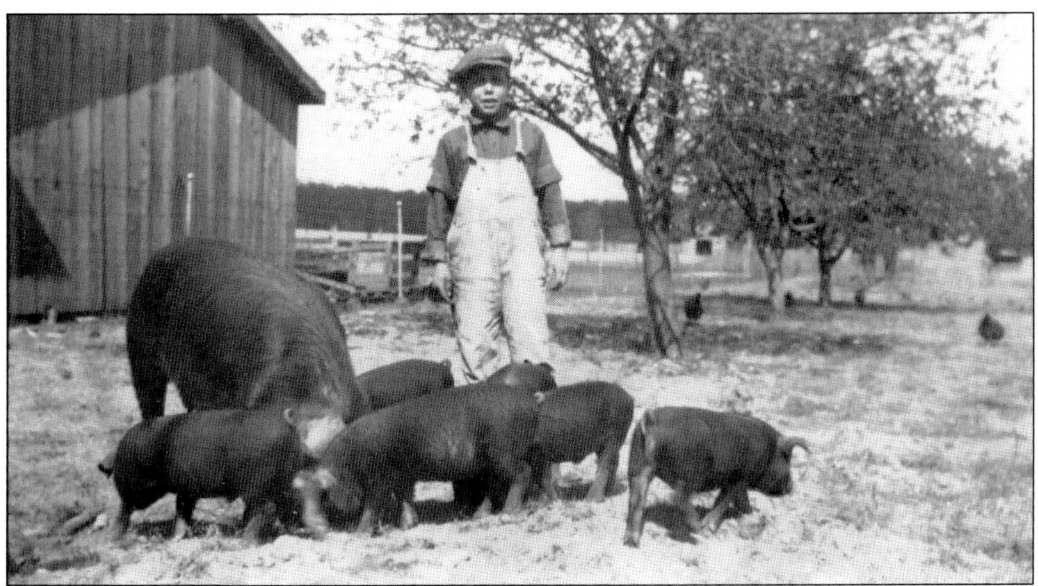

A young boy on the Savedge Farm is pictured with his prized pigs in the 1920s. (Courtesy of Mary Alma Savedge.)

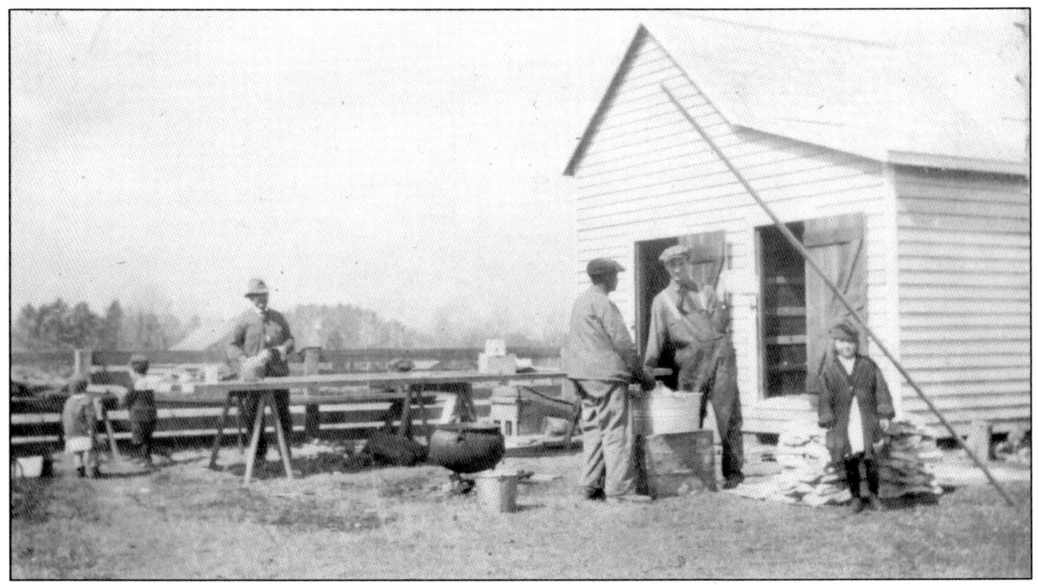

Pictured during "hog killing" time with several Savedge children, from left to right are George A. Savedge, Willie Winfield, and Nicolas Savedge. This was another time when farm neighbors helped each other. Hogs were killed, butchered, smoked, preserved, and used as the major meat sources for the family. (Courtesy of Mary Alma Savedge.)

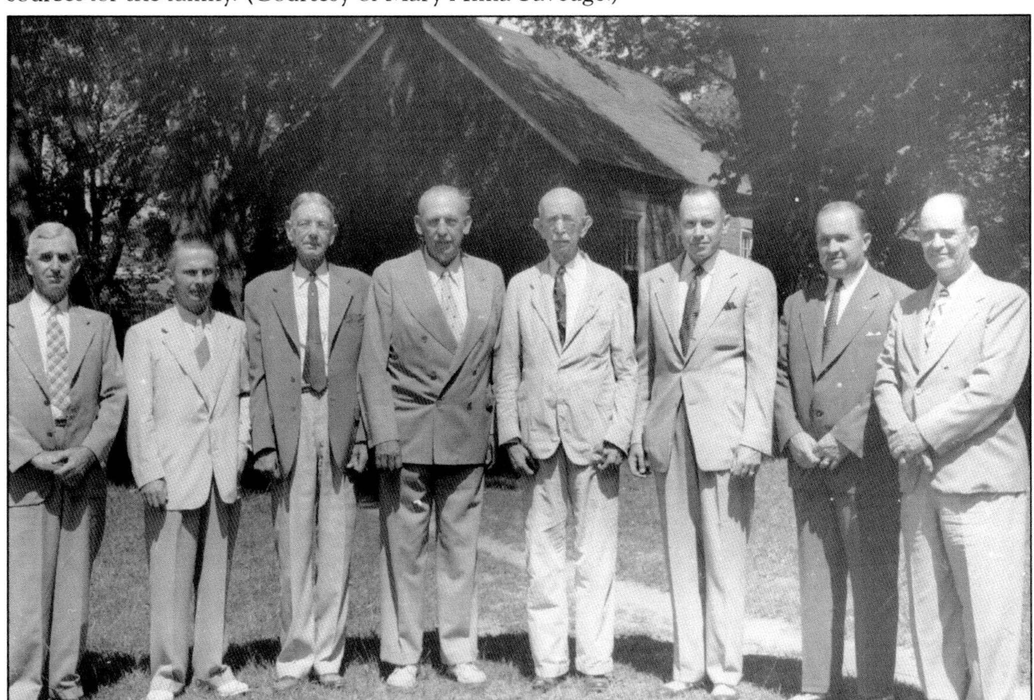

Surry County government officials are pictured standing on the courthouse lawn in the early 1950s. From left to right are C.M. Ellis, supervisor from the Blackwater District and chairman of the board; Ernest W. Goodrich, attorney for the commonwealth; Gordon C. Berryman, commissioner of the revenue; A.H. Ochsner, supervisor from the Guilford District; S.B. Barham Jr., clerk; A.T. Sowder, treasurer; P.H. Cox, supervisor from the Cobham District, and E.O. Cockes, sheriff.

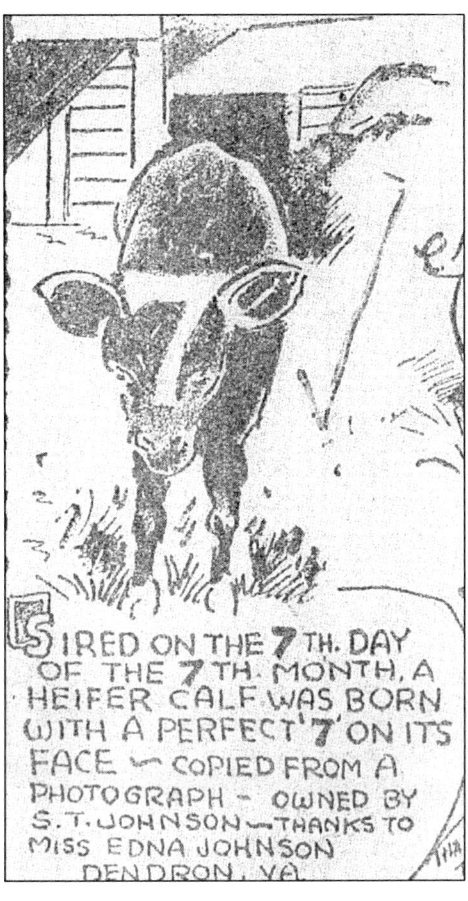

Edna Johnson, daughter of Sidney and Ruth Johnson, of Marl Spring Farm near Dendron, submitted this image of a calf born with a perfect *7* on its forehead. It was featured and won the weekly prize in "Old Dominion Oddities" by FoXo in the January 12, 1941, edition of the *Richmond Times-Dispatch*. (Both, courtesy of Robert L. Bartlett.)

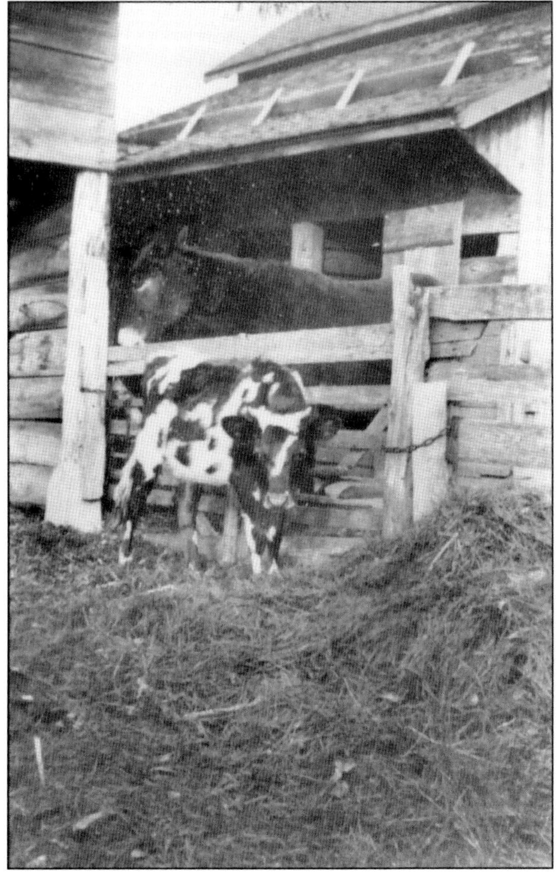

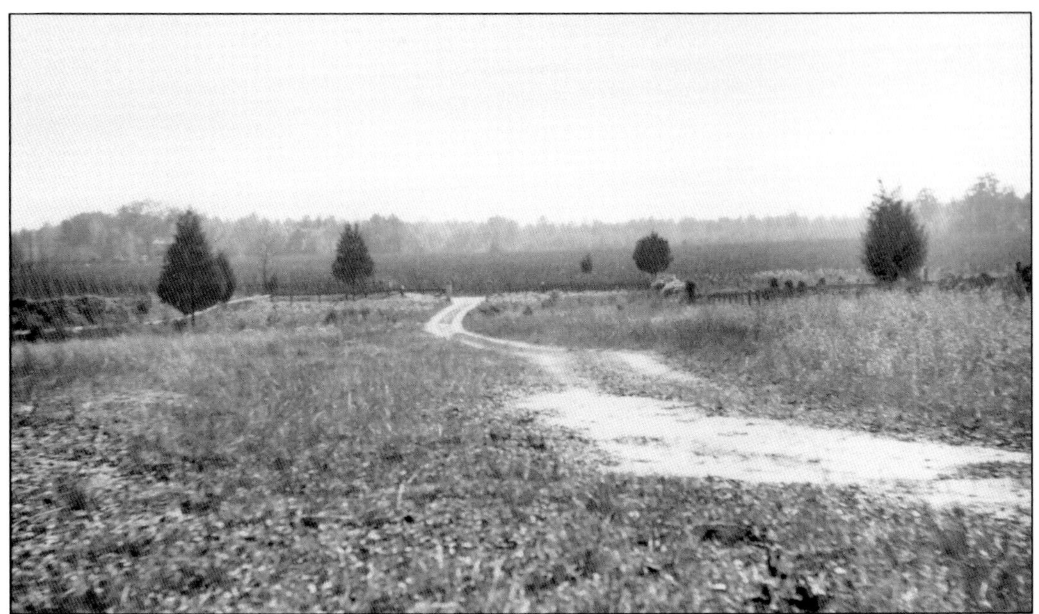

The peanut crop is shown in the field in front of the house at Marl Spring Farm in 1947. The driveway leads down to New Design Road. The house across the road on the left was built by Sidney Johnson for his wife's father, William Thomas Rogers. (C. Lawrence Bartlett photograph, courtesy of Robert L. Bartlett.)

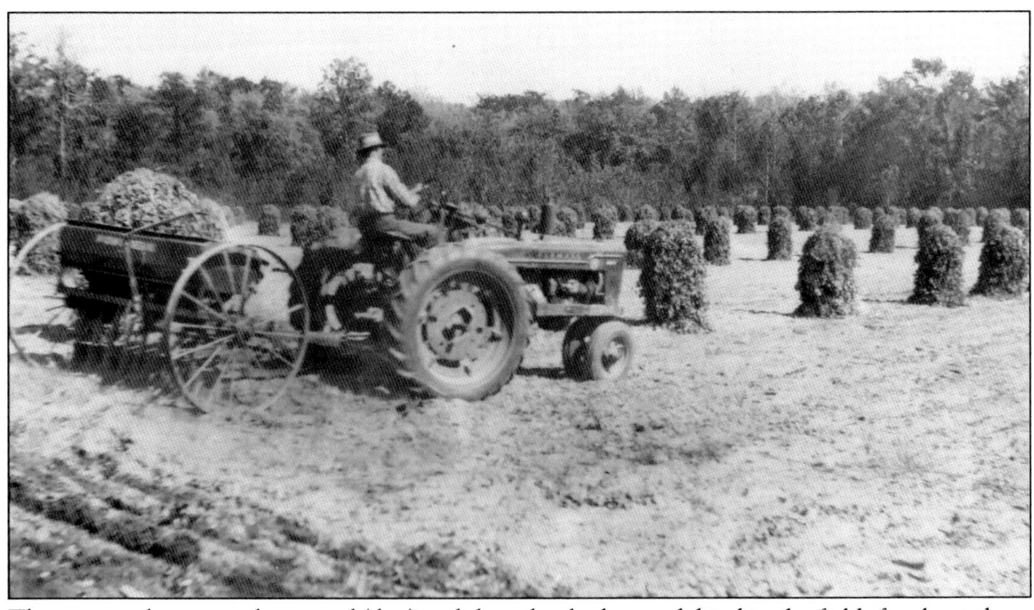

The peanut plants were harvested (dug) and then shocked up and dried in the fields for about three weeks before picking. In this view, the shocked and dried plants are being gathered and moved to a central location in the field. The peanuts were then separated (picked) from the plants using a mechanical picker. (C. Lawrence Bartlett photograph, courtesy of Robert L. Bartlett.)

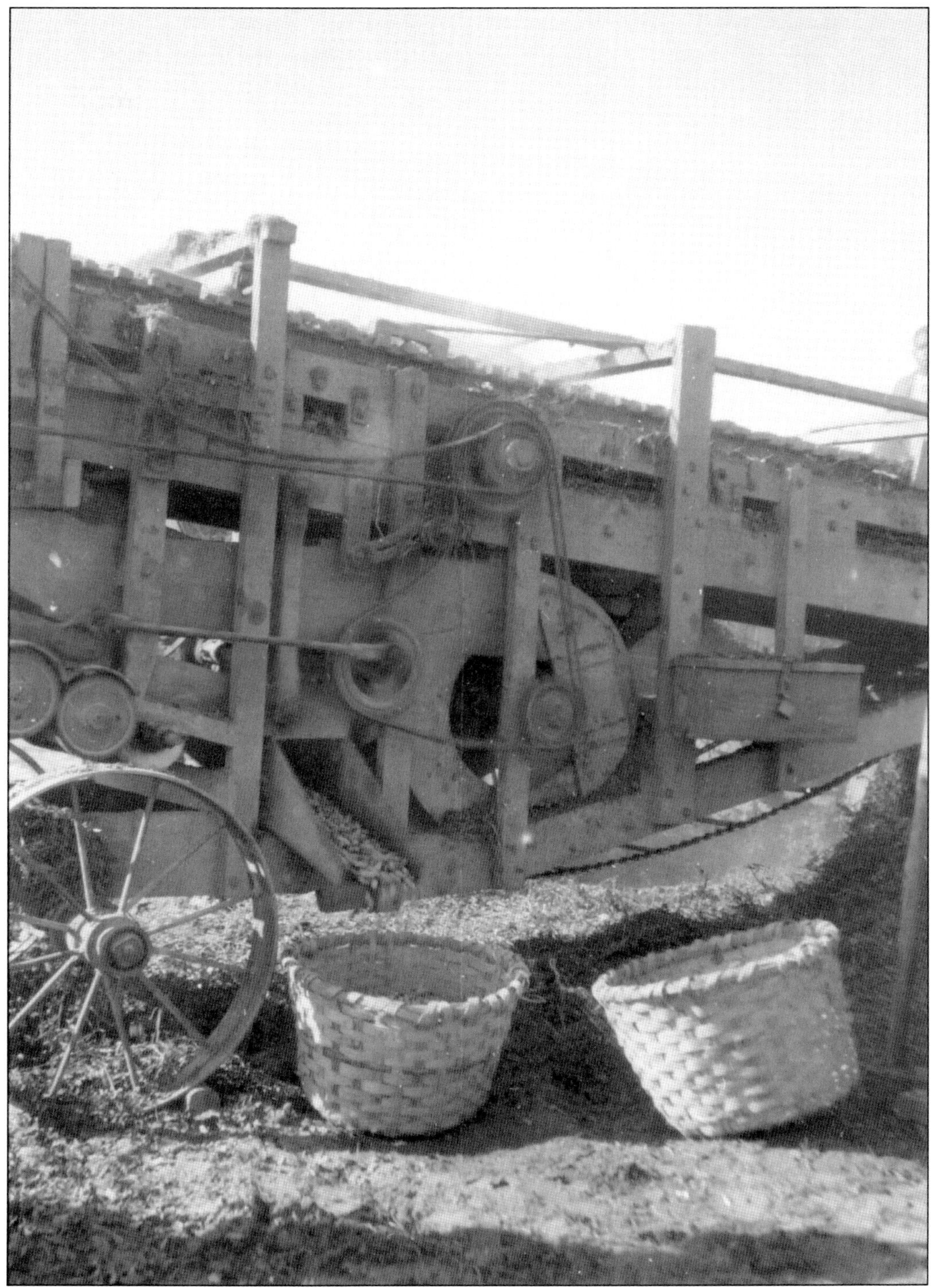

This artistic photograph shows a mechanical peanut picker at Marl Spring Farm in 1942. The dried plants and peanuts were fed into the picker, and the peanuts fell into the baskets. They were then poured into burlap bags for market. (C. Lawrence Bartlett photograph, courtesy of Robert L. Bartlett.)

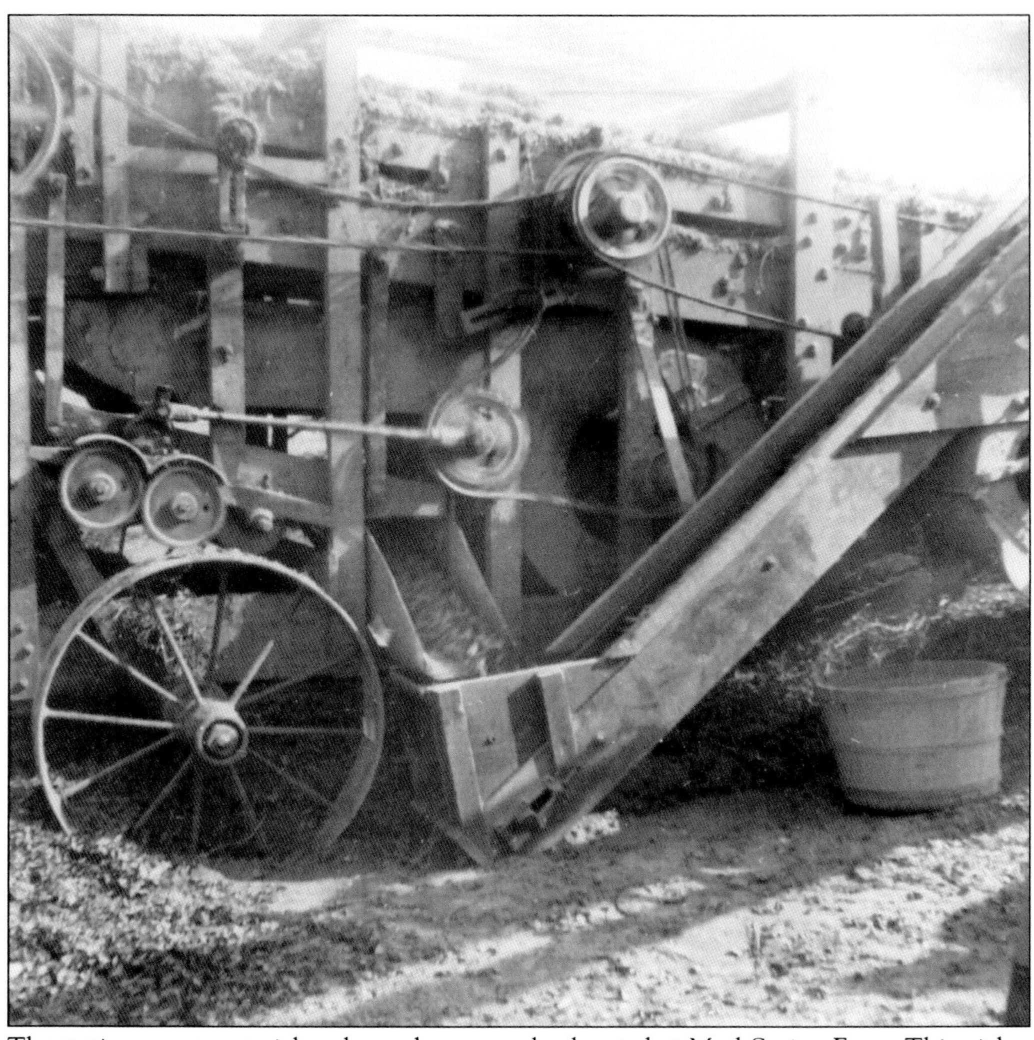

The stationary peanut picker shown here was also located at Marl Spring Farm. This picker was equipped with a conveyor belt that moved loose peanuts to a waiting truck that most likely transported them to the Planters Peanut Plant located in nearby Suffolk. (C. Lawrence Bartlett photograph, courtesy of Robert L. Bartlett.)

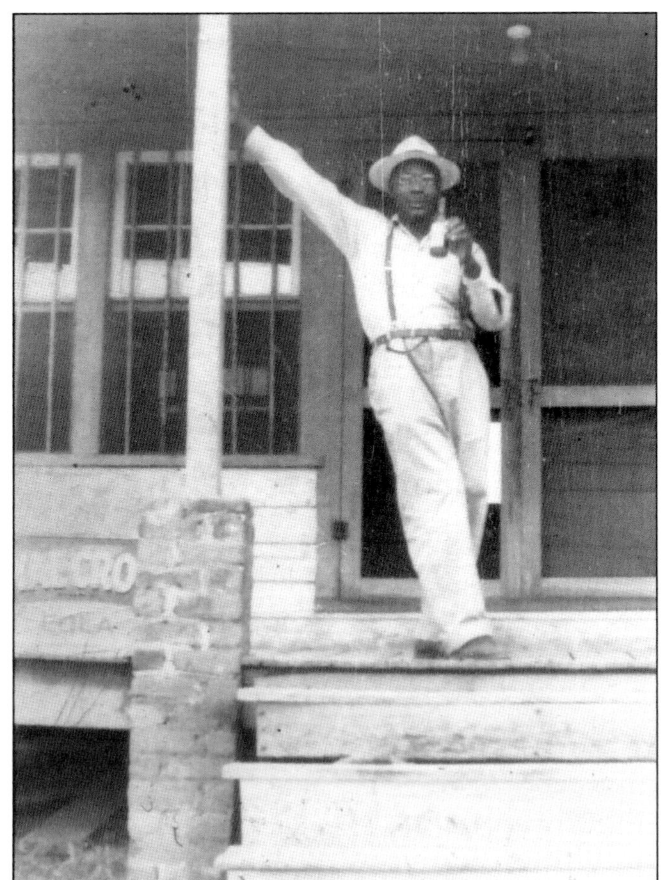

Robert Lee Holmes (1892–1980) established a general store in the Carsley community in the 1930s and ran the establishment until the late 1970s. Holmes was a descendant of Surry County freedmen and also operated a farm. The store was a favorite meeting and socializing place for the black community at Carsley. (Courtesy of James M. Harrison.)

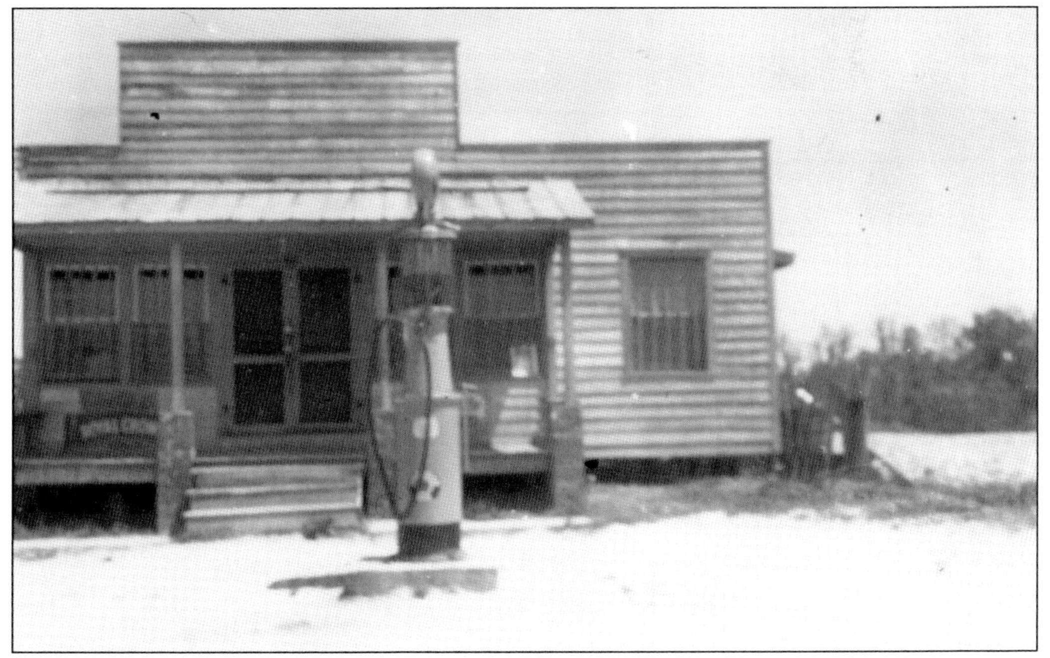

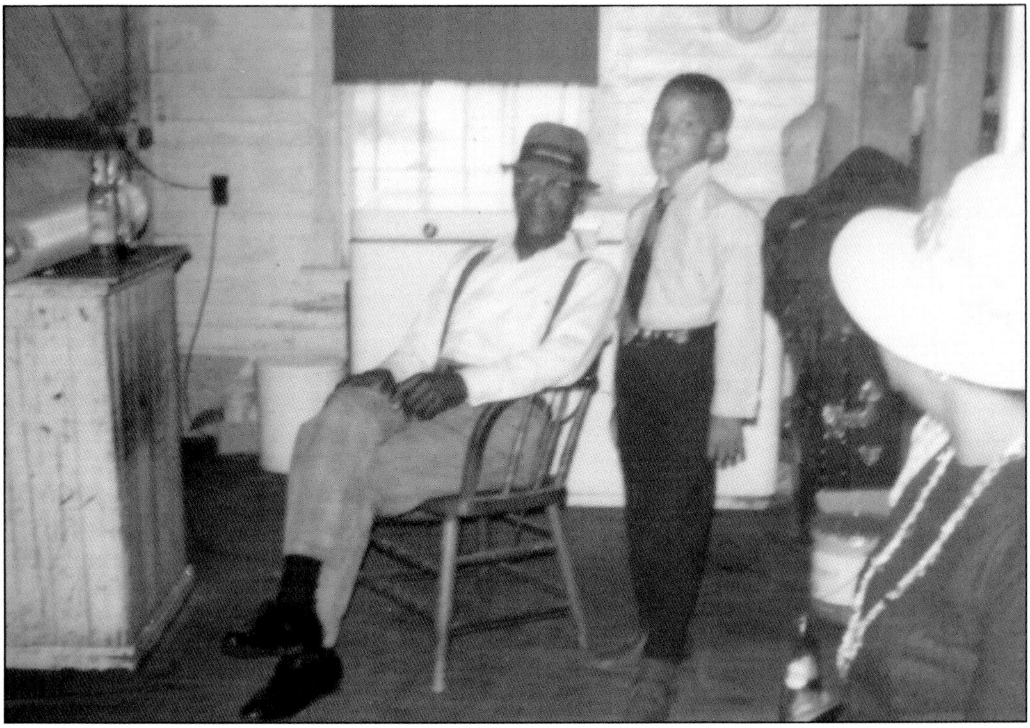

Robert Lee Holmes is pictured inside his store with great-grandson Benjamin Francis around 1969. Mabel Holmes, one of his seven daughters, is also pictured. Benjamin is the grandson of Holmes's daughter Essie Mae Holmes McQueen. He was visiting from Queens, New York, and Mabel from Newport News, Virginia. (Courtesy of James M. Harrison.)

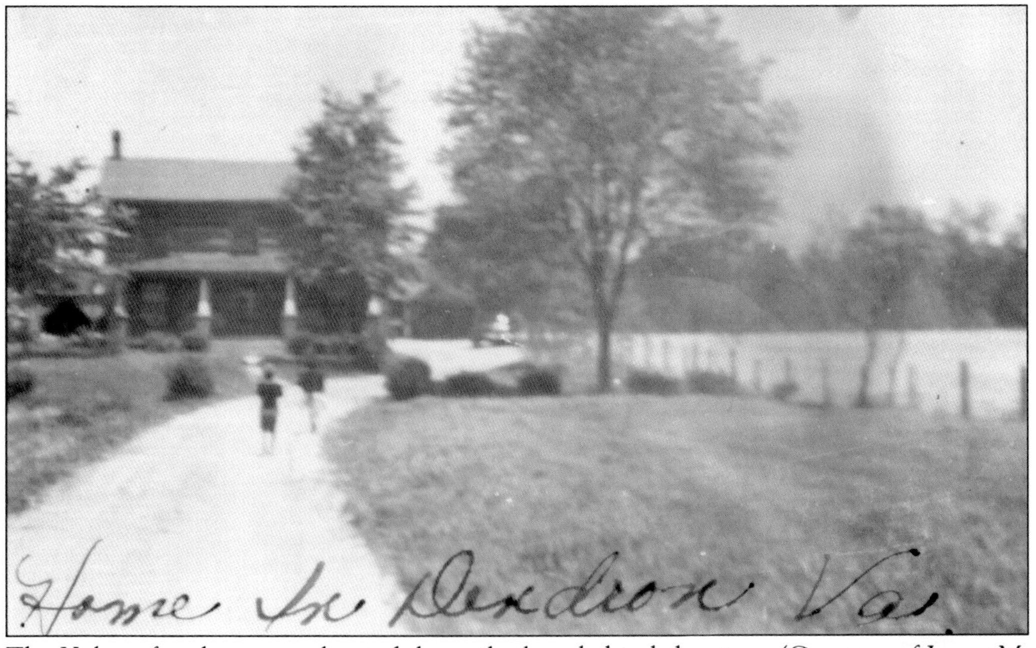

The Holmes farmhouse was located down the lane behind the store. (Courtesy of James M. Harrison.)

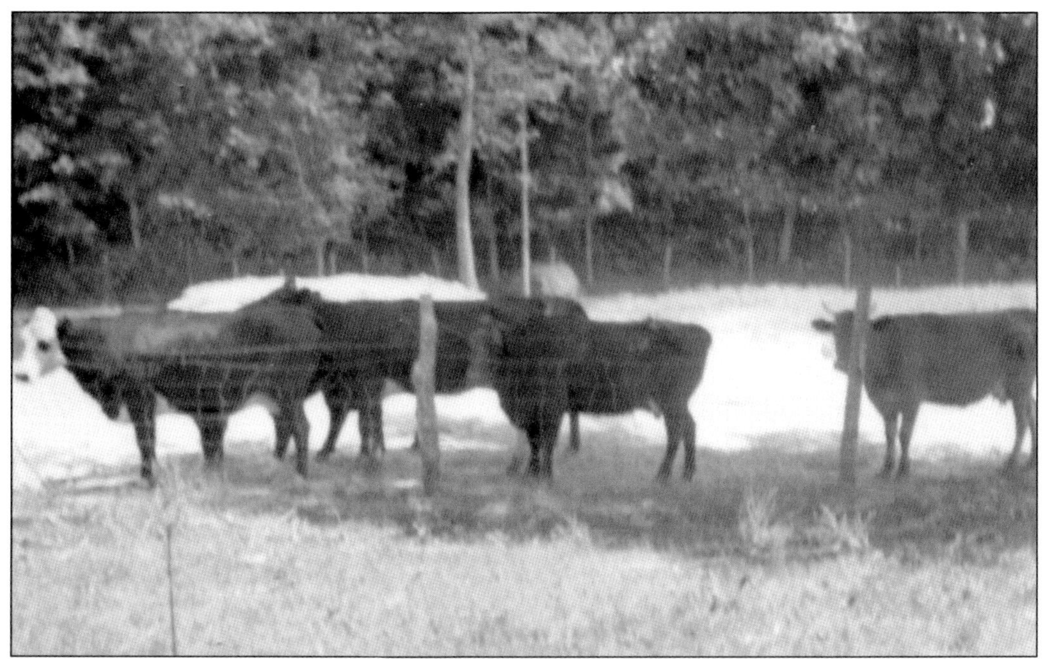

Pictured here are animals on the Holmes Farm. A young James Harrison is most likely showing a relative where the pigs live. The pigs were raised for market as well as for consumption by the family. Cows were also raised on the farm. A favorite cow of Holmes's grandchildren was Old Black Eye, named for the black circles around her eyes. (Courtesy of James M. Harrison.)

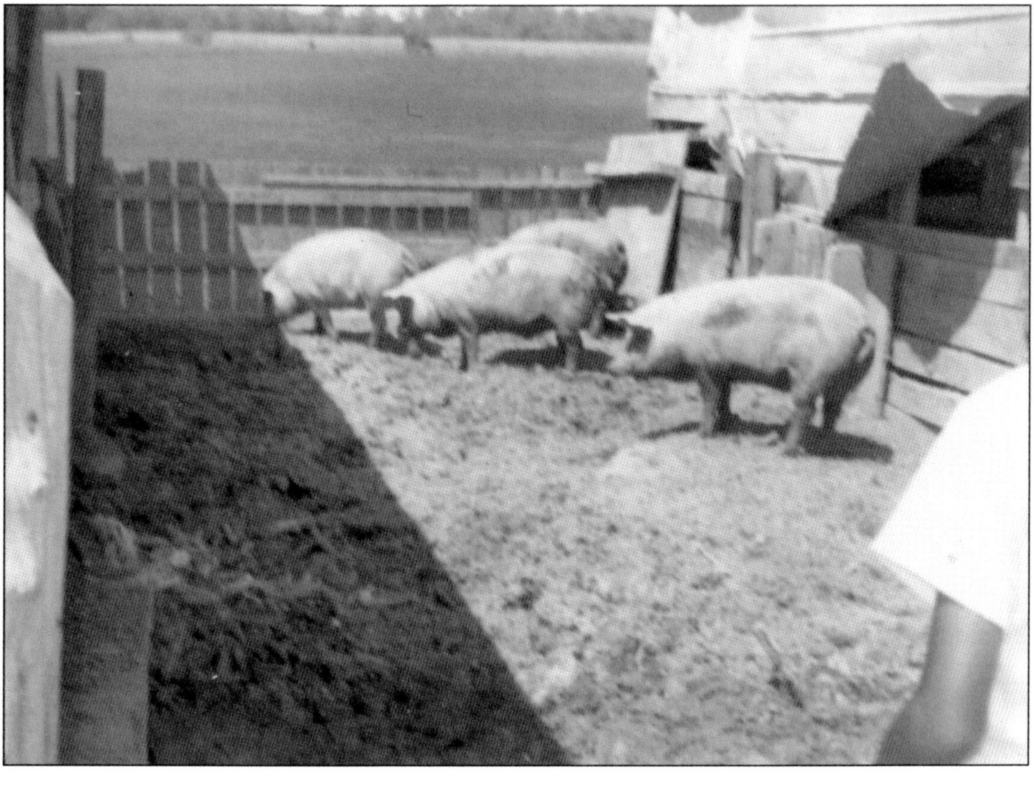

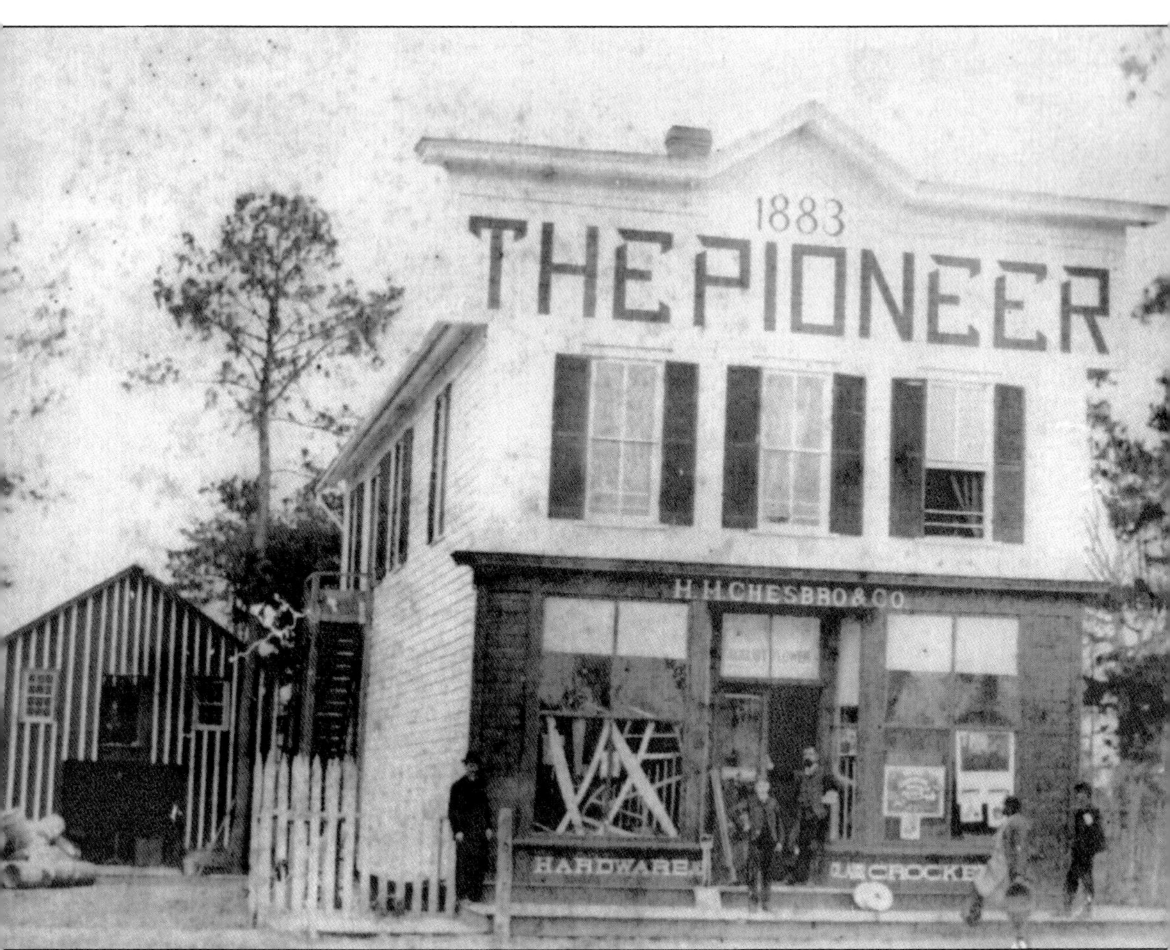

The Hale Hiram Chesbro Store in Claremont is pictured in 1883. In 1895, Chesbro and his wife, Hattie, sold 36 acres, which included several buildings and a wharf, to Dr. John J. Smallwood for his expansion of Smallwood Institute.

Three

Schools and Churches

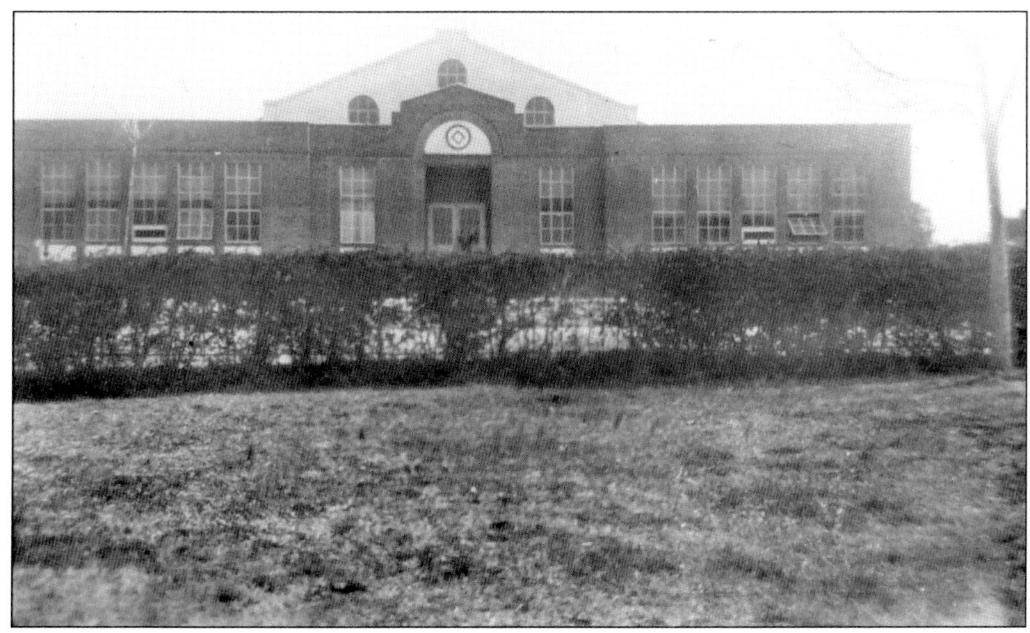

Shown is Surry High School, which opened around 1946 after Dendron High School and many of the one-room and smaller schools in the county closed. Surry County Training School, the high school for black students, remained open in the town of Dendron. (Courtesy of Claude Reeson.)

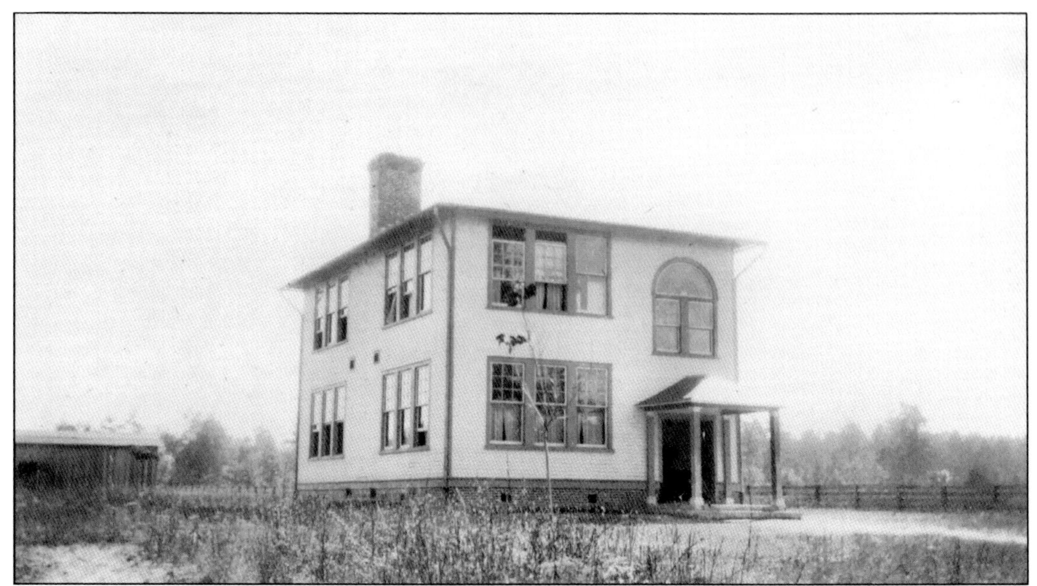

The Robert E. Lee School in Surry served as an elementary school next to the first Surry High School. It was in operation during the 1940s and 1950s. (Courtesy of Claude Reeson.)

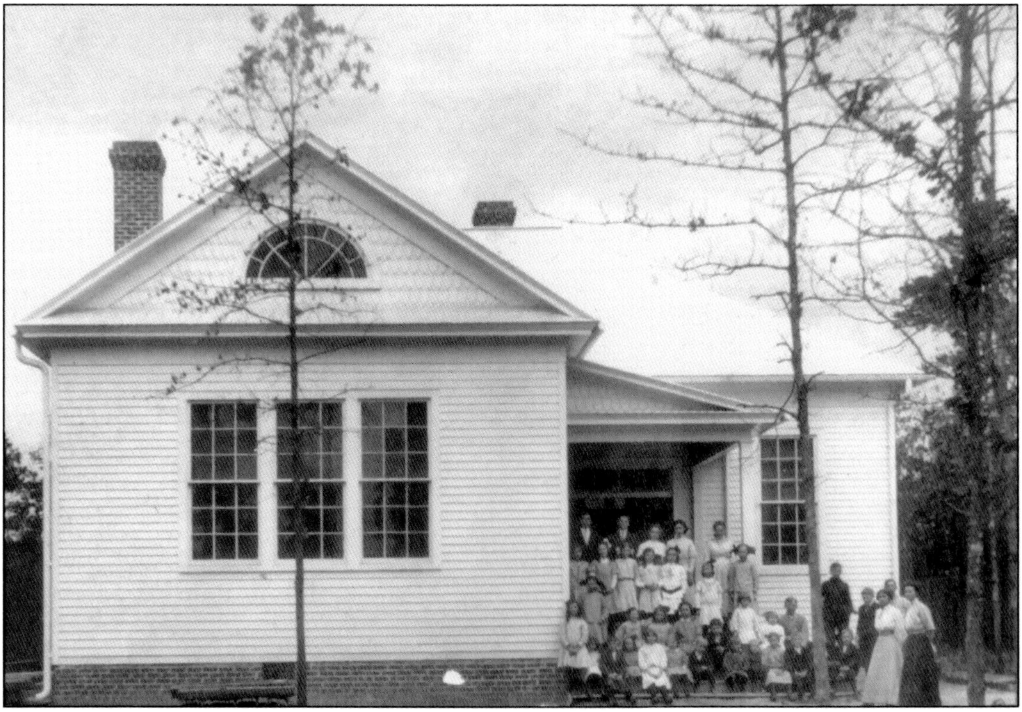

Pictured around 1925 is Savedge School with teachers and students outside. (Courtesy of Claude Reeson.)

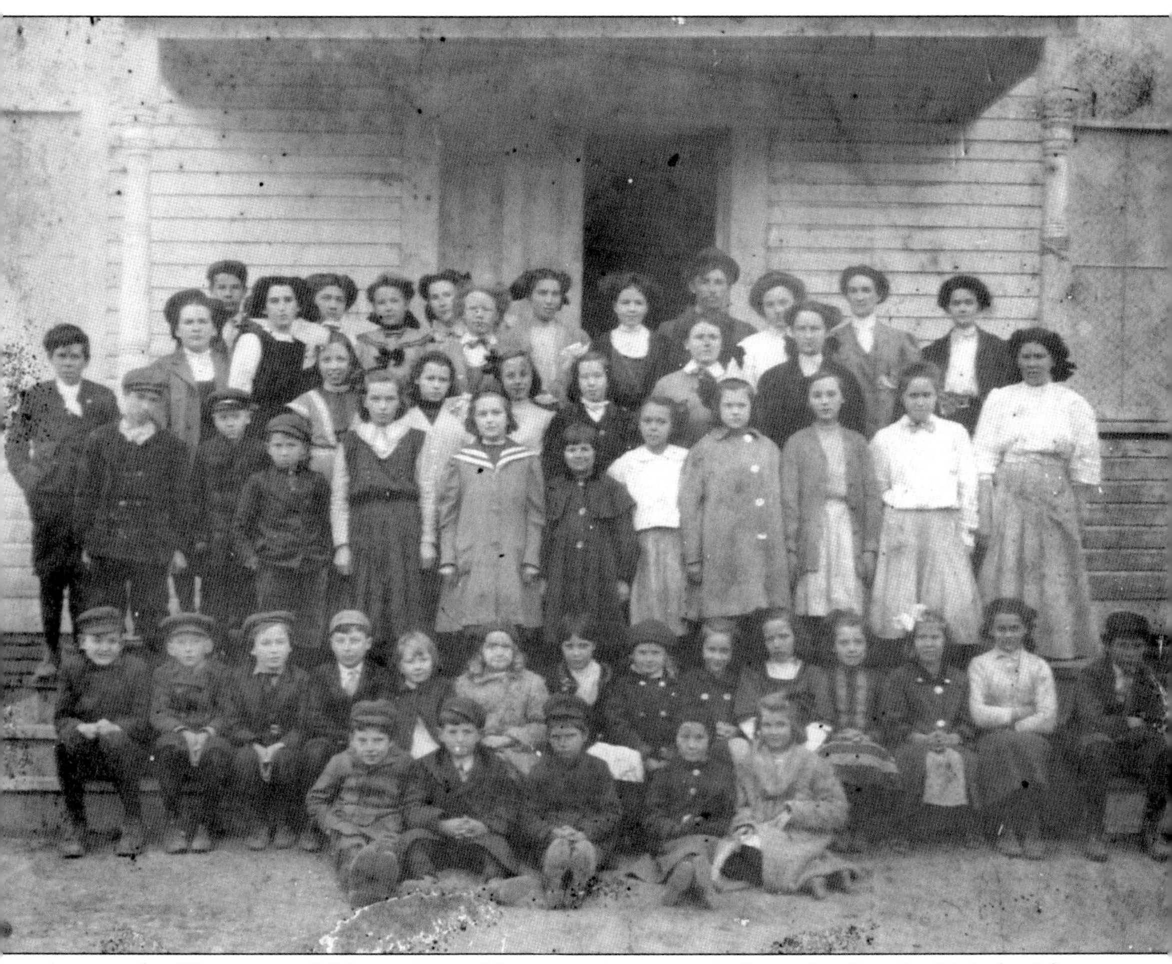

Among the Claremont children pictured here are, in no particular order, Rosalind Marks, Ida Belding, Sadie Rich, Ethel Mills, Florance Topping, Eva Brockwell, Ruth Arrington, Elsi Lovell, Eva Arrington, Alice Topping, Awbry Colgin, and Walker Lee Marks.

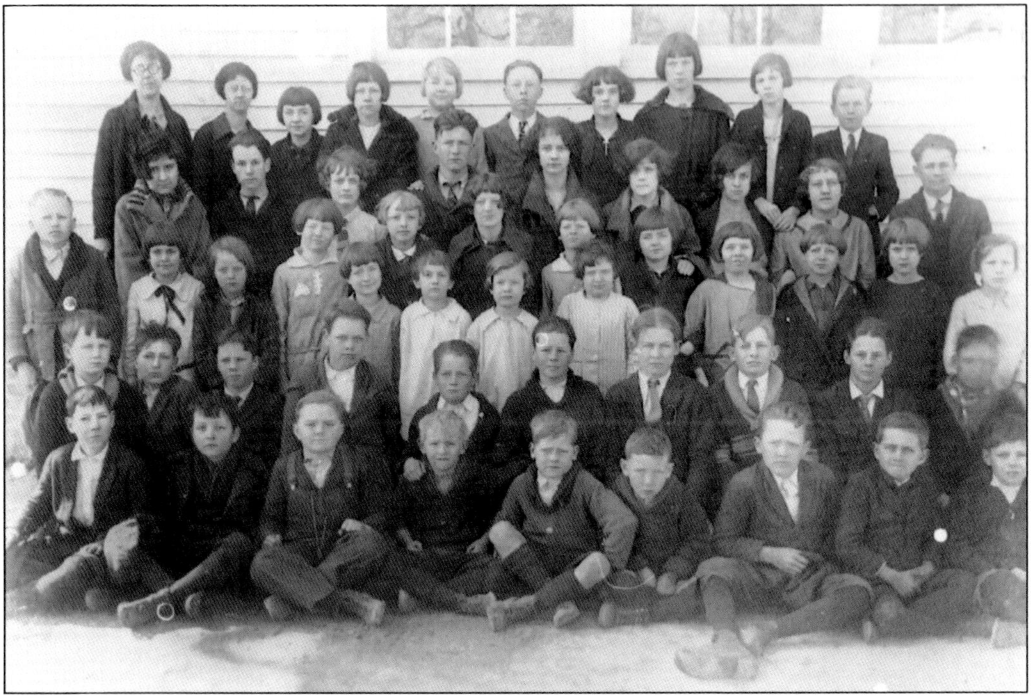

This 1925 image shows a group of students with their teacher outside the Savedge School near Carsley.

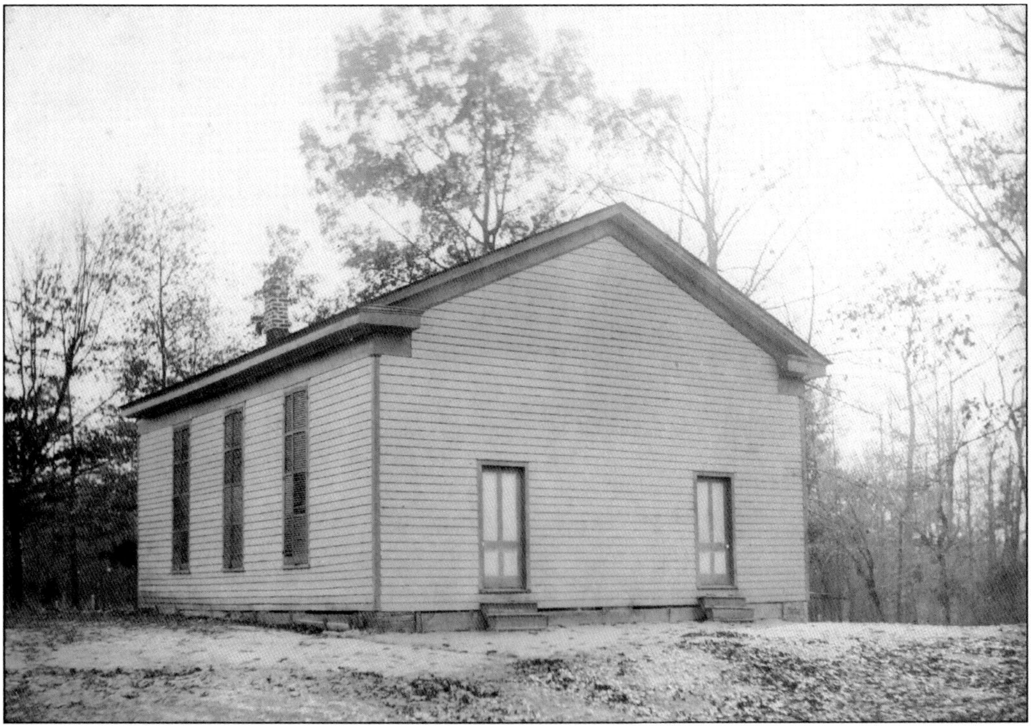

Union Christian Church was founded near Dendron in 1882. It still stands today and is a well-kept structure. (Courtesy of Katherine Johnson Fox.)

Claremont Agricultural High School

SCHOOL OFFICIALS.

State Superintendent Public Instruction,
HARRIS HART, Richmond, Va.

County Superintendent, L. N. SAVEDGE, Alliance, Va.

School Board:

F. W. BRECK, Chairman, Claremont, Va.
W. B. SHAW, Clerk, Claremont, Va.
W. P. MARKS, Claremont, Va.

Teachers—1917-18.

Principal and Agricultural Instructor....A. T. Lewark
Asst. Principal and Domestic Science...Louise Stanton
Second Assistant High School.............Irma Gray
Grammar Department..................Susan Yates
Intermediate Department...........Littie Brockwell
Primary Department.................Lillian Elliott

1918-19.

Principal...........................M. W. Lewark
Assistant Principal High School.........————
Agricultural Instructor................A. T. Lewark
Domestic Science ....Leona Reeves
Grammar Department..................Susan Yates
Intermediate.........................Minnie Lewark
Primary...........................Littie Brockwell
Primary........................Elizabeth Primrose

Featured here is an early-1910s annual report to patrons of the Claremont Agriculture High School. The school experienced growth between 1914 and 1917 when residents developed more confidence in the local school and stopped sending their children away for high school work. In 1914, Claremont Agriculture High School had seven grades and offered two years of high school courses. The school had one teacher for the high school department and three for the other grades. By the 1917–1918 term, the school was accredited and offered four years of high school work. Along with the growth in student body from 11 in 1914 to 30 in 1917, the school received donations of money, materials, equipment, and supplies from Charles Strotz, owner of Swan's Point Plantation, and Dr. A.J. Ochsner, of Chicago, Illinois.

1917.

Agriculture Notes.

$ 3,000,000,000 = Ill health tax in U.S.
1,049,500,000 = Insect tax in U.S.
500,000,000 = Rat Waste in U.S.
600,000,000 = Weed tax in U.S.
335,000,000 = Education tax in U.S.
($ Unestimable) = Fungi tax in U.S.

Rotation of crops in Virginia

No. 1 Corn - Wheat - Grass (3, 5 or 7 yrs.)
no. 2. Corn - Clover (under) cowpeas - wheat - grass (5-6-7 yrs.) Western Section.
No. 3. Wheat - cowpeas - oats - rye (under)
No. 4. Peanuts - rye - corn - grass - clover etc.
No. 5. Potatoes - cowpeas - corn - rye or clover.
No. 6. Early cabbage - cowpeas - corn - rye.
No. 7. Rye or vetch or crimson clover - corn wheat, soy beans.
No 8. Buckwheat - corn - wheat - soy beans - potatoes.
No. 4, 5, & 6 are Eastern Va.,
No. 7 & 8 are mountainous Va.

At Claremont Agricultural High School, as detailed in the notes above, students were given lessons in the Virginia taxes and the rotation of crops throughout the different regions with their varied land types.

Feeding Young Chicks.

During the first week chicks should never be allowed all they will eat. If permitted to have all they will eat, it will bring about bowel disorder at once.
Never feed new born chicks any thing until they show signs of wanting food, and nothing should be given them until 48 hours after they hatch.

If they start picking at things earlier than this very small quantities of easily digested food may be given.
One of the best feeds is a mixture of equal parts of stale bread crumbs and corn meal with hard boiled egg, using about six parts of the breadcrumb mixture to one part of the hard boiled egg with crust shell included.

There is enough moisture in the egg to make the mixture sufficiently moist.
This mixture should be fed and nothing else for the first three days in small amounts 5 times a day.
It is recommended that large sheets of heavy brown paper should be used for

Another page of notes from Claremont Agriculture High School discusses the proper feeding of young chicks. One of the best feeds for the chicks was a mixture of stale bread crumbs, cornmeal, and hard-boiled eggs still in the shell.

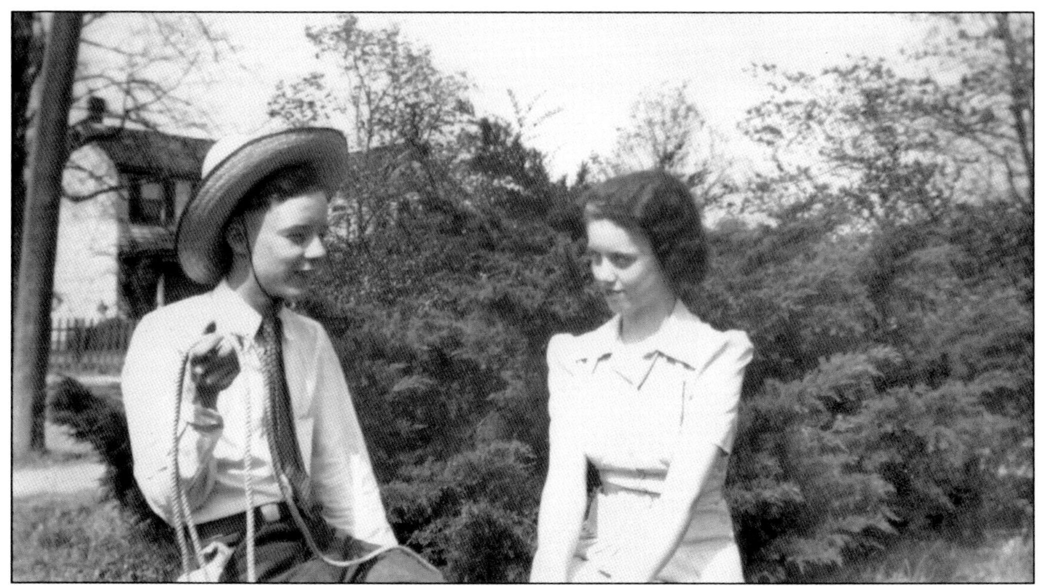

Jim Atkins and Celia Emory practice for the play *Sweet Sioux City Sue* at Dendron High School around April 1946. (Courtesy of Celia E. Parsons.)

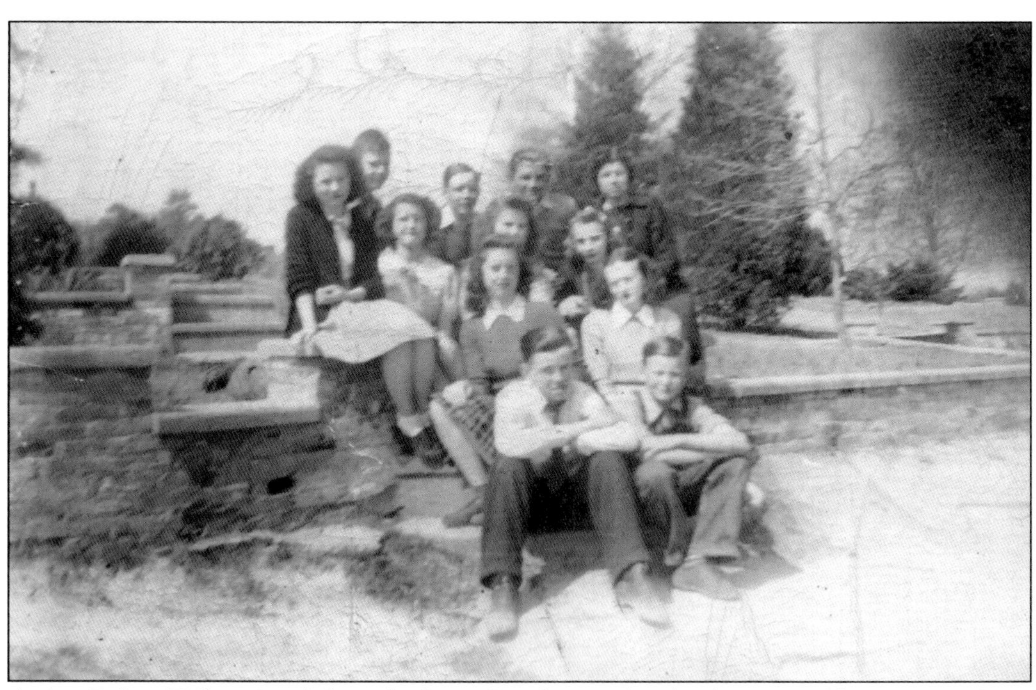

Audrey Bishop Williams's eighth-grade class at Dendron High School is pictured here in 1946. From left to right are (first row) James Lee Savedge and Alton Pittman; (second row) Celia Emory and Dorothy Joyner; (third row) Marjorie Lowe, Esther Butler, Myrtle Goodrich, and Lillian Harrup; (fourth row) Fields "Sonny" Cobb, James Atkins, Earl Holdsworth, and Audrey Williams.

Audrey Bishop Williams was a well-known teacher at Dendron High School and other schools in the area. (Courtesy of Celia E. Parsons.)

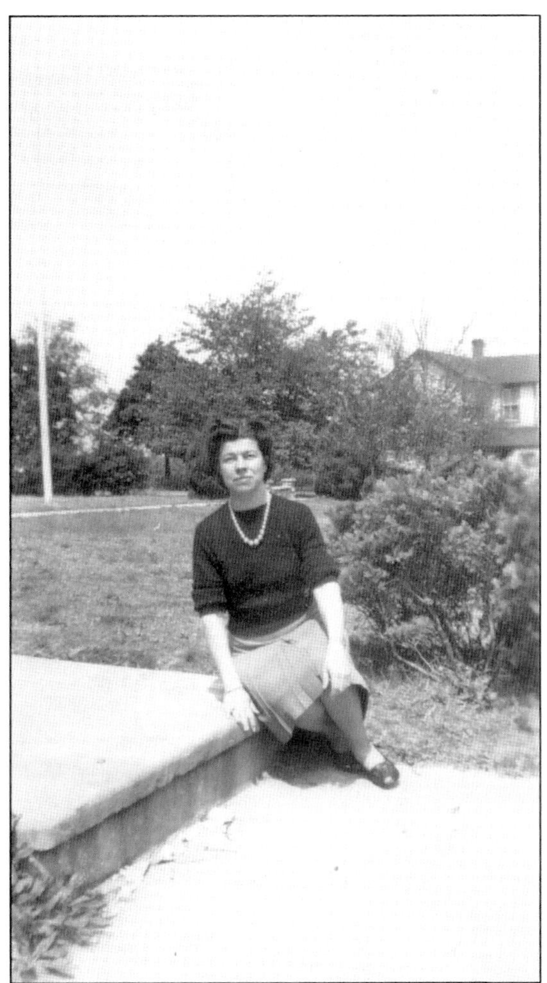

Dendron schoolchildren are featured here around 1945. The children participated in the Schools at War Program, which coordinated the efforts of schools to provide supply and equipment funds for the US military between 1941 and 1945. The program was jointly sponsored by the Treasury Department and the Office of Education. School-based projects and activities varied by location and scale. The 100-percent stamp buyers here probably purchased 10¢ and 25¢ war stamps for their stamp books that were eventually exchanged for US savings bonds. (Courtesy of Celia E. Parsons.)

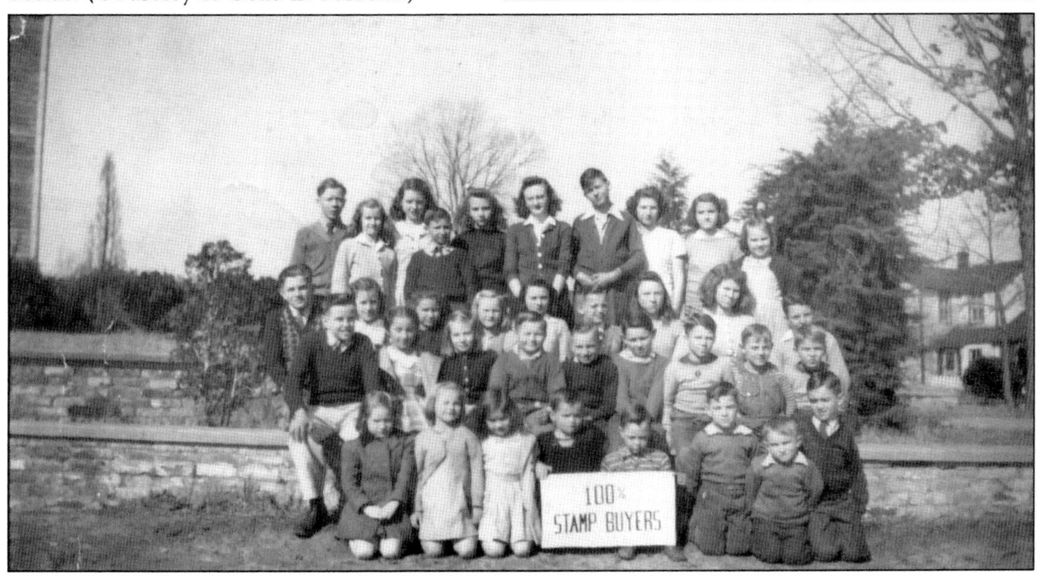

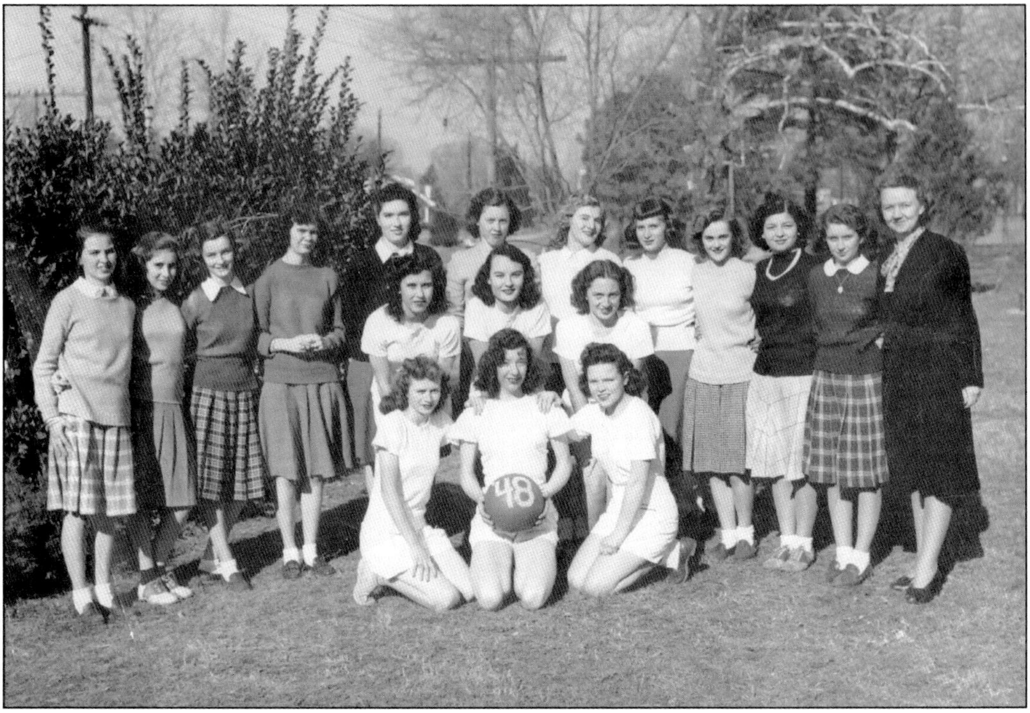

Shown is the Surry High School girls' basketball team of 1948. Dorothy "Dot" Ingram Hewit is holding the basketball. (Courtesy of Celia E. Parsons.)

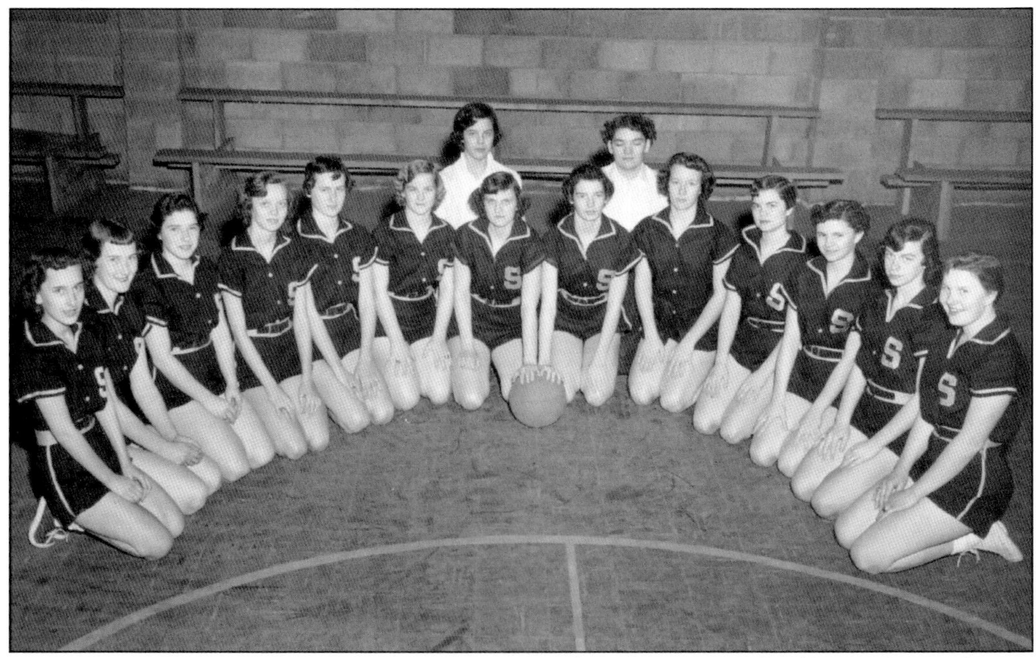

A 1940s Surry High School girls' basketball team includes, from left to right, (first row) Pat Johnson, Annetta Seward, Emily Gail Berryman, Norma Judkins, Jackie Seward, Alice Johnson, Emma Jane Buhls, Lorena Baker, Helen Britt, Margaret Freeman, Betty Burrow Berryman, Barbara Ruth Bell, and Shirley Babb; (second row) Judy Greco and Deanne Cofer.

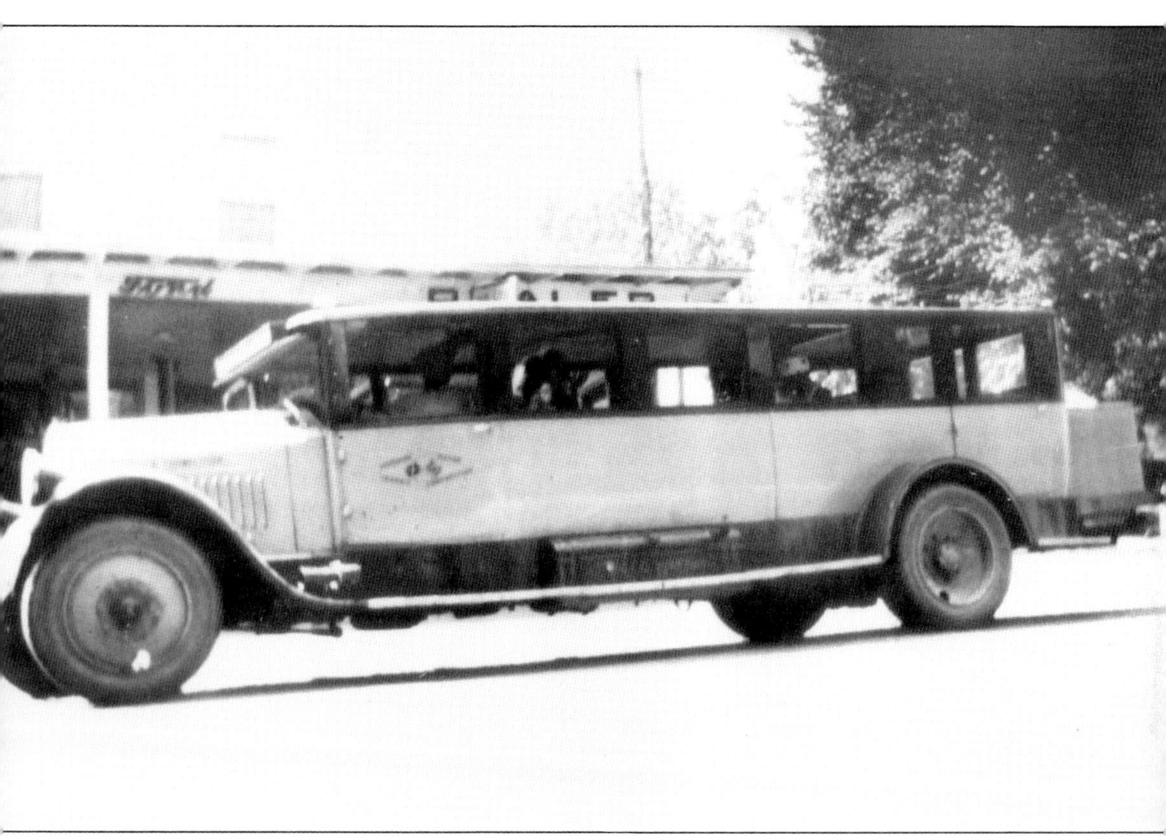

This 1930s school bus transported Claremont students to centralized schools in other parts of the county.

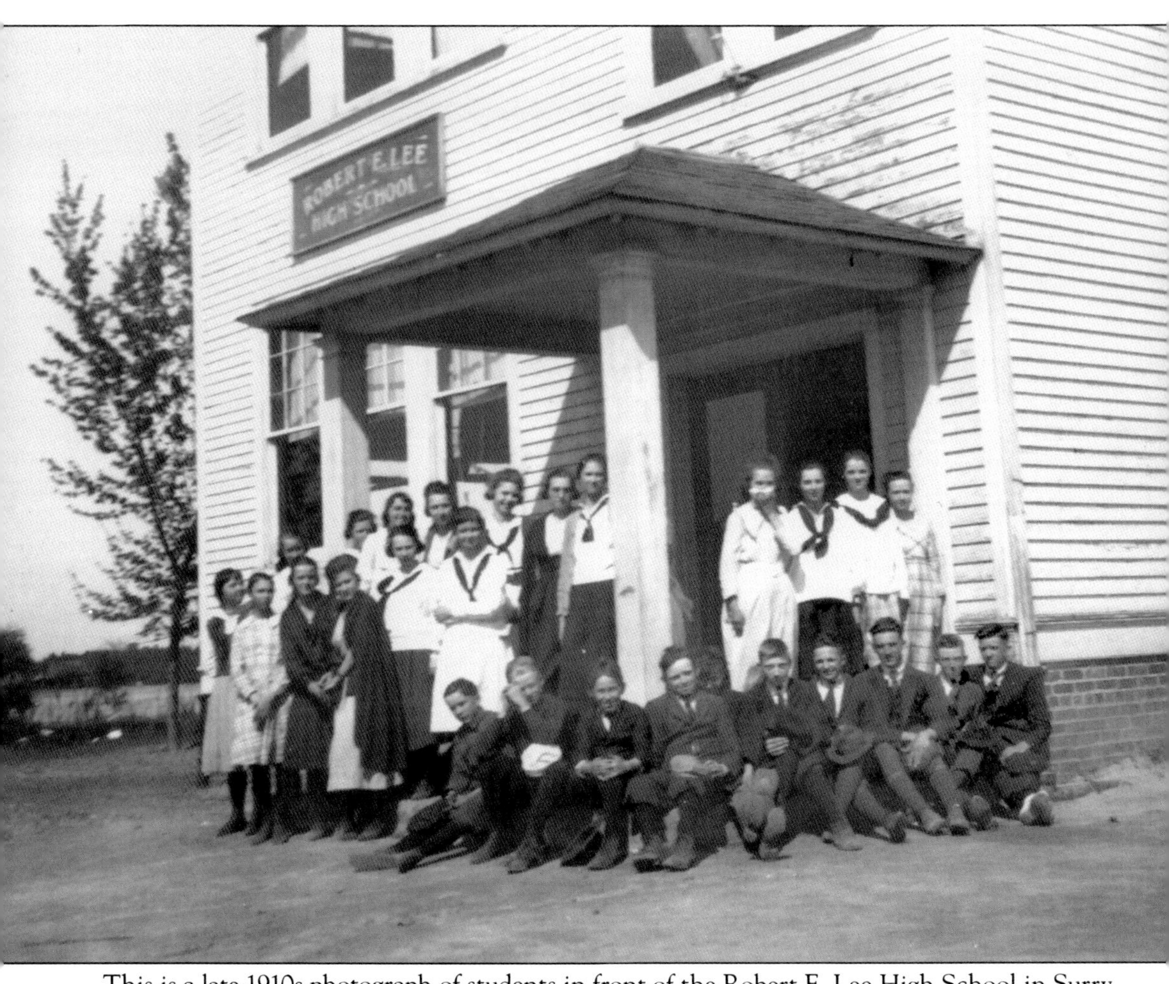

This is a late-1910s photograph of students in front of the Robert E. Lee High School in Surry.

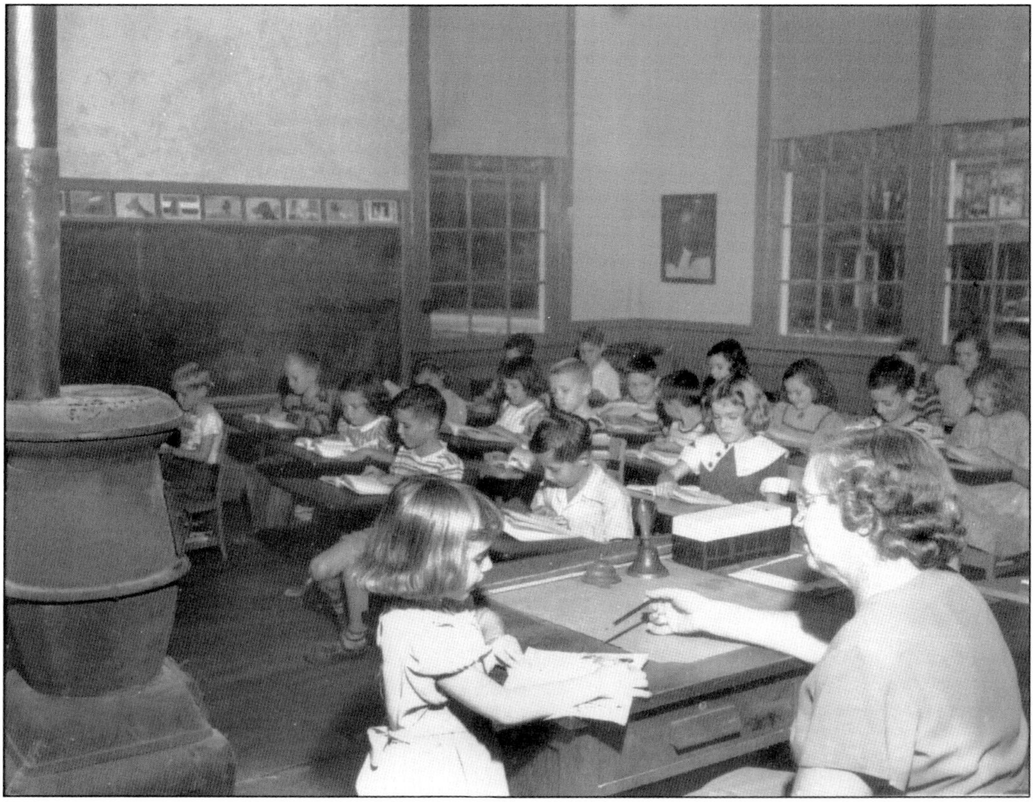

In October 1953, Dendron Elementary School was the only all-white, one-room school left in the county. The lower grades remained in Dendron after the high school and grades four through seven were moved to the Surry courthouse between 1946 and 1948. The teacher is Mary West Thompson. Donna Leigh Slade, the student at Thompson's desk, is demonstrating her reading skills. (Courtesy of Donna Slade.)

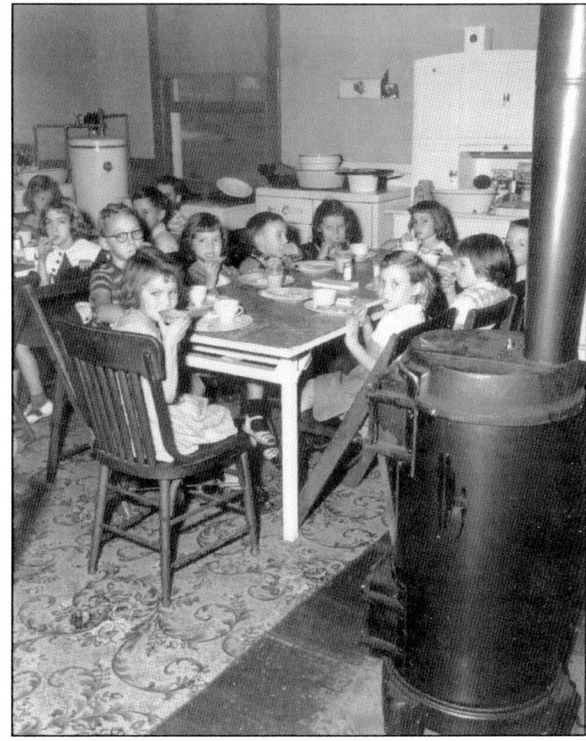

The lunchroom and kitchen at Dendron Elementary School are shown here. The students seated at the front table, clockwise from the young man with glasses, are Shelton Stewart, Joanie Goodrich, Richard Barfield, Ruthie Livesay, Donna Slade, Richard Burt, Mary Humphrey, Peggy Casper, and Sara Jean Collier. (Courtesy of Donna Slade.)

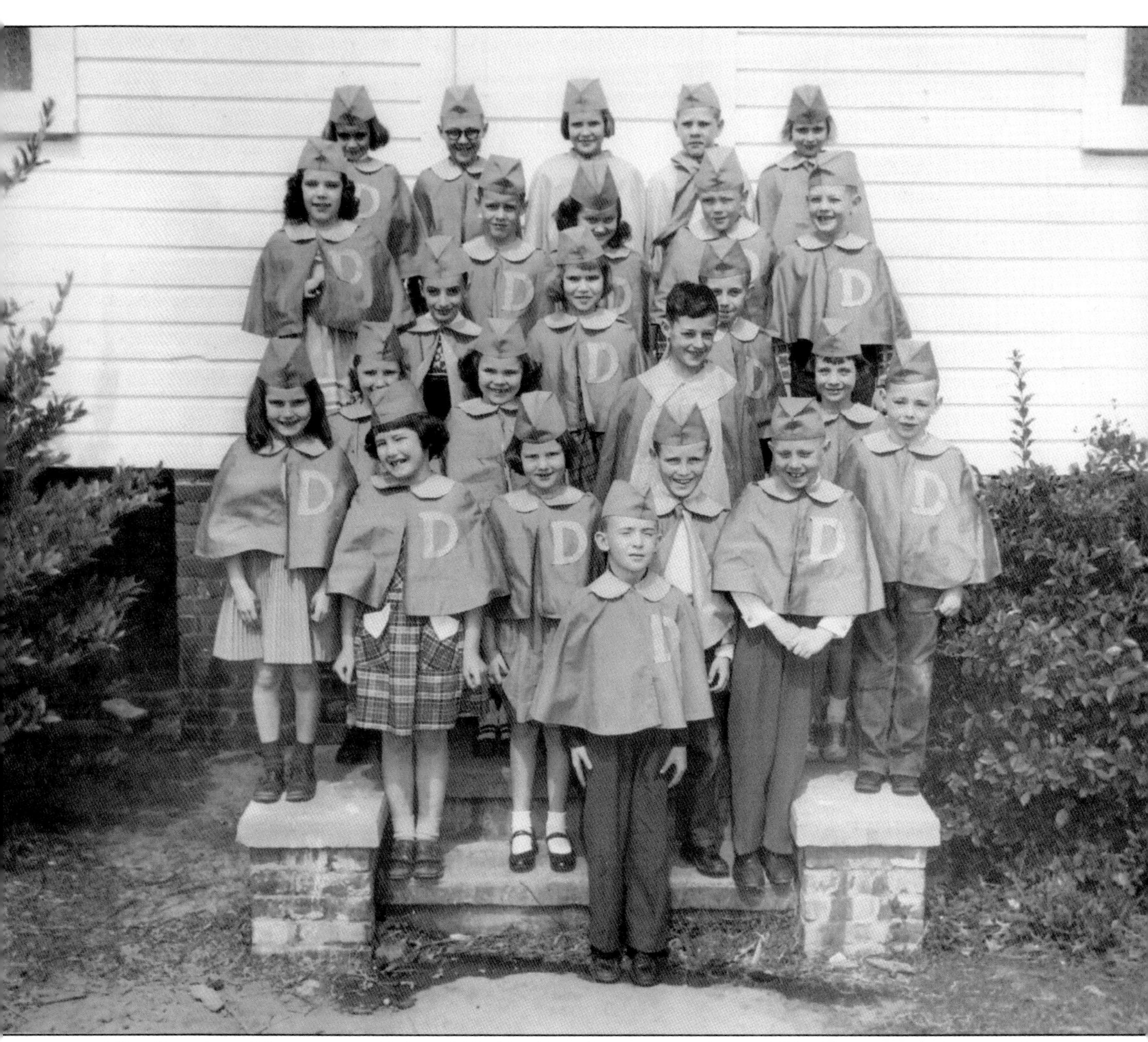

The Dendron Elementary School Kiddie Band is pictured in 1953. The members are, from left to right, (first row) Richard Barfield; (second row) Alice Ruth Cofer, Joanie Goodrich, Tommy Casper, and Wyatt Slade Jr.; (third row) Ruthie Livesay, Judy Barton, Barbara Hite, Robert Johnson, Mary Humphrey, and Richard Burt; (fourth row) Johnny Rollins, Christine Collier, and Roy Collier; (fifth row) Jennifer Taylor, David Spruill, Anne Pittman, Johnny Spratley, and Barry Threewitts; (sixth row) Donna Slade, Shelton Stewart, Peggy Casper, Don Padgett, and Joyce Casper. (Courtesy of Donna Slade.)

Form C. No. 3—50M

CONTRACT WITH TEACHERS

This Article of Agreement, between the SCHOOL BOARD OF Claremont,

State of Virginia, of the first part, and Miss Ellen Carlsen

of the second part;

WITNESSETH, That the said party of the second part subject to the authority of the said school board and under the supervision and control of the division superintendent agrees to teach in the schools administered by the said school board under the following conditions; to-wit:

1. The said teacher or party of the second part shall open and close school on regular school days at such hours as the school board may designate, and shall give daily recess with appropriate supervision in accordance with the recess schedule adopted by the school board, provided the school day shall consist of not less than five hours or more than six and one-half hours exclusive of the noon hour recess, when such is provided.
2. The said teacher shall obey all school laws and regulations and all rules made in accordance with the law by the said school board and shall make promptly and accurately all reports required by the superintendent of schools.
3. Said teacher shall exercise care in the protection and upkeep of the school property, furniture and fixtures and shall promptly report to the superintendent needed repairs or necessary added facilities or supplies.
4. In schools in which no regular janitor is employed the arrangement for keeping the school clean and in sanitary condition is to be stipulated below under special covenant.
5. The said teacher hereby swears or affirms allegiance and loyalty to the Government of the United States.
6. The school board or party of the first part shall deduct monthly from the salary of the said teacher a sum equal to one per centum of the salary, to be placed to the credit of the Retired Teachers Fund and to be applied as provided by law.
7. The said school board reserves the right to change the teacher from one teaching position to a different teaching position, provided on the recommendation of the division superintendent the efficiency of the school system may require such a change, and provided further that no reduction in salary may be made because of such change.
8. The said board reserves the right to dismiss the teacher or party of the second part for just cause, an opportunity on request being granted for a hearing, paying for services rendered in accordance with this agreement to date of dismissal. In the event the public school funds be exhausted and the board finds it necessary on this account to shorten the school term, said board may terminate this contract after giving reasonable notice to the party of the second part. In case schools are closed temporarily on account of an epidemic or for other necessary cause the board may pay the teacher for time lost, or may extend the school term.
9. The said school board or party of the first part agrees to pay said teacher or party of the second part, $ 85.00 per school ~~or calendar~~ month for a term of Nine (9) school ~~or calendar~~ months, beginning on Sept 4th, 1923, for a lawful school, for services rendered, payable on the last day of each school ~~or~~ calendar month or as soon thereafter as possible.

SPECIAL COVENANTS.

1. With reference to care and cleanliness of school building in which no janitor is employed.

2. With reference to time lost by teacher on account of sickness or for other cause.

The said board shall determine in each case whether such time lost shall be paid for or not.

3. Other covenants.

The special covenants on the reverse side hereof also are hereby mutuall agreed upon and form a part of this agreement.

In witness whereof, the parties hereunto have set their hands and seals, this seventh day of July 1923

M J Lovell [L. S.]
Chairman of the Board

H W Winston [L. S.]
Clerk of the Board

Ellen Carlson [L. S.]
Teacher

This interesting document is a 1923 teacher contract for Ellen Carlsen, of Claremont. The contract did not provide for sick days but included some paid holidays. A note with Miss Carlsen's contract detailed a supplement of $15 per month for the school term. The additional money increased Carlsen's salary from $85 to $100.

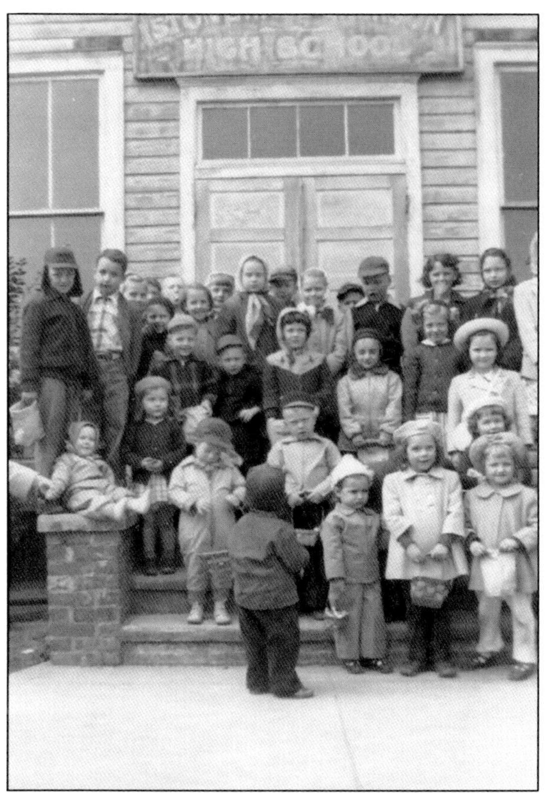

Standing in front of the Stonewall Jackson High School building (also known as Dendron High School) are children after they have enjoyed the Dendron Methodist Church–sponsored Easter egg hunt. The photograph was taken in the early 1950s and features, in no particular order, Donna Slade, Jennifer Taylor, Judy Mae Barton, Woody Cofer, Billy Spruill, Robert Johnson, Ruthie Livesay, Judy Burt, Wyatt Slade Jr., Johnny Rollings, Alice Ruth Cofer, Linda Cofer, Nancy Barrett, Betty Ann Goodrich, Mae Cofer, Otelia Rollings, and Lucille Johnson. (Courtesy of Donna Slade.)

The Spring Grove Methodist Church was built during the 1880s and served the community for years. The Spring Grove Ladies Aid Society sponsored many fundraisers to pay for building repairs over the years. The church was eventually torn down in the 1980s. A small cemetery is located just northwest of the old church lot. (Courtesy of Claude Reeson.)

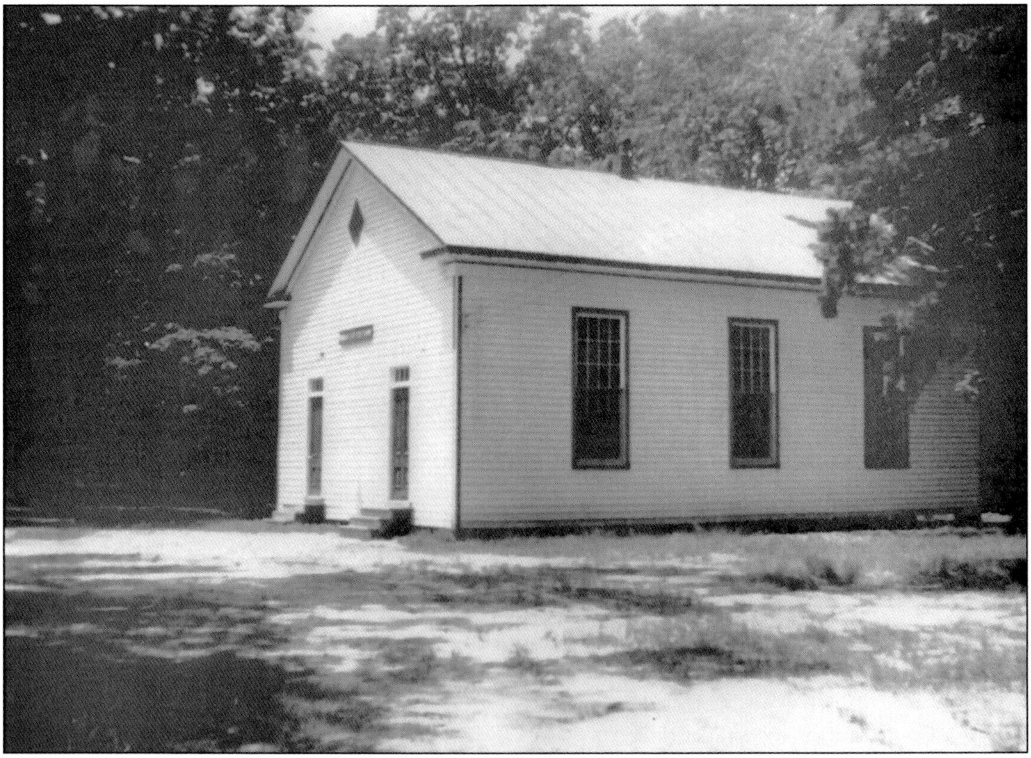

The old Lebanon Church marker on Route 10 near Surry identifies the site where the first Christian church in America was organized. In 1794, the Reverends James O'Kelly and Rice Haggard and about 30 other Methodist ministers withdrew from the newly organized Methodist Episcopal church. They were certain that the officials of the Methodist Episcopal church denied local church governance and religious liberty.

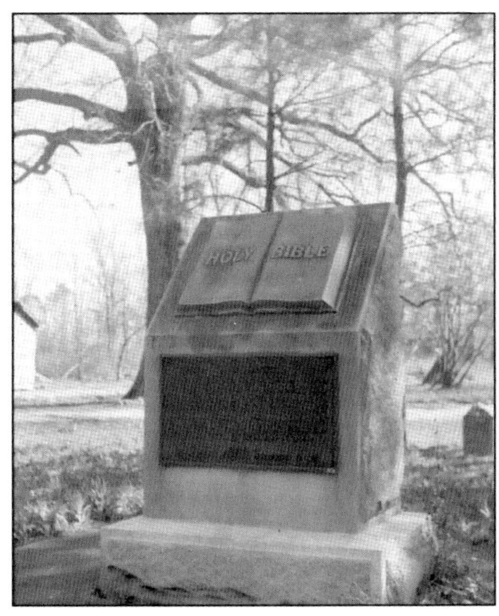

Pictured here in the 1960s is the New Lebanon Christian Church at Elberon. It was organized in 1881 and for many years was known as "Cockes' Church." New Lebanon earned this popular name because of the three Cockes brothers who were very active in church activities.

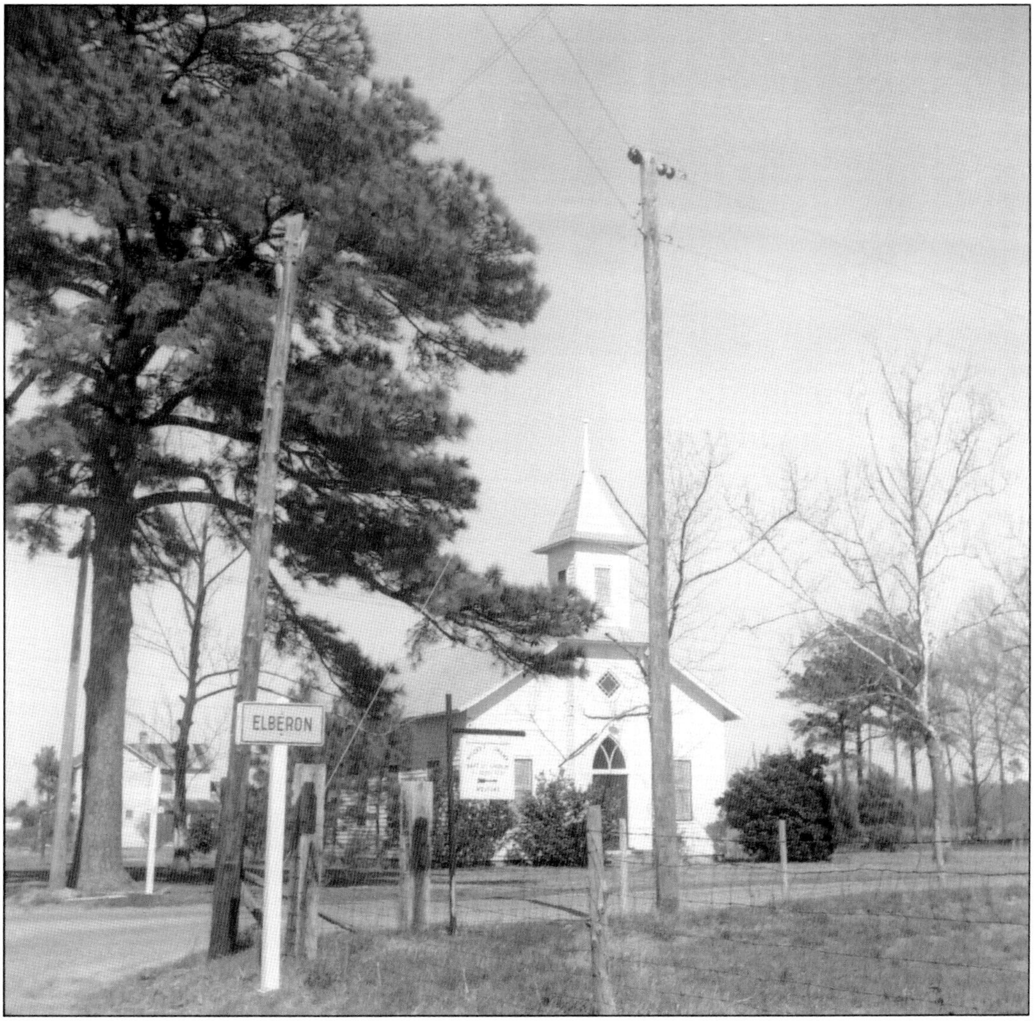

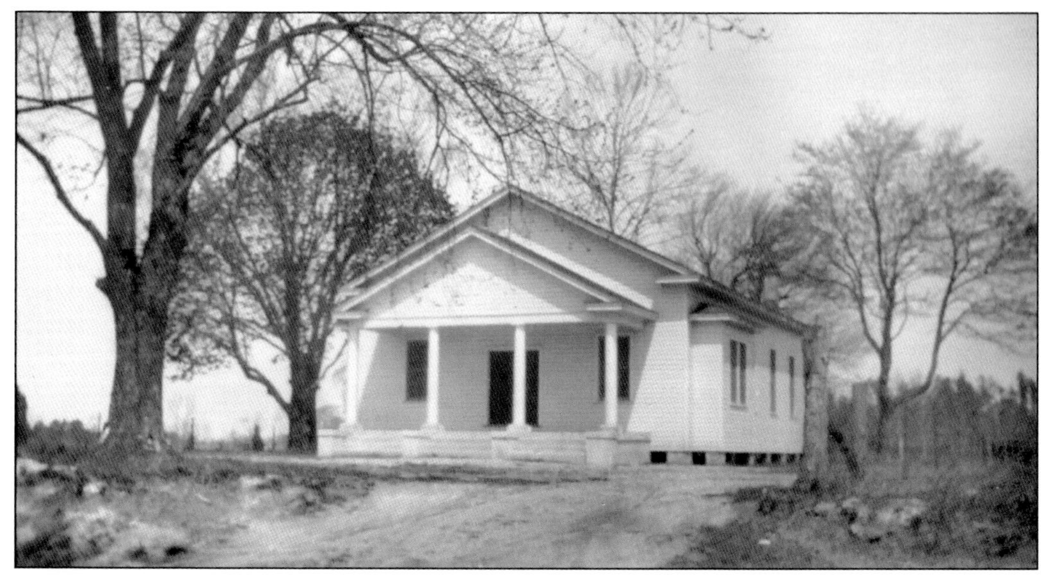

Pictured here is the early construction of Surry Methodist Church, which was organized in 1924. (Courtesy of Mary Alma Savedge.)

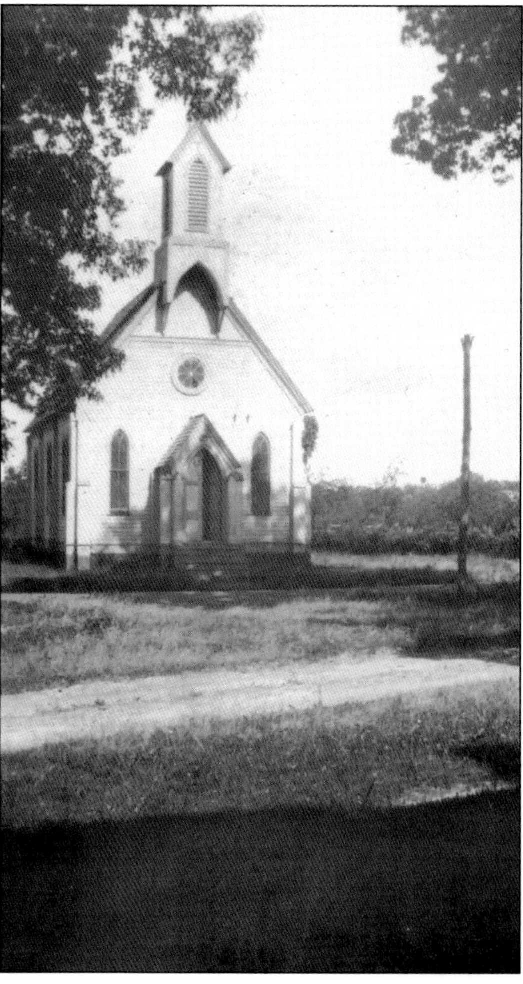

This 1920s photograph shows St. Paul's Episcopal Church–Surry, which was organized in 1885. (Courtesy of Mary Alma Savedge.)

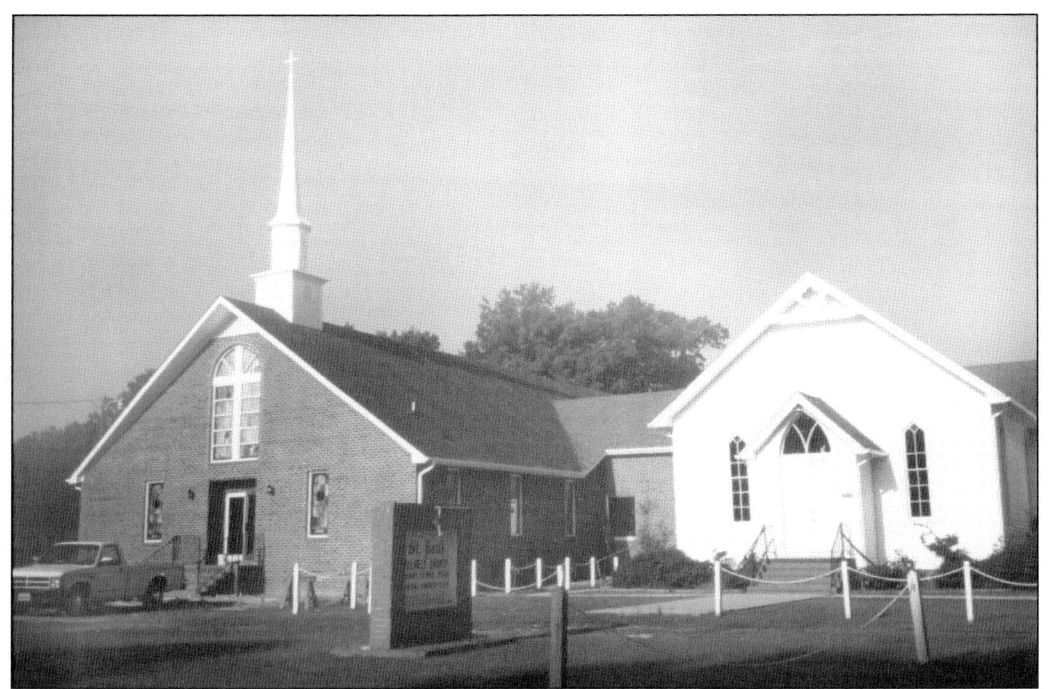

St. Paul's Apostolic Church completed an expansion and renovation. The white building served as sanctuary and was formerly Moorings Methodist Church. St. Paul's purchased the property after Moorings consolidated with another church.

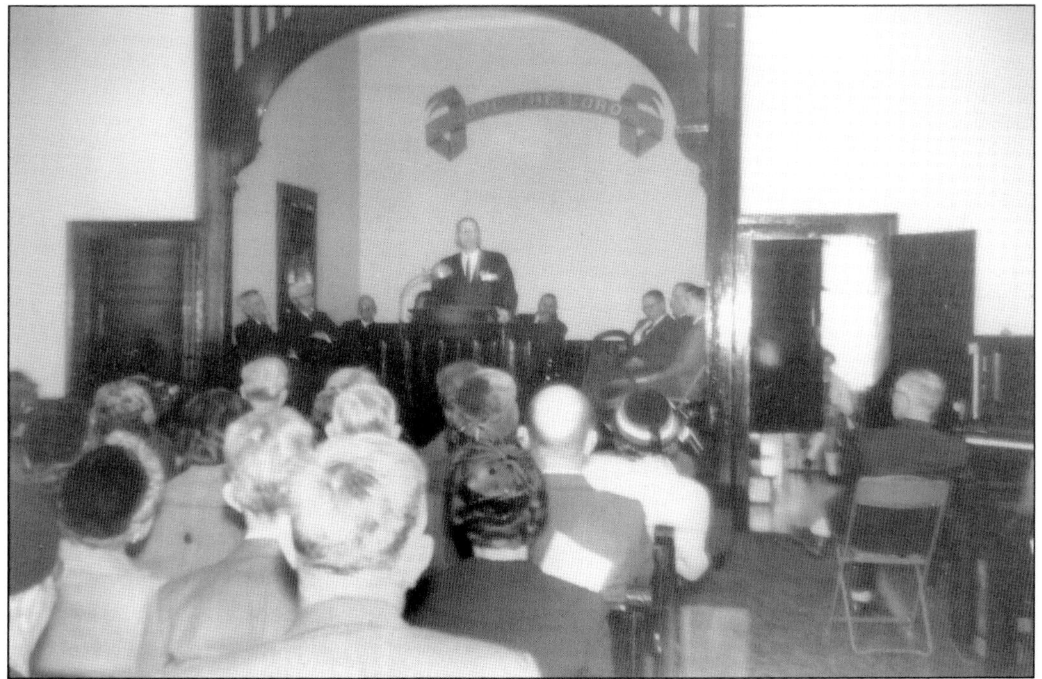

Shown here is a 1950s service at Spring Grove United Methodist Church. The church was built around 1880, and it was town down in the 1980s after the congregation dwindled. (Courtesy of Claude Reeson.)

MINUTES

Of The

Sixty-Sixth Annual Session

Of The

Lebanon Virginia Baptist Association

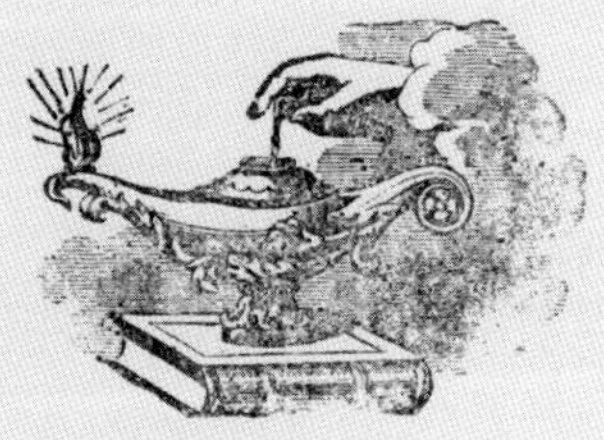

Held With

Mt. Nebo Baptist Church, Surry, Va.

Wednesday and Thursday

September 14 - 15, 1949

The Association Adjourned to Convene in its next Annual Session with the Jerusalem Baptist Church, Waverly, Virginia, September 13 – 14 1950

Shown here is the Lebanon Virginia Baptist Association minutes for session 66 on September 14–15, 1949. (Courtesy of James Harrison.)

LEBANON VIRGINIA BAPTIST ASSOCIATON 9

Rev. R. L. Davis	Surry, Virginia
Rev. S. R. Williams	Smithfield, Virginia
Rev. G. A. Ruffin	Richmond, Virginia
Rev. C. S. Askew	Zuni, Virginia
Rev. Thomas Ash	Portsmouth, Virginia

LIST OF LICENTIATES

Rev. Jonathan Thomas	Smithfield, Virginia
Rev. W. B. Harriston	Spring Grove, Virginia
Rev. H. P. Johnson	Dendron, Virginia
Rev. Wm. Taylor	Smithfield, Virginia
Rev. Robert Parham	Windsor, Virginia
Rev. Purnell Holloway	Smithfield, Virginia

LIST OF DELEGATES

Cypress	Deacons Russell Savedge & Richard Molton
Clarks Memorial	Dea. S. H. Hilton
1st Bapt. Dendron	Deacons Berkley Green & Edward Byrd
Emmanuel	Bro. James H. Hall & Miss Mary M. Parker
Lebanon	Dea. Arthur Lunsford & Rev. W. B. Harrison
Little Zion	Dea. Charlie Spratley & Dea. John T. White
Jerusalem	Sister Maggie A. Mason & Rev. G. A. Ruffin
Golden Hill	Dea. W. H. Evans
Mt. Nebo	Rev. E. D. Harrell, Dea. W. S. Winfield & Bro. Joseph Howell
Harrison Grove	Mrs. Martha Rogers
Ash Grove	
Shiloh	Dea. A. L. Johnson
Sandy Mt.	Dea. John D. Tynes
Popular Lawns	Deacons John Lane & D. L. Haskett
Lebanon, (P. G.)	
Ferguson Grove	Rev. S. R. Williams
Jones Grove	Rev. G. W. Johnson & Rev. J. C. Allmond
Gravel Hill, Surry	Dea. G. E. Mason & Bro Sheppard Johns
1st Gravel Hill	Dea. Miles Bradby & Rev. J. D. Marshburn
Swans Point	Dea. G. T. Braxton
Morning Star	Dea. D. B. Jones
Mt. Sinai	Deacon's Ross Hakin & A. H. Godwin
Rising Star	

Bacon Castle, Virginia 1949

September 14, Morning Session

The Lebanon Virginia Baptist Association met in its Sixty-sixth Annual Session with the Mt. Nebo Baptist Church of Surry, Virginia. Devotionals at 9:30 a. m., were conducted by Rev. B. J. Luster.

Opening hymn was led by Choir "Is My Name Written There." Scripture Lesson Matt. 17: 1-13. Which was followed with prayer by

The Lebanon Virginia Baptist Association was founded around 1883 for the purpose of spreading "the Redeemer's Kingdom upon the earth by doing all in its power for home and foreign missions encouraging and fostering education interest among our people, devising and recommending means for increasing the harmony and spiritual powers of the churches and Sunday School." The association took the name of Lebanon Baptist Church, and its membership included regular Baptist churches throughout Surry County. The annual session was held each year in September and included sermons, reports of auxiliary activities, workshops, and leadership training. The inspirational sermon at this 1949 session was delivered by Rev. William B. Harrison, and his subject was "Being at Ease in Zion." Delegates from the various churches included Dea. Russell Savedge, Dea. Arthur Lunsford, Dea. Miles Bradby, Rev. S.R. Williams, and Rev. J.D. Marshburn. (Courtesy of James Harrison.)

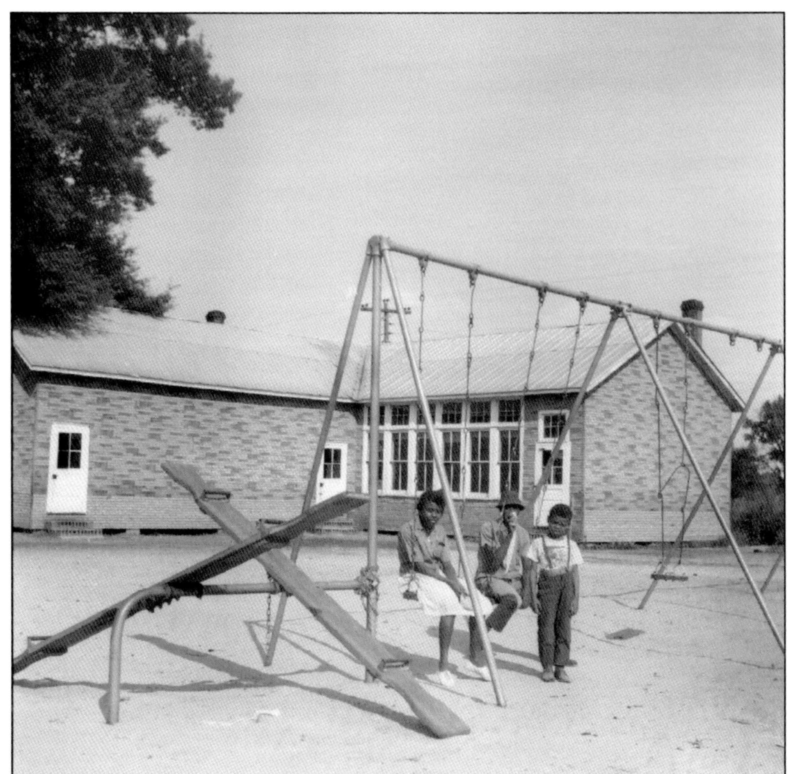

Children are shown on the playground in front of the elementary building at the Surry County Training School complex in Dendron.

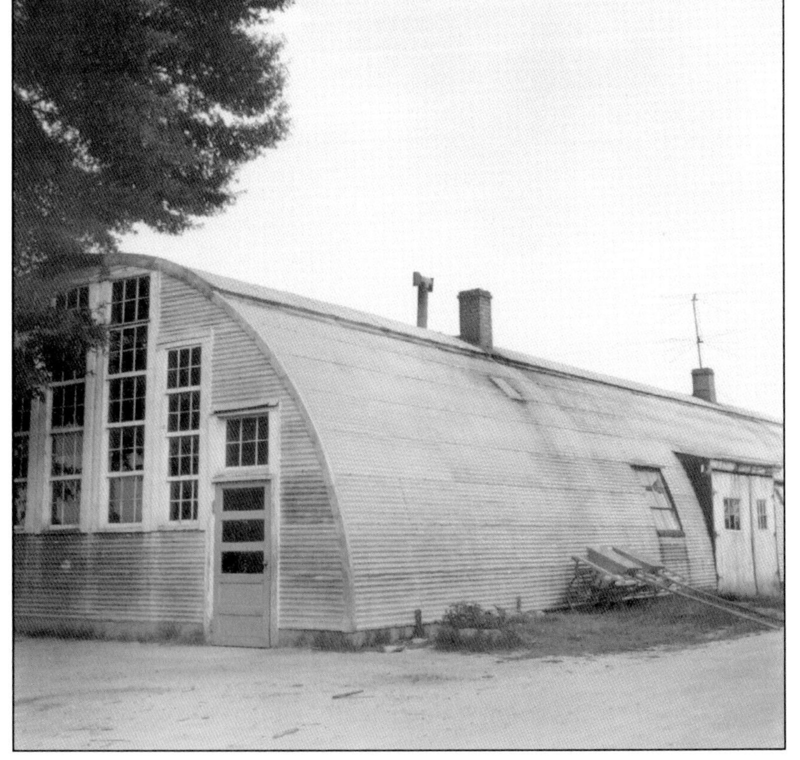

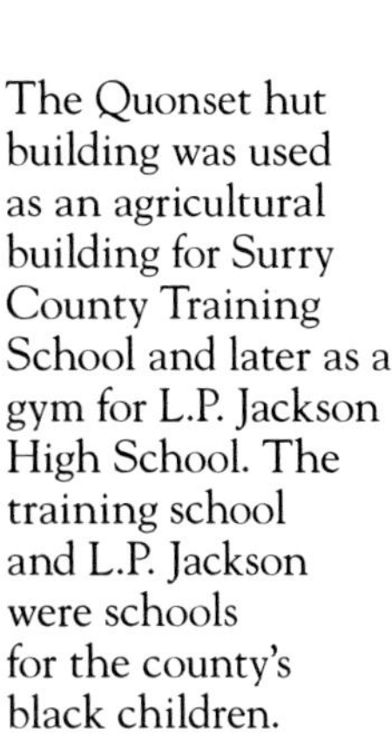

The Quonset hut building was used as an agricultural building for Surry County Training School and later as a gym for L.P. Jackson High School. The training school and L.P. Jackson were schools for the county's black children.

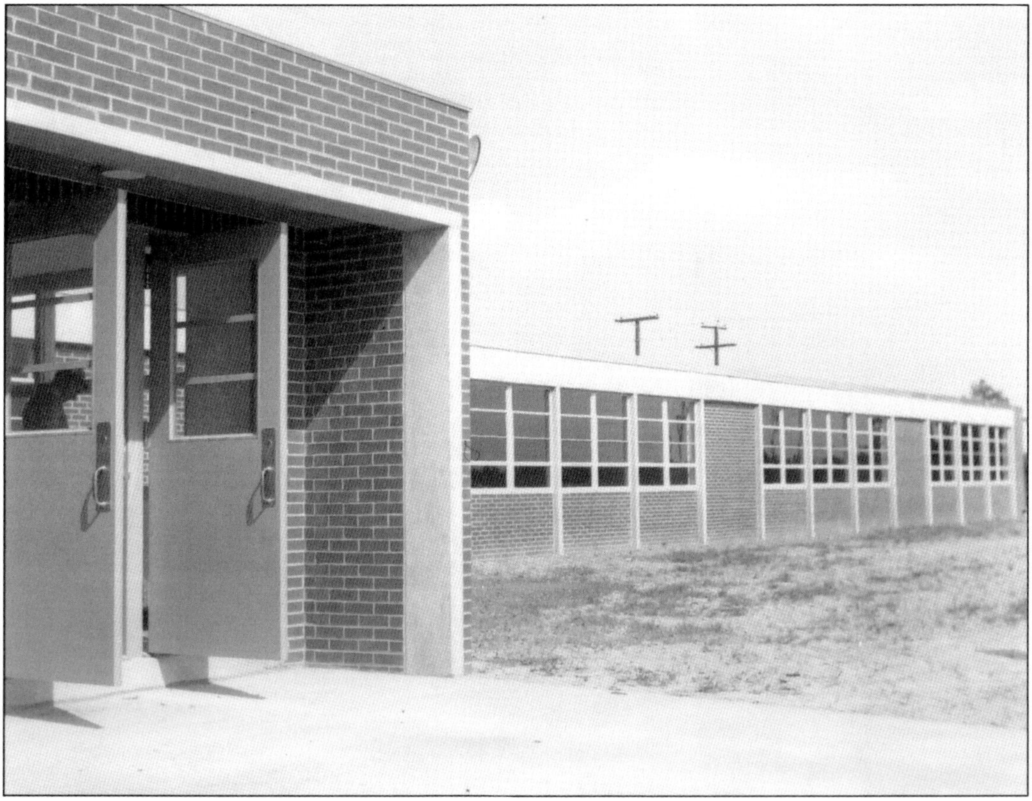

In 1960, a new brick elementary school was opened in Dendron next to L.P. Jackson High School. School officials include, from left to right, superintendent of schools M.B. Joyner, Mrs. Herman T. Cooper, and E.F. Huber.

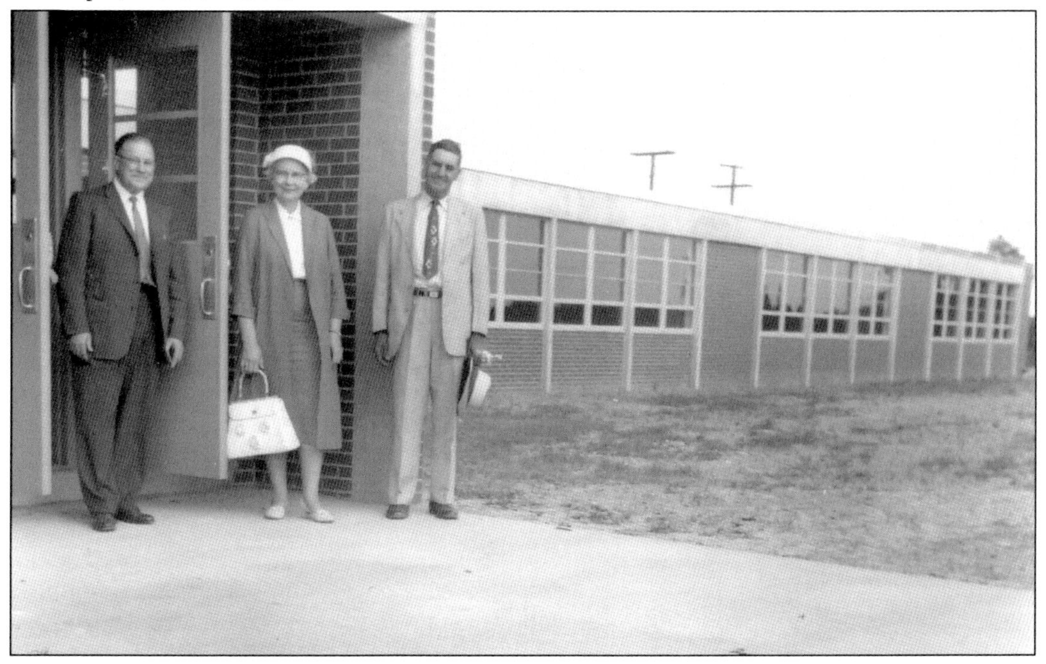

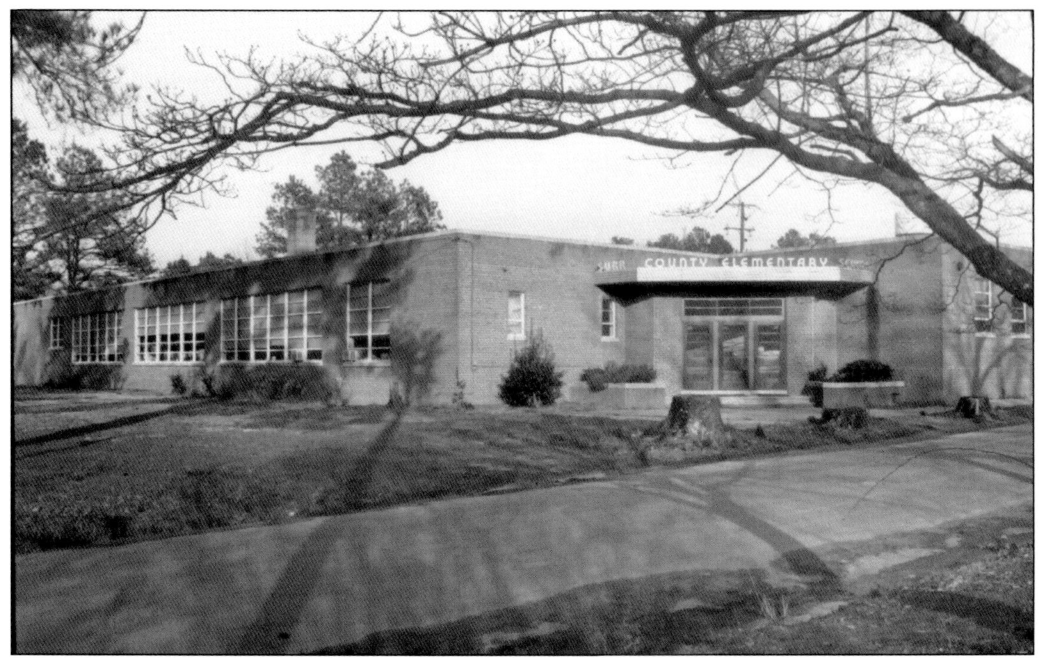

Surry County Elementary School in the town of Surry is shown in this 1970s photograph. The school opened to serve students after one-room schools closed throughout the county. (Courtesy of Surry County Public Schools.)

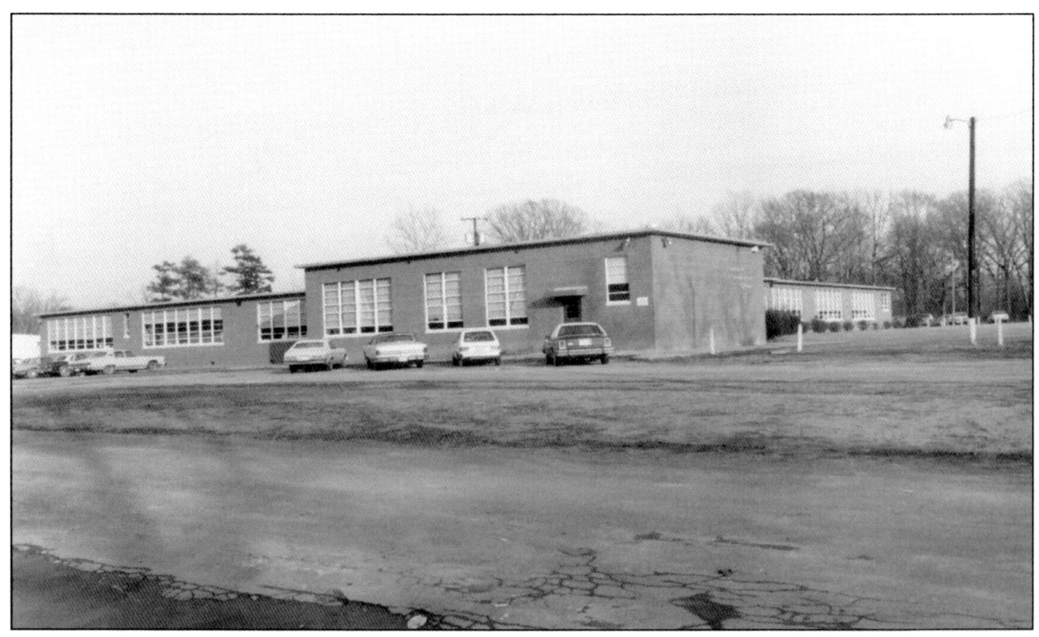

Lebanon Elementary School on Lebanon Road was opened in the late 1950s and closed in the 1980s when the consolidated Surry Elementary School was opened on Hollybush Road. (Courtesy of Surry County Public Schools.)

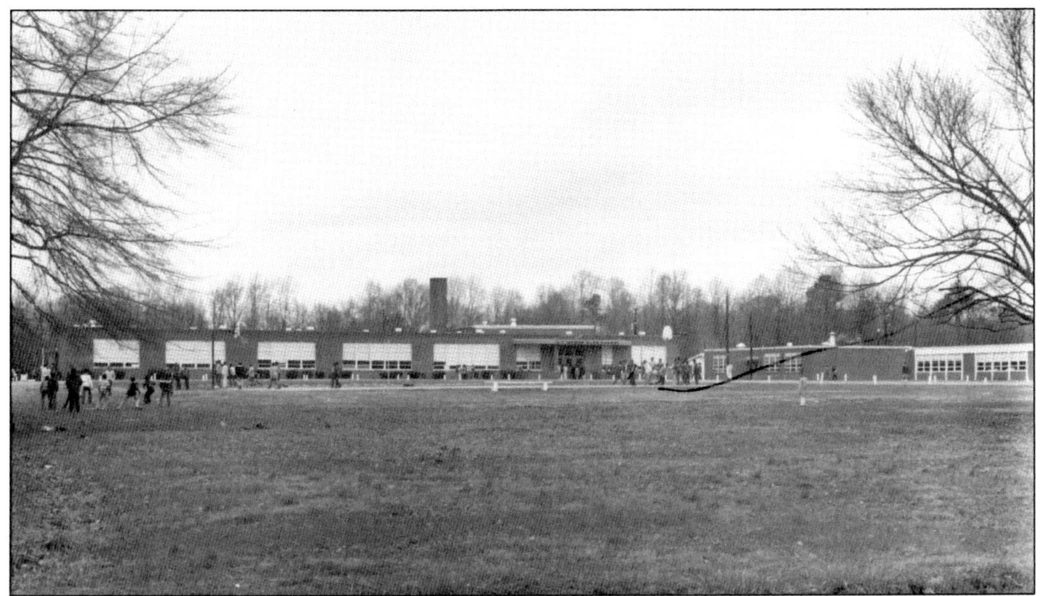

L.P. Jackson High School opened in 1950 to replace Surry County Training School. The school was named for Luther Porter Jackson (1892–1950), a history professor at Virginia State College in Petersburg, Virginia. He was one of Virginia's most important civil rights activists of the 1930s and 1940s. (Courtesy of Surry County Public Schools.)

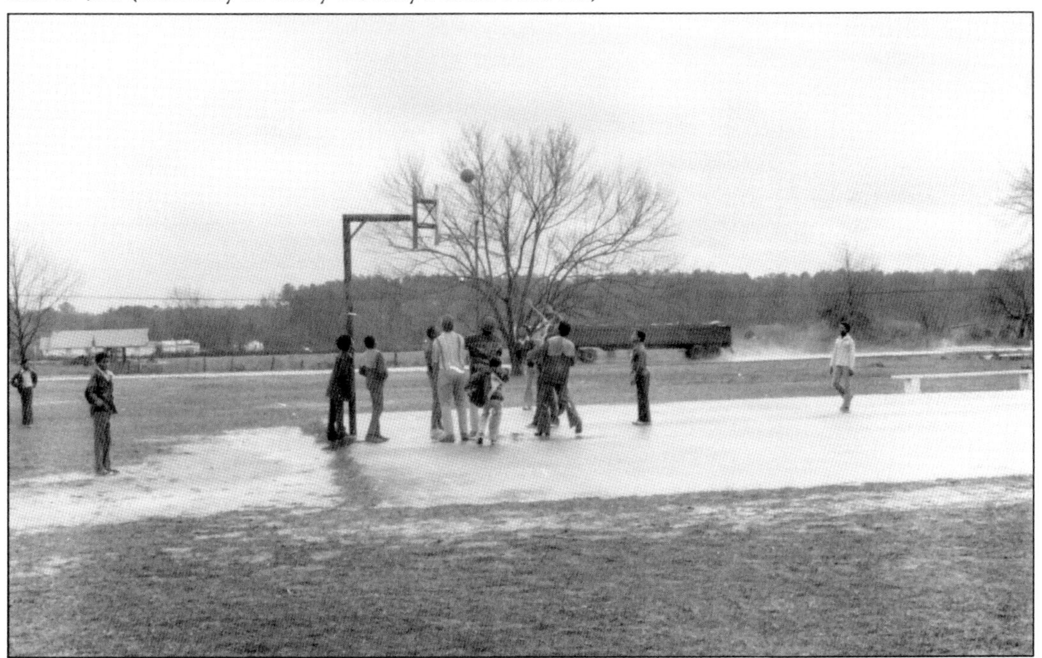

The outdoor basketball court at L.P. Jackson High School was nothing but packed dirt until the early 1960s when asphalt was laid over it to provide a hard surface. In a February 14, 1999, *Daily Press* article, the basketball team of 1969–1970, William Warren, Mario Newby, Joe Ellis, Benjamin Warren, coach George Reynolds, and others, remember how extraordinary the Cougars were despite having to practice and play mostly outdoors in varying weather conditions. (Courtesy of Surry County Public Schools.)

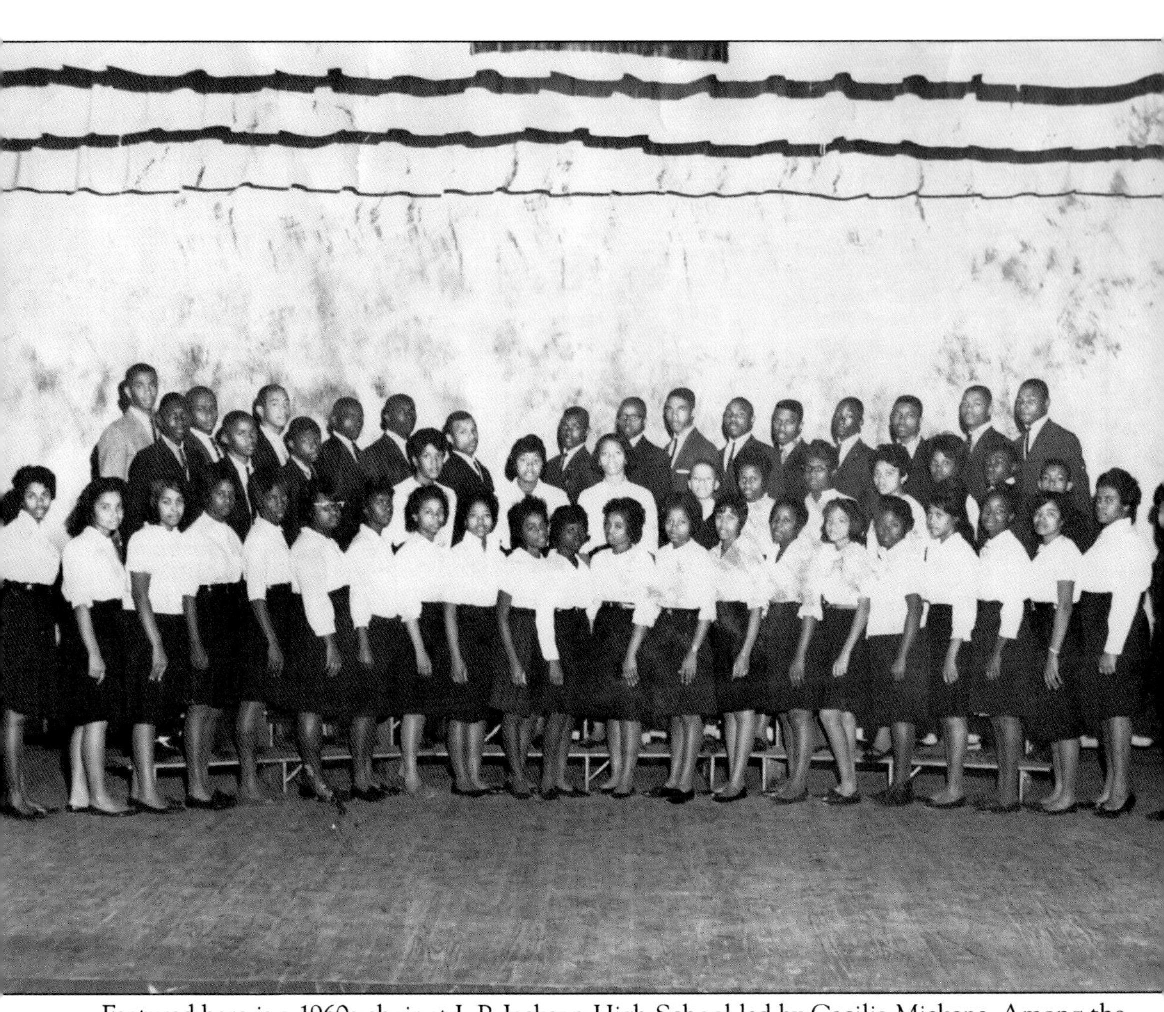

Featured here is a 1960s choir at L.P. Jackson High School led by Cecilia Mickens. Among the students in the choir are Carolyn Harrison Jones and Barbara Harrison Mallory. (Courtesy of Surry County Public Schools.)

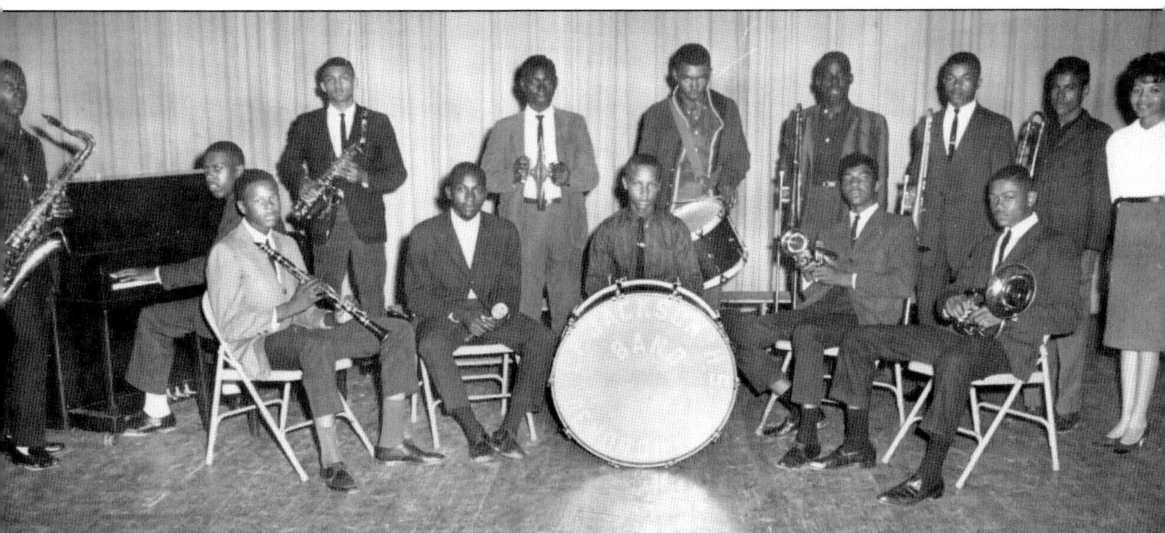

In the 1960s at L.P. Jackson High School, music teacher Cecilia Bacon Mickens organized a jazz band that played at school functions. Pictured from left to right are (seated) Bernard Edler (piano), Richard Parham, unidentified, John Anderson, Wardell Price, and Waymon Parson; (standing) Pernell Fields, Carl Overby, Earnest Williams, Theodore Lunsford, Russell Doswell, Echo Bailey, Dennis E. Harrison, and Cecilia Mickens. (Courtesy of Surry County Public Schools.)

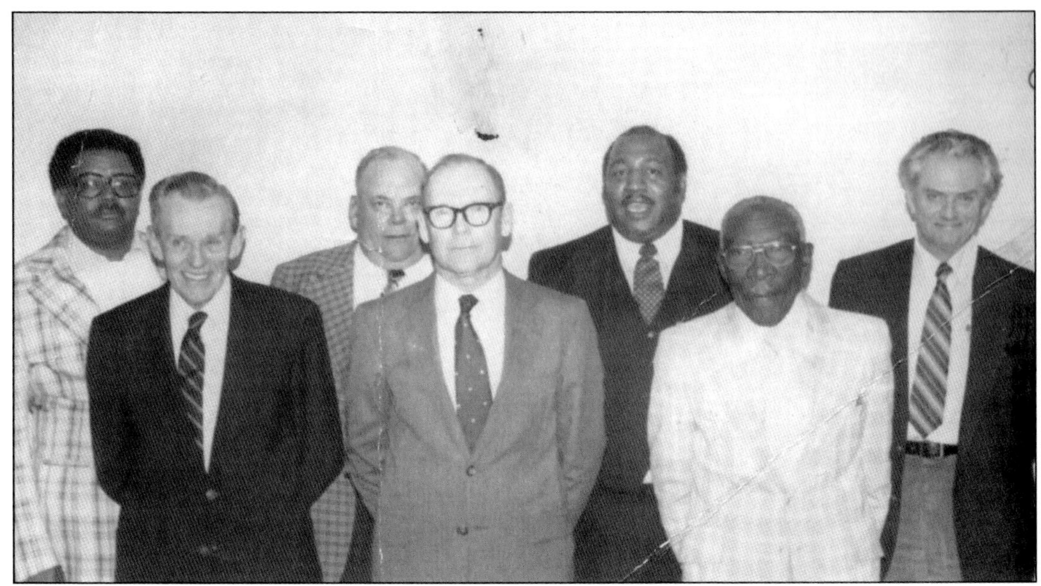

Dr. Clarence P. Penn (pictured third from right) became superintendent of Surry School in 1977 and served for over 20 years. The quality of education improved considerably for all Surry students during his tenure. Taken after a board meeting, this photograph features, from left to right, Surry School Board members Rufus Blount, Col. Nelson Ritchie, Bailey Ashby, Noel Taylor, Dr. Penn (superintendent), Newton M. Taliaferro, and Dr. Jeremy Irons. (Courtesy of Surry County Public Schools.)

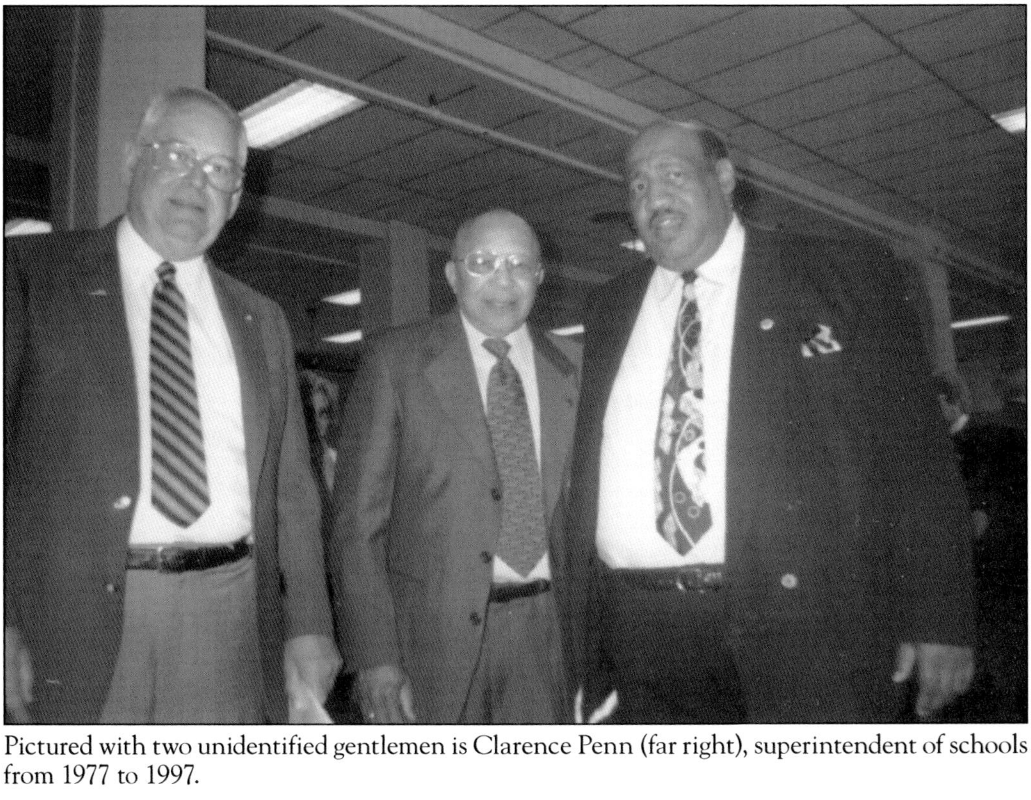

Pictured with two unidentified gentlemen is Clarence Penn (far right), superintendent of schools from 1977 to 1997.

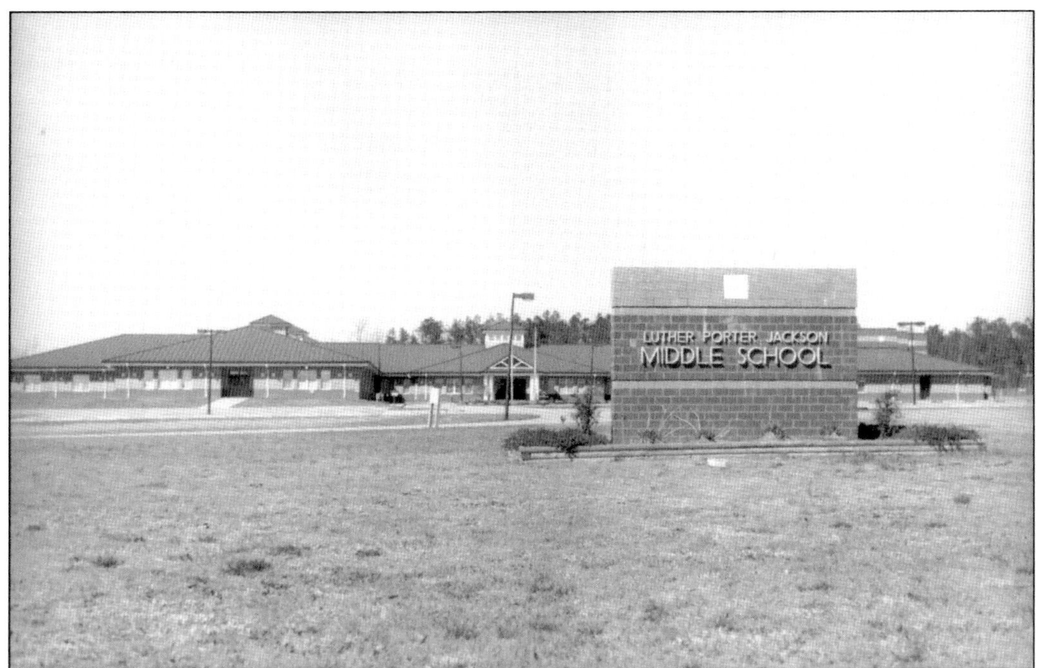

Luther Porter Jackson Middle School opened in 1995 and was the third and last school built at the intersection of Hollybush and New Design Roads.

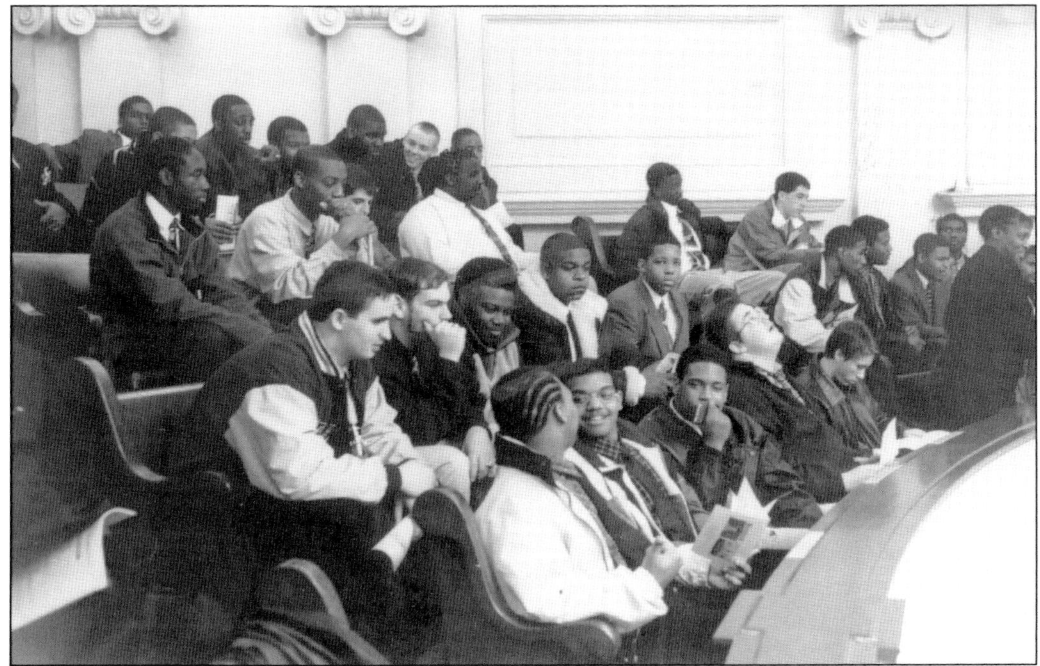

Members of the Surry County High School football team are pictured here in 2000 at the Virginia General Assembly in Richmond. They await the reading of a resolution that recognizes the team for winning the state championship and having a perfect season in 1999.

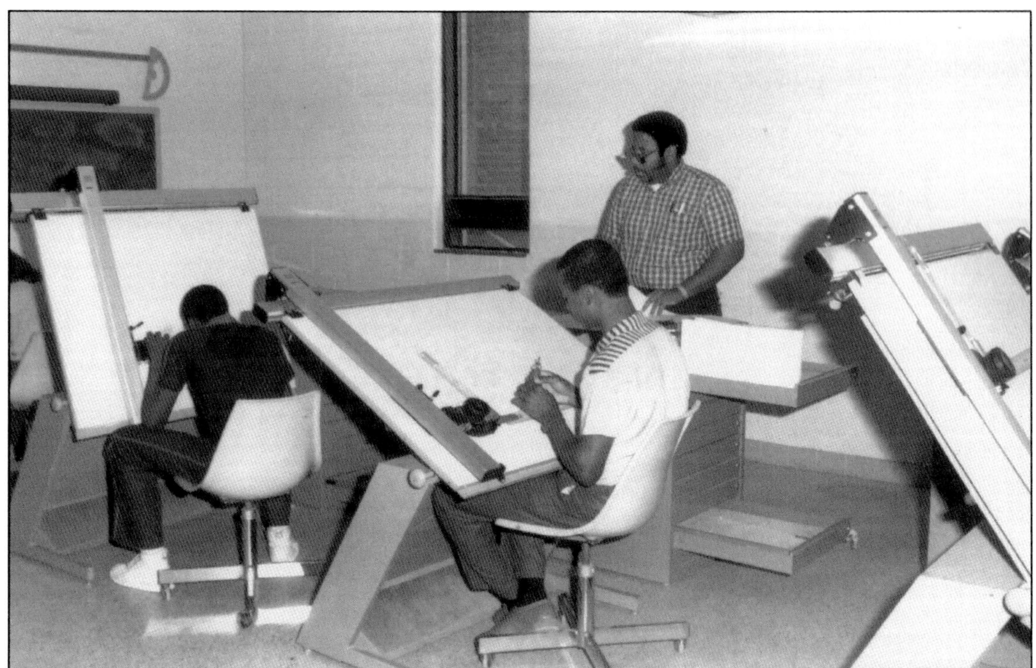

Coach Larry "Bear" Jones was a teacher, coach, award-winning Technology Student Association (TSA) sponsor, mentor, confidant, and educator at Surry County High School for over 30 years. He is pictured with one of his 1970s drafting classes. (Courtesy of Surry County Public Schools.)

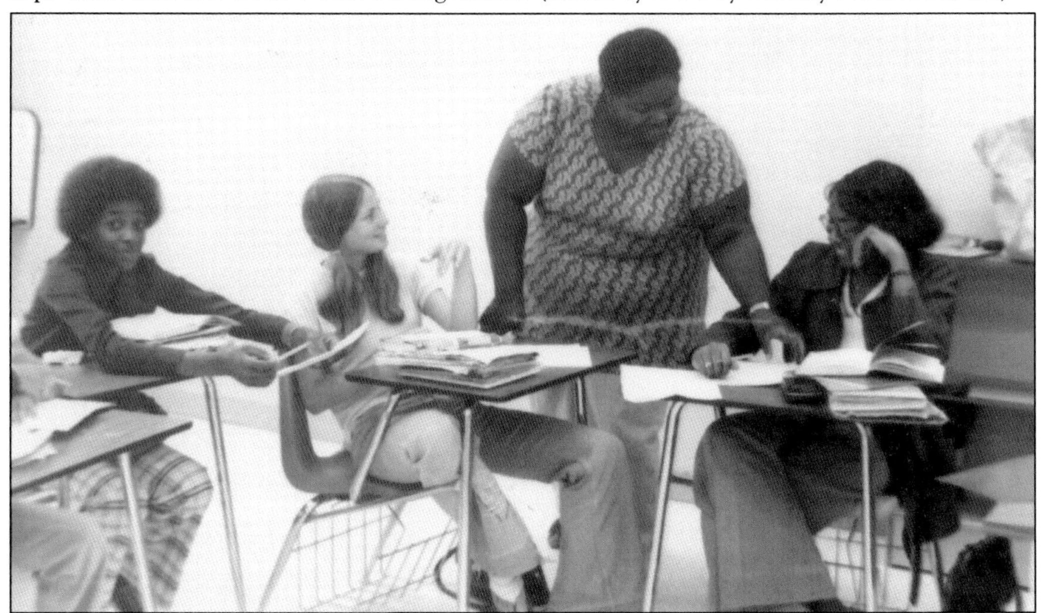

Edna Ford Powell is pictured teaching a trigonometry class at Surry County High School in 1977 with, from left to right, students Sarah Washington Mayo, Patsy Hopper Rush, and Deborah Harrison Dawson. Powell has been a teacher in Surry County since 1972 and currently teaches trigonometry, advanced mathematics, advanced placement calculus, and physics. Powell is a teacher who demands the best from her students and is a constant support and role model for present and past pupils. (Courtesy of Surry County Public Schools.)

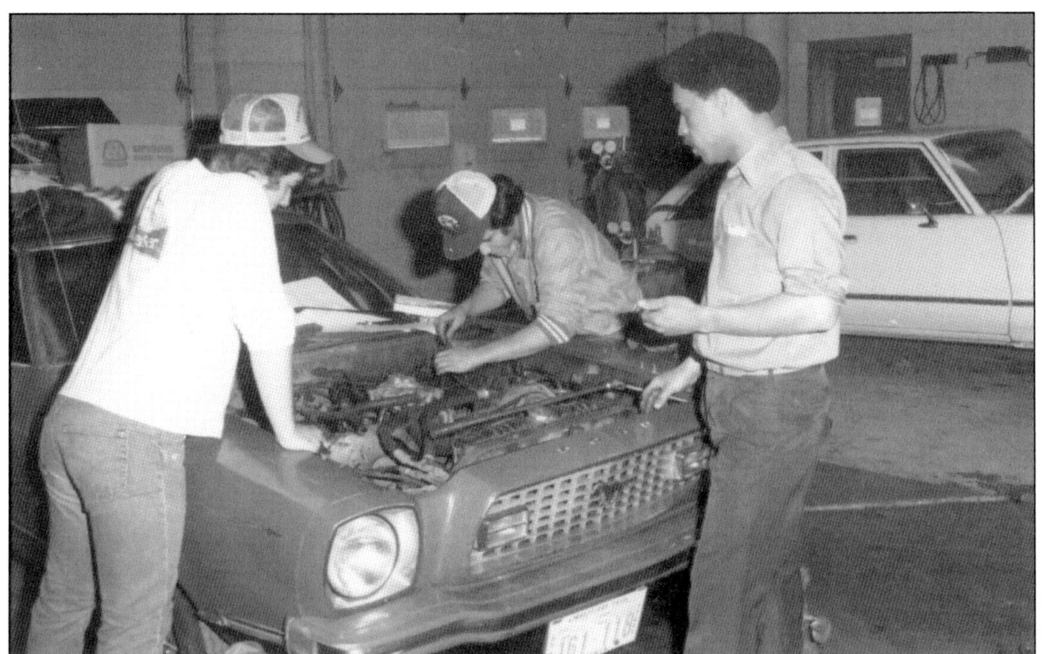

Pictured here around 1979, Elwood Wooden Jr. has taught automobile mechanics at Surry County High School since the mid-1970s. He is a methodical and detailed-oriented teacher who has inspired many students to pursue careers in automobile mechanics. He is also an US Air Force veteran. (Courtesy of Surry County Public Schools.)

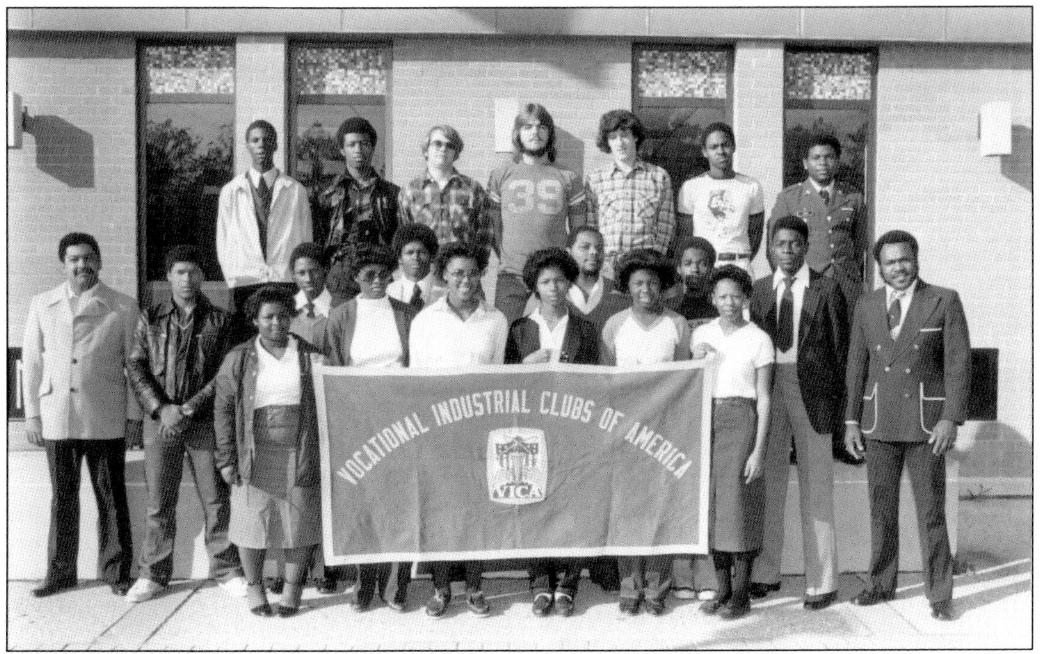

Pictured here is the award-winning Surry County High School Vocational Industrial Clubs of America (VICA) in the late 1970s. Rodney Thomas and Stacey Byrd are two of the students pictured. Giron Wooden Sr. (far left) and Allan T. Parson (far right) were the two sponsors. (Courtesy of Surry County Public Schools.)

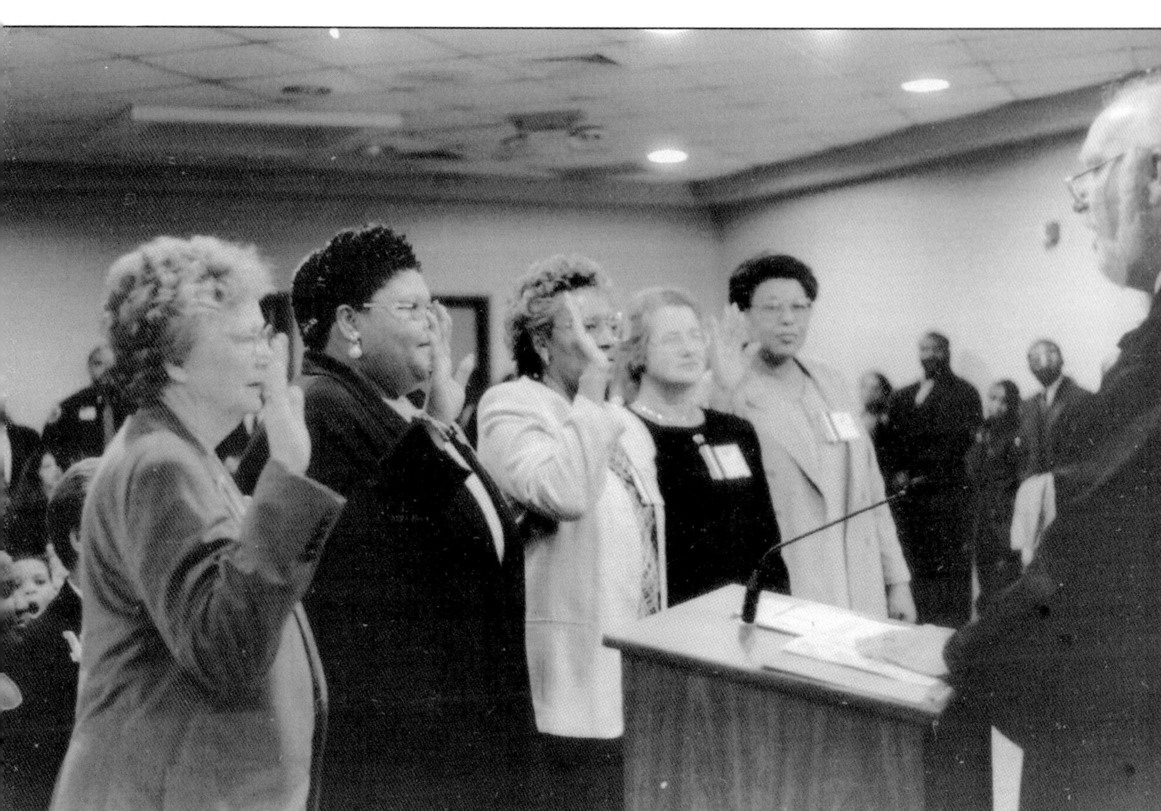

In a history-making moment, a photographer captured the swearing in of the first elected and first all-female school board in Surry County. In previous years, board members were appointed by local government officials. The women were elected to the board in November 1999. Pictured from left to right are Iva Seward, Jackie Hardy Ricks, Gladys Harris, Stephanie Headley, and Gloria Bailey Brown.

Four

People and Places

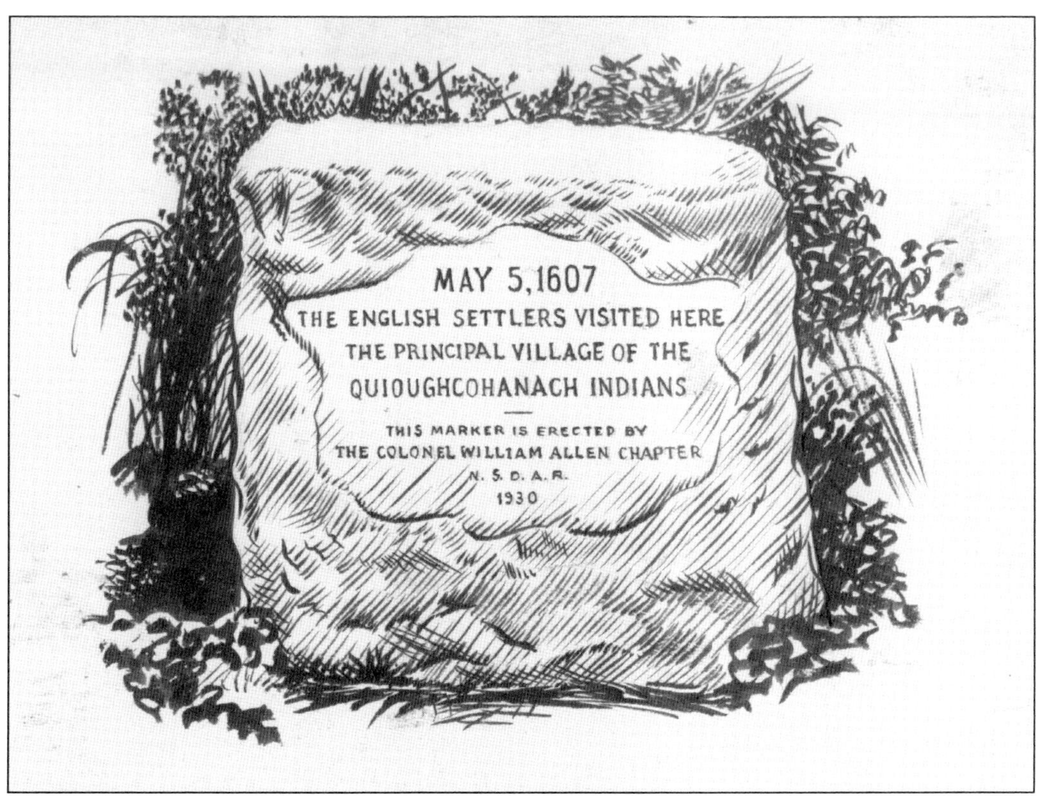

This pencil sketch was done for the 300th anniversary of the founding of Surry County. It is located at Claremont and indicates that English settlers arrived on the south side of the James River before establishing a permanent settlement at Jamestown.

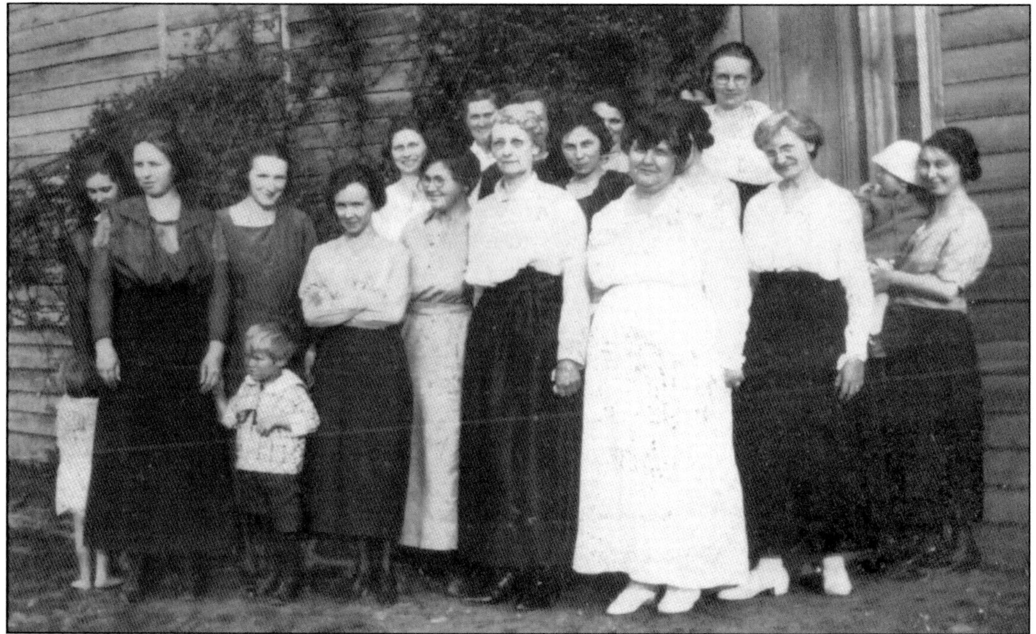

The Spring Grove Ladies Aid Society was formed in 1905 to pay for repairs to the Spring Grove Methodist Church. This 1900s image features, from left to right, unidentified, Eva Haff Barnes with a young boy, unidentified, Emily Barnes Baugh, two unidentified women, J. Huber, Mrs. Mook, Mrs. Utgard, Ortive Haff, Florence Sobel Huber, Mrs. Setchin, and Nell Geyer Reeson. The club remains strong, and even though the church no longer stands, members support the community with fundraisers. The club name was changed to the Spring Grove Community Club, and they celebrated 100 years of service in 2005.

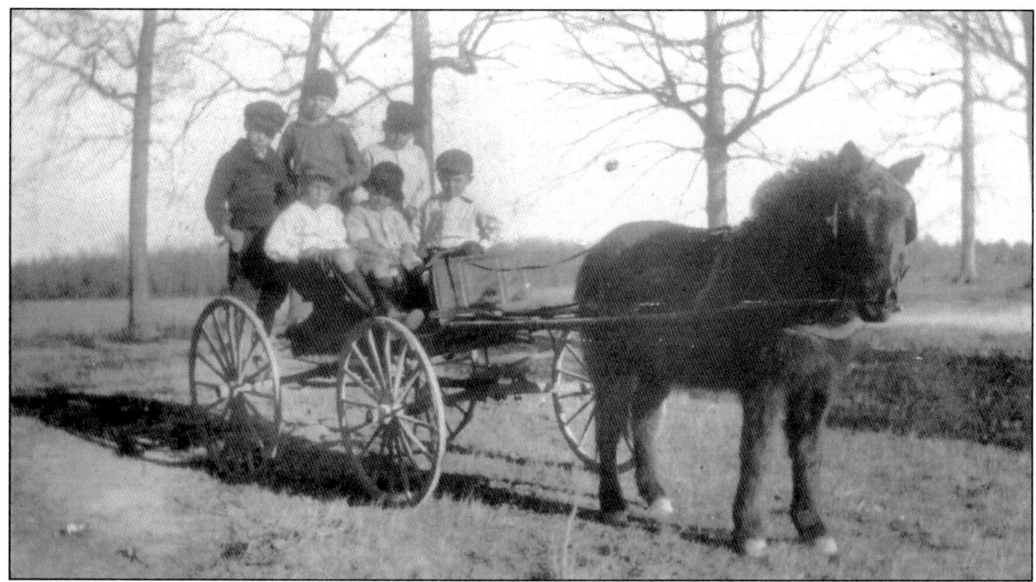

The Spring Grove children featured here are the three Reeson brothers, the Baugh brothers, and Sonny Utgard. Frisz, the black pony, belonged to the Baugh family and was known to chase the train as it came through Spring Grove—whether it had a rider or was pulling a cart. (Courtesy of Claude Reeson.)

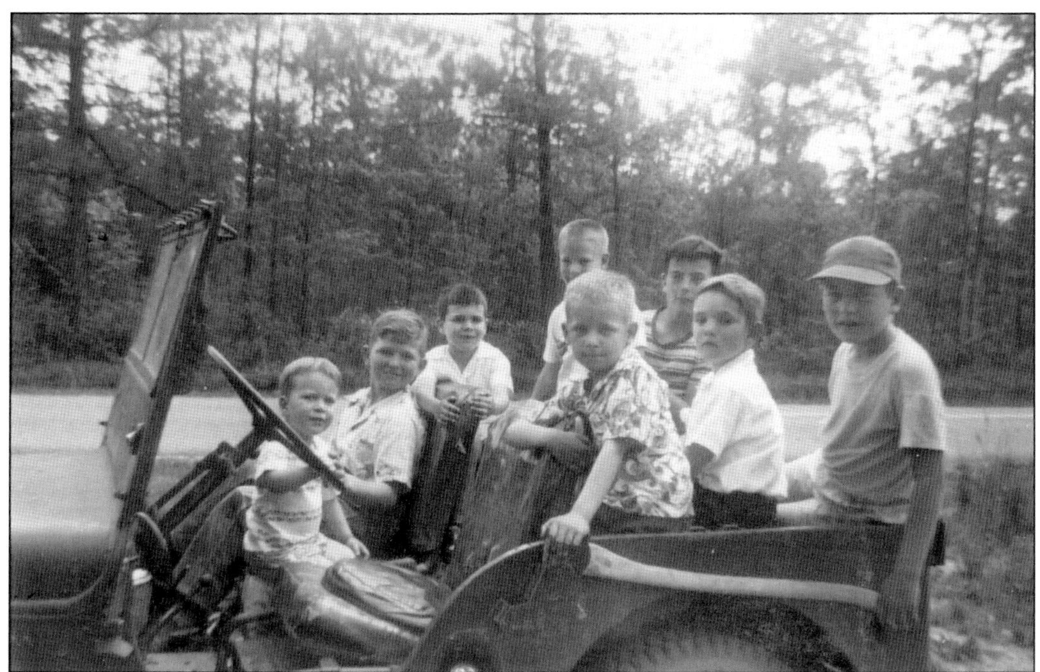

Sunday afternoon, May 2, 1954, finds a group of Spring Grove children playing on this 1947 Jeep. From left to right are Mike Reeson, Phillip Chappell Jr., David Barnes, James Fields, Archie Scarborough (in rear), Claude Reeson, Wayne Chappell, and Jerry Reeson. (Courtesy of Claude Reeson.)

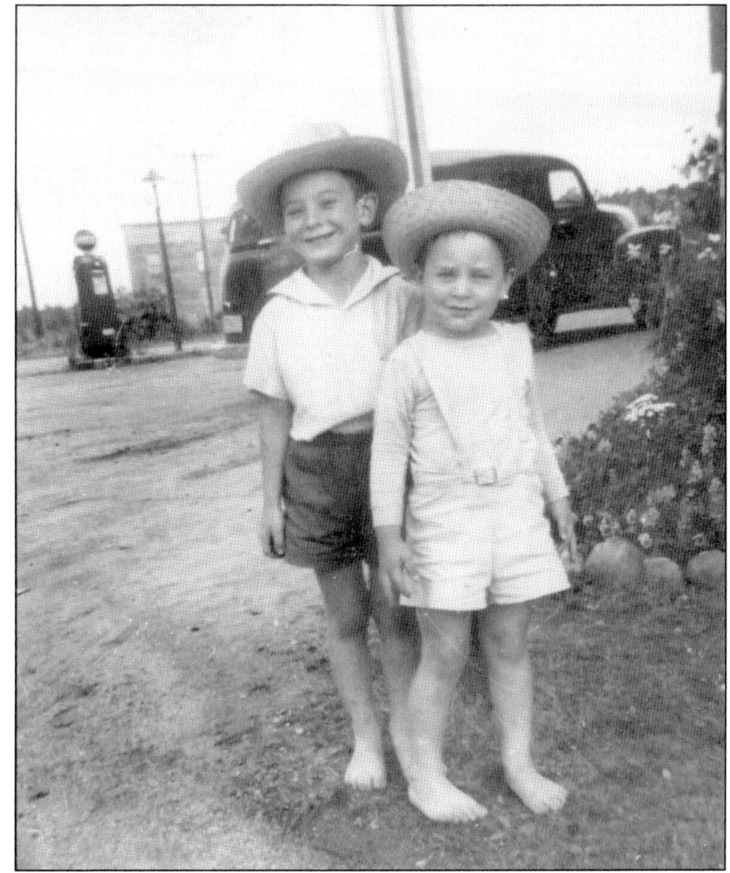

Claude (left) and William "Jerry" Reeson are pictured in July 1949 at the corner of the Spring Grove post office. In the background is the black-panel mail truck driven by Thurman Elliott, who delivered mail to Savedge, Spring Grove, and Clarement. Also in the background is the Spring Grove Hotel. (Courtesy of Claude Reeson.)

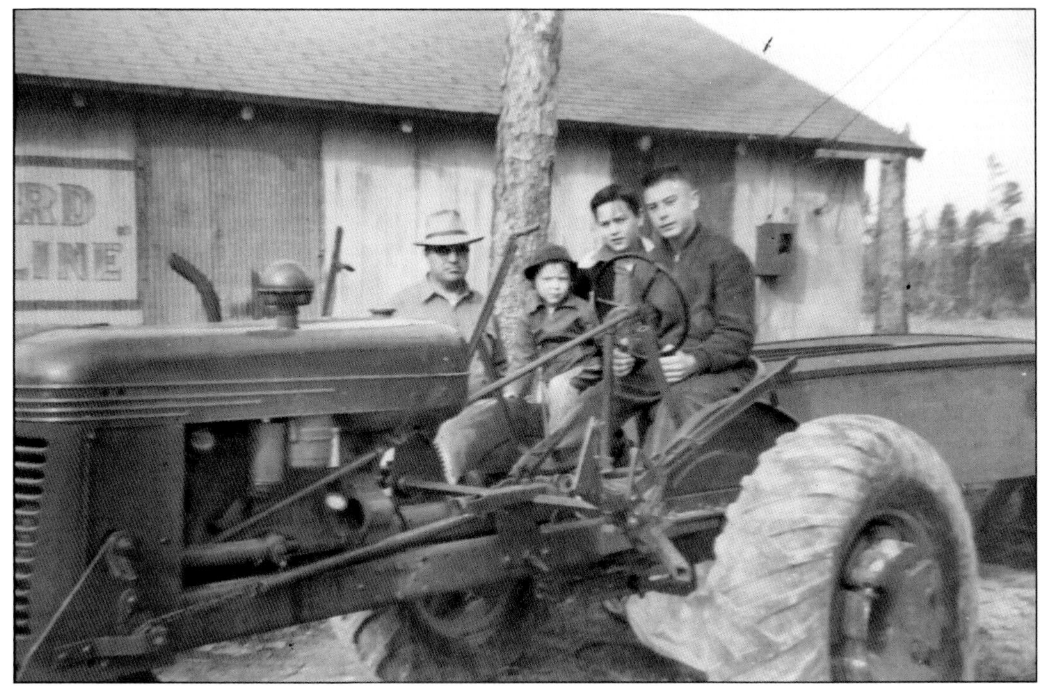

This April 1956 photograph features the Reeson family with their 1930 Avery tractor. From left to right are Willis, Mike, Jerry, and Claude Reeson. (Courtesy of Claude Reeson.)

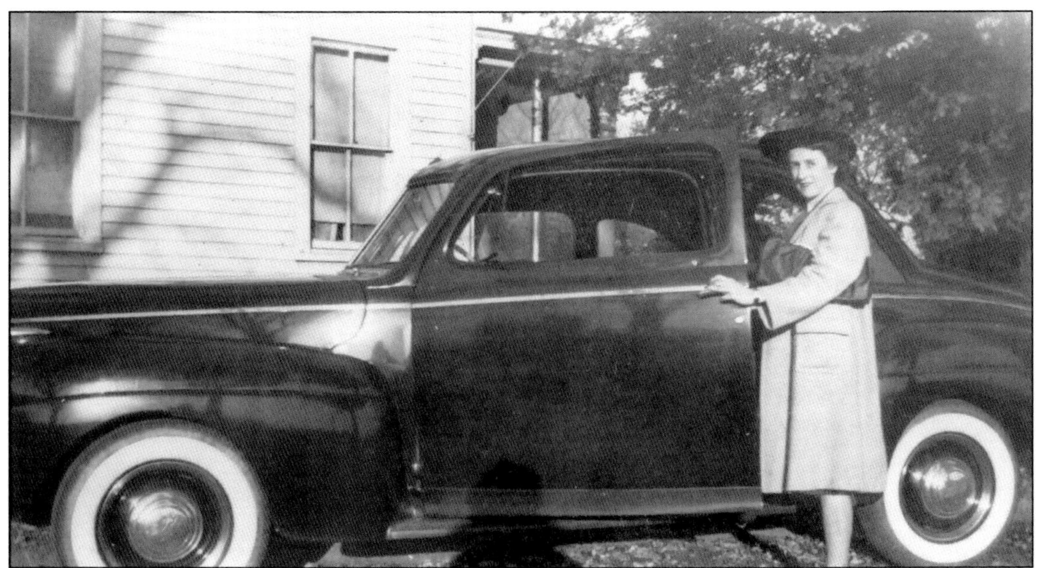

Willie Gwaltney, postmistress at Spring Grove from 1942 until the 1980s, is shown with her 1942 Ford Coupe. (Courtesy of Claude Reeson.)

James Garland Cooper was the mail carrier at Savedge until the station closed and his route was moved to Spring Grove. In this photograph, he is standing beside his 1947 Ford mail car with a full mailbag on his shoulder. He retired in the 1960s. (Courtesy of Claude Reeson.)

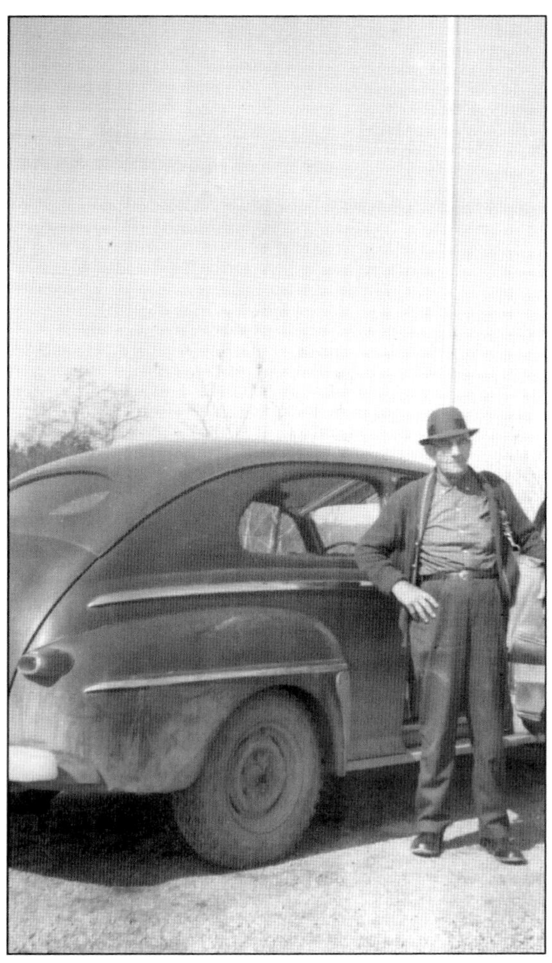

John Baugh celebrated his 21st birthday on February 20, 1907, with a reception where "no dancing" was allowed. (Courtesy of Claude Reeson.)

Mr. and Mrs. W. W. Baugh
cordially invite you to attend the reception given in
honor of the twenty=first birth=day
anniversary of their son
John C. Baugh,
at their residence, Spring Grove,
Wednesday evening, February 20th, 1907.
NO DANCING.

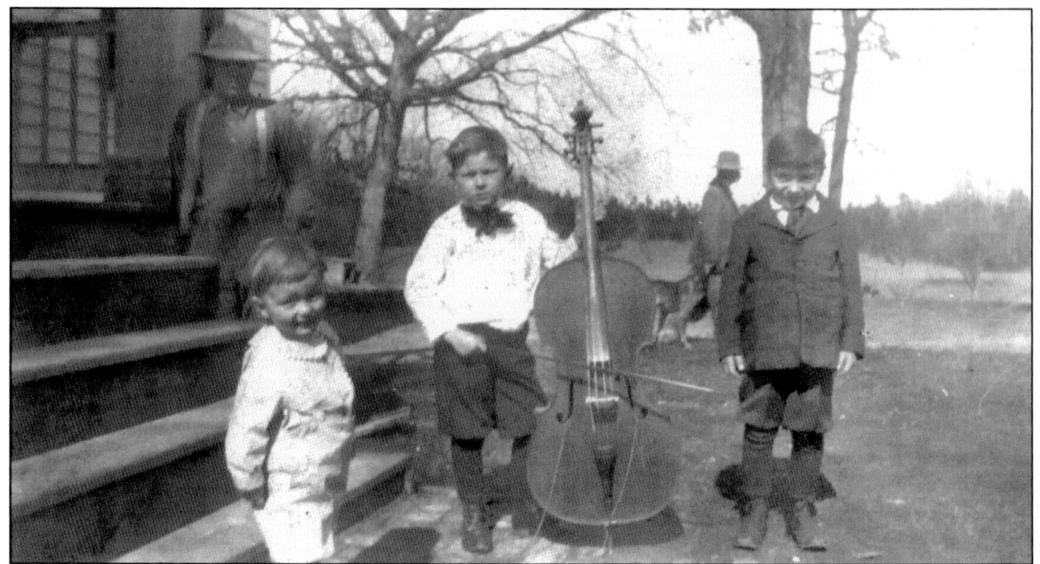

Standing at the front steps of the Reeson home are, from left to right, Tim, Claude, and Willis Reeson. The two gentlemen in the background are unidentified. The family owned the home from 1895 to 1950. (Courtesy of Claude Reeson.)

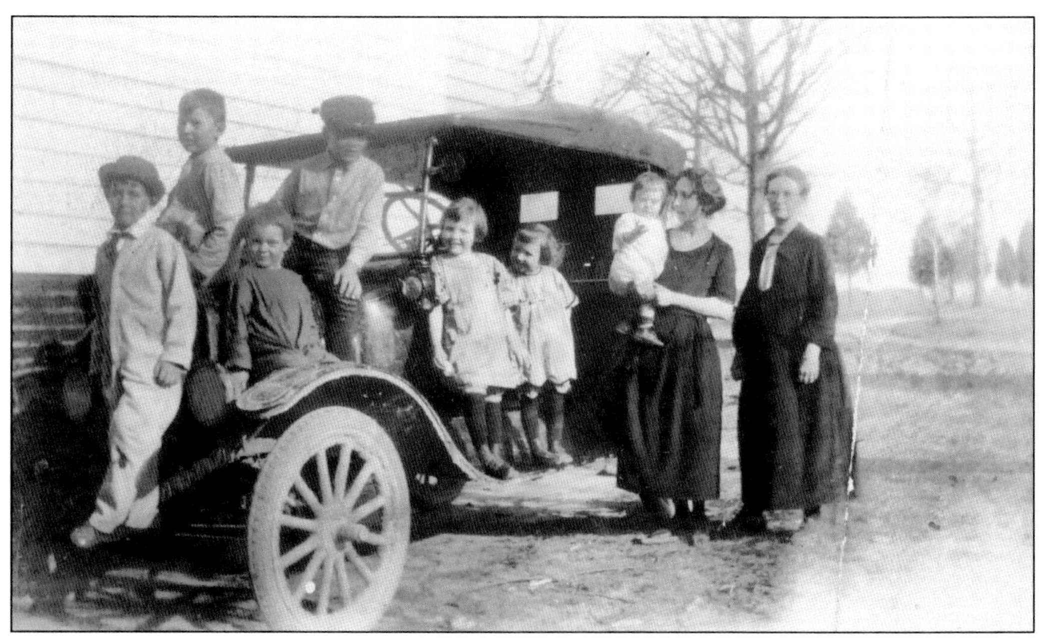

Family and friends of the Reesons gather for a group photograph at Spring Grove. (Courtesy of Claude Reeson.)

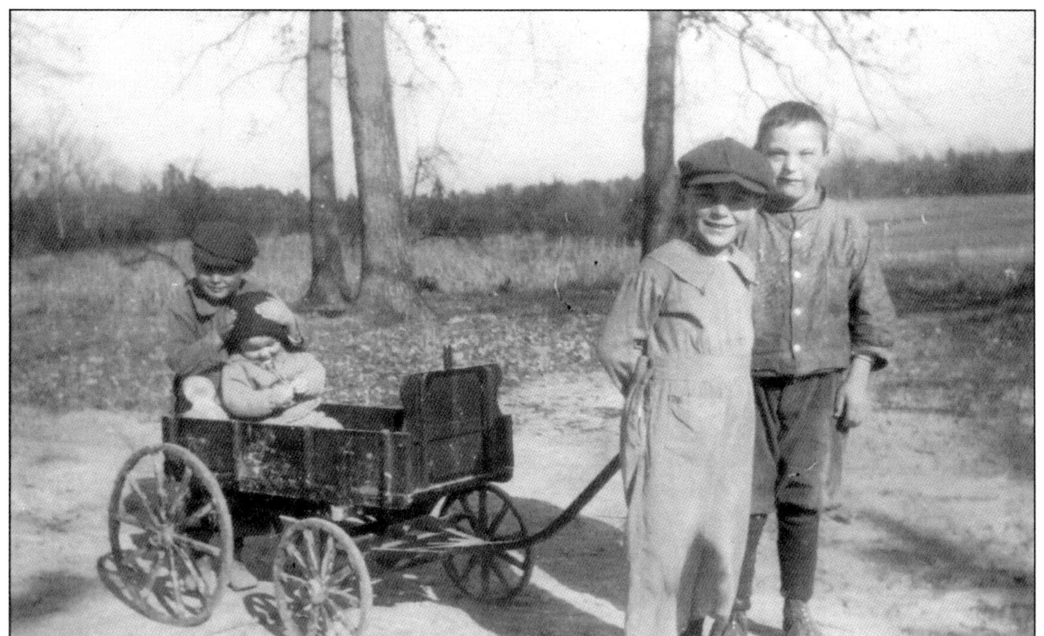

The Reeson children are featured in this January 1921 photograph taken at Spring Grove. Bob (far left) and Tim Reeson are in the wagon, with Willis Reeson (center) and their uncle Joe Geyer (right) pulling the wagon. (Courtesy of Claude Reeson.)

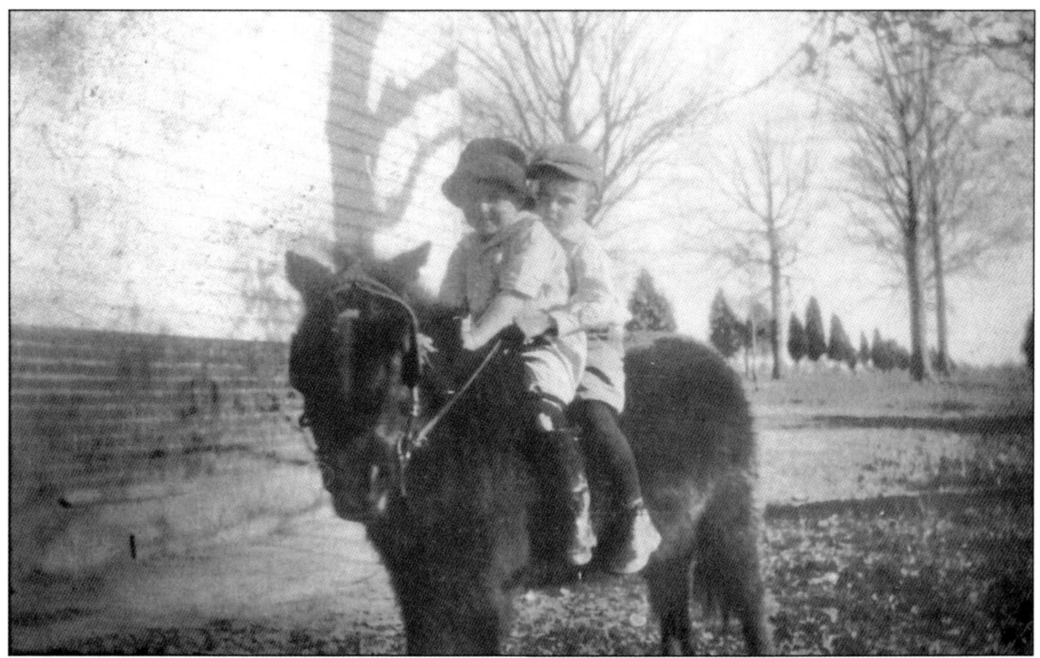

Tim Reeson (left) and Buddy Baugh are riding Fritz, the famous black pony, at the Reeson home in this December 1923 image. (Courtesy of Claude Reeson.)

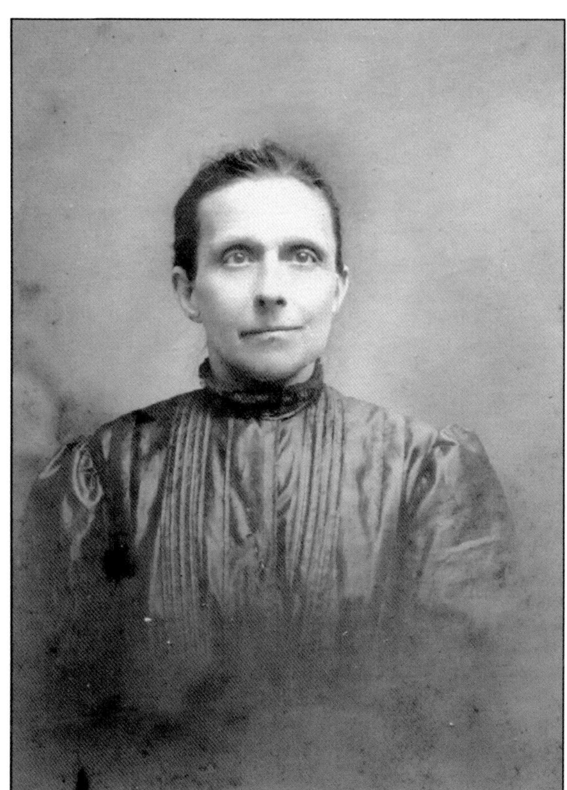

Emerreta Burgess Bishop is pictured in April 1907. She was mother of James Robert Bishop and well known throughout the Dendron community. (Courtesy of the Dendron Historical Society.)

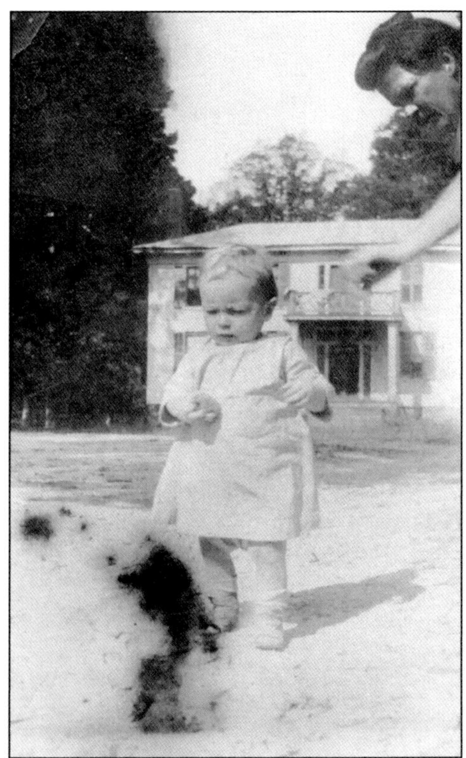

The Reeson family are longtime residents of Spring Grove. In this October 1920 photograph, a very young Tim Reeson is playing in front of the home place. (Courtesy of Claude Reeson.)

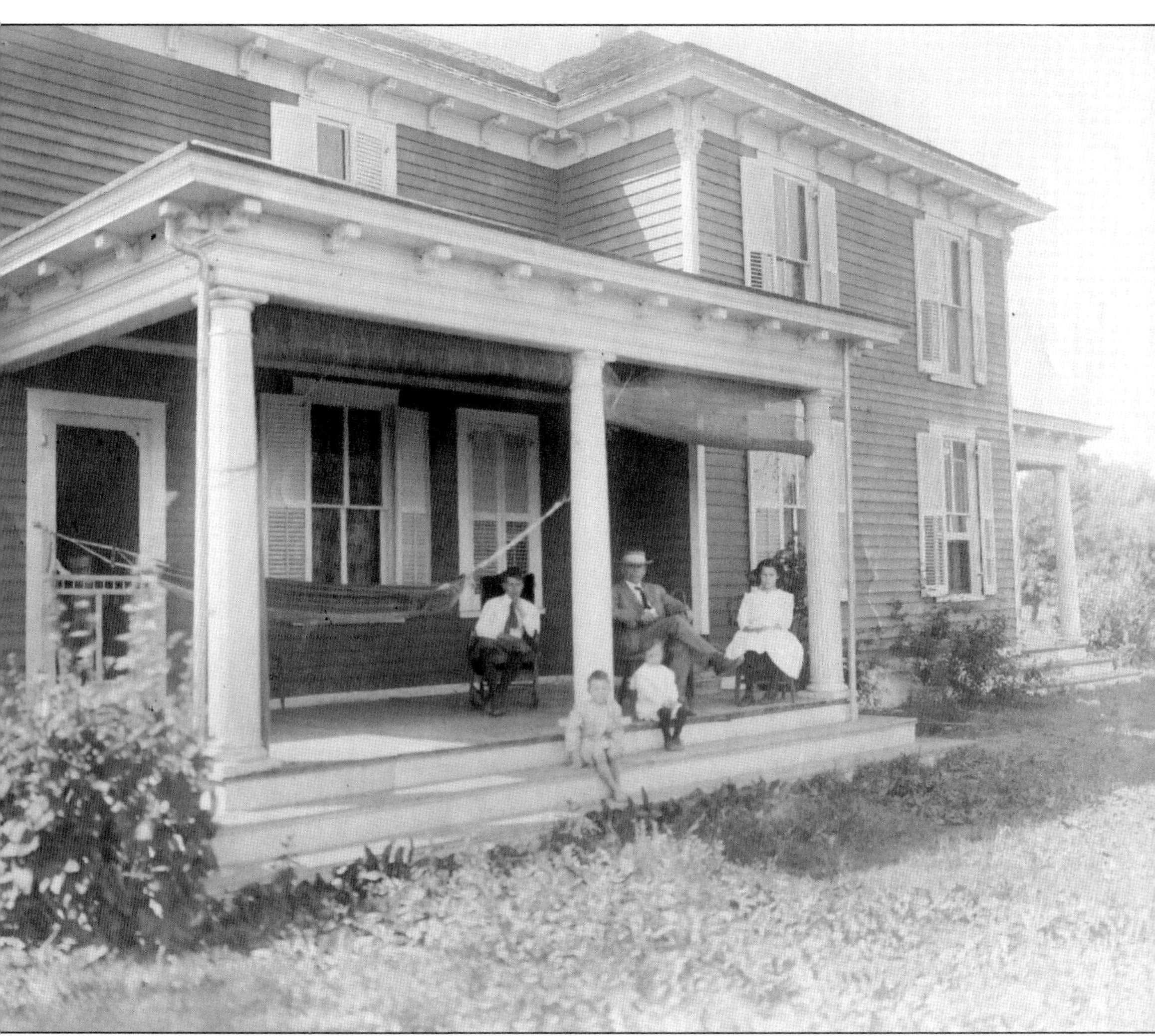

The Hopper house in Claremont is pictured on their recently completed porch around 1909 or 1910. James Robert Hopper is sitting in the center, and son James Lewis Hopper is at the left. Daughter Aois Hopper appears right, and sitting on the stairs are sons James (left) and Hal Hopper.

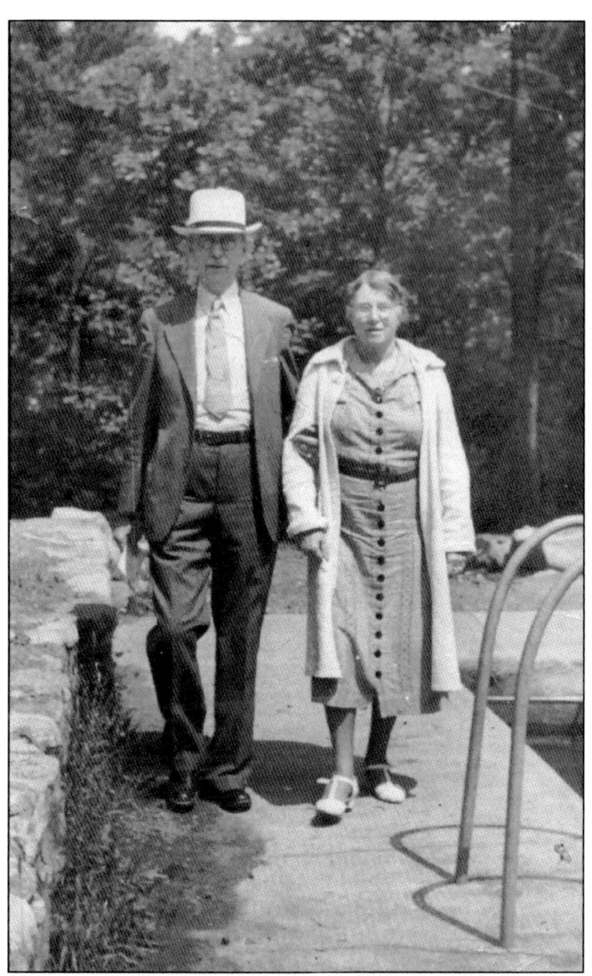

Around 1903, Sidney B. Barham Jr. was a merchant at Runnymede in Surry County. He was the son of Dr. S.B. Barham, who referred to him as "Sid." The younger Sidney, "Sid," is pictured here with his wife, Annie T. Barham.

Rosabelle Scammel, the great-grandmother of Henry Burleigh Holdsworth Jr., uses the spinning wheel in this image by award-winning photographer Lorena Wilcox Leath, who was born in Surry County in 1902. Her work mostly captured rural life in southeast Virginia. Leath died in 1991, and her heirs donated her collection of slides, photographs, and awards to the Surry County Historical Society. (Courtesy of Mary Grace Padgett.)

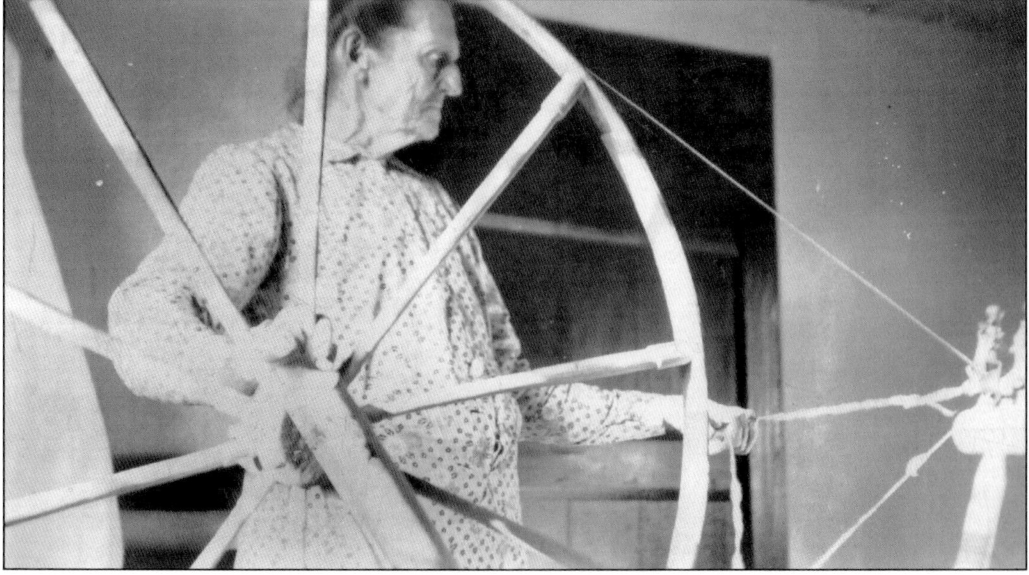

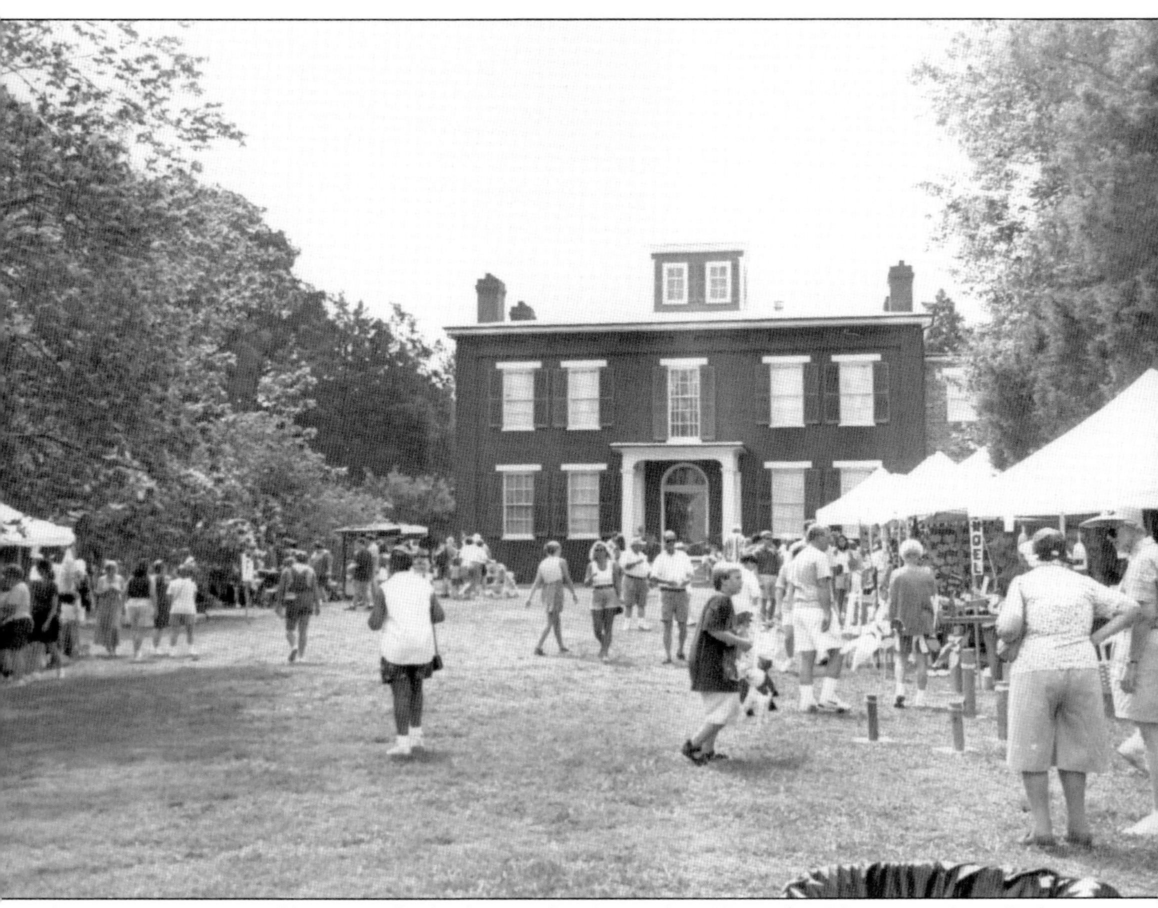

The Stewart Mansion (shown in the background) is located at Chippokes Plantation State Park. The event taking place is the July 1999 Pork, Pine, and Peanut Festival. The festival began in 1976 as a project of the Surry County Bicentennial Committee. It is scheduled for the third weekend in July and celebrates the three cash crops that have been Surry's livelihood since the 1600s.

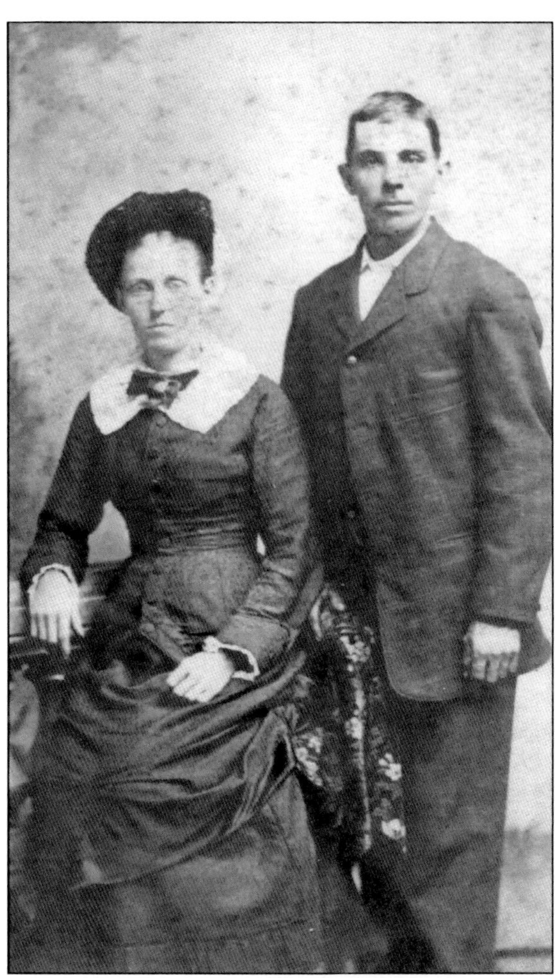

John Henry Holdsworth and Agusta Scammel Holdsworth are pictured shortly after their marriage. They are the grandparents of Henry Burleigh Holdsworth Jr. (Courtesy of Mary Grace Padgett.)

John and Agusta Holdsworth are pictured during their later years. (Courtesy of Mary Grace Padgett.)

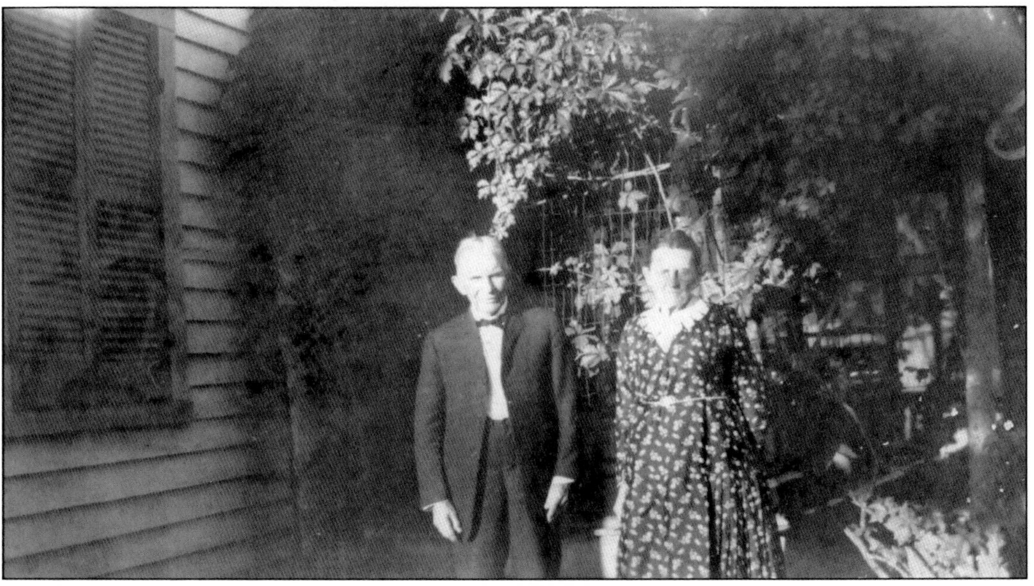

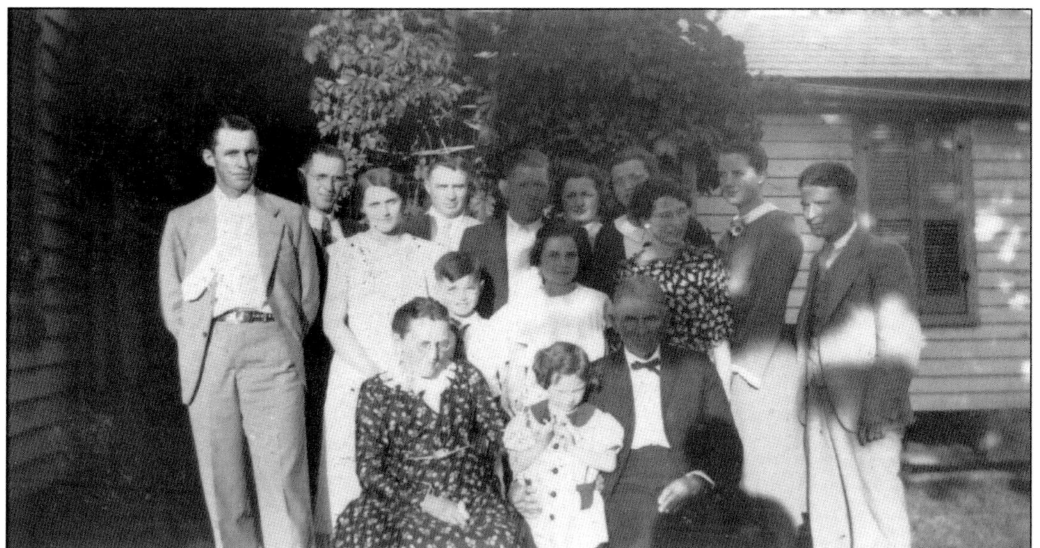

John and Agusta Holdsworth are pictured with their children and grandchildren. Henry Burleigh Holdsworth Jr. is the child standing behind Agusta. (Courtesy of Mary Grace Padgett.)

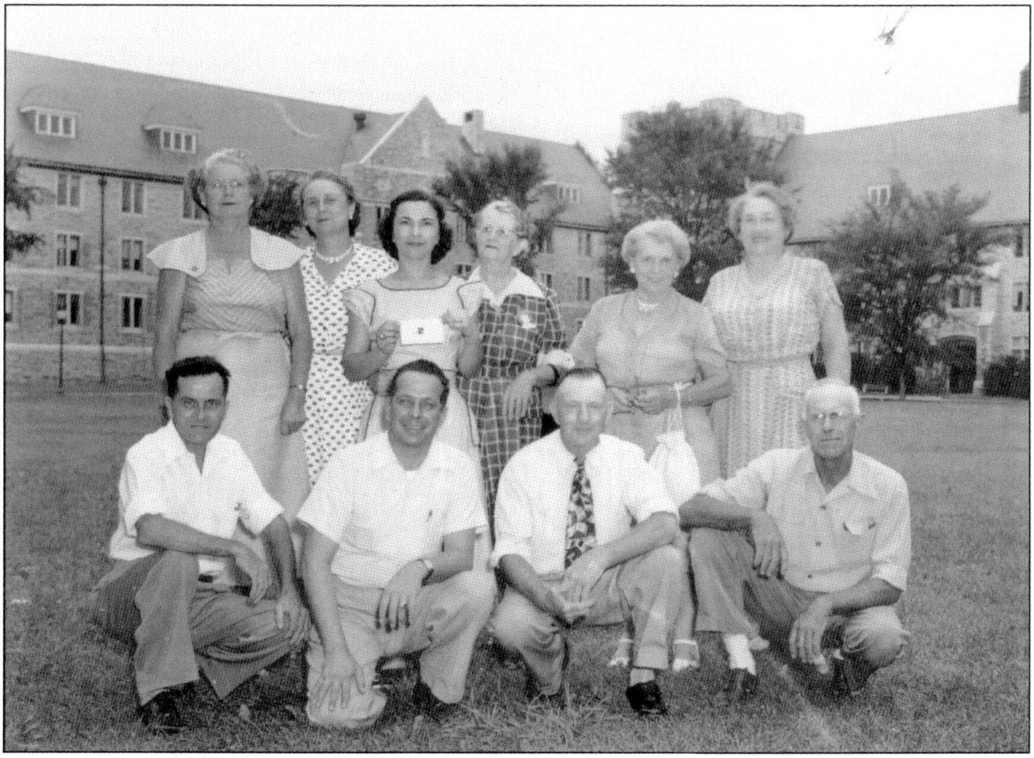

From July 30 to August 1, 1952, Surry representatives attended the Institute for Rural Affairs Conference at Virginia Polytechnic Institute in Blacksburg, Virginia. From left to right are (first row) Claude Menzel (county agent), E.L. Rawls, F.C. Laine, and H.O. Burgess; (second row) Annie W. Price (Bacon's Castle), Opal S. Jennings (Surry Home agent), Mrs. R.J. Slade Jr. (Dendron), Mrs. O.D. Belding, Edna Kimball (Claremont), and Mrs. H.O. Burgess (Carsley). (Courtesy of Donna Slade.)

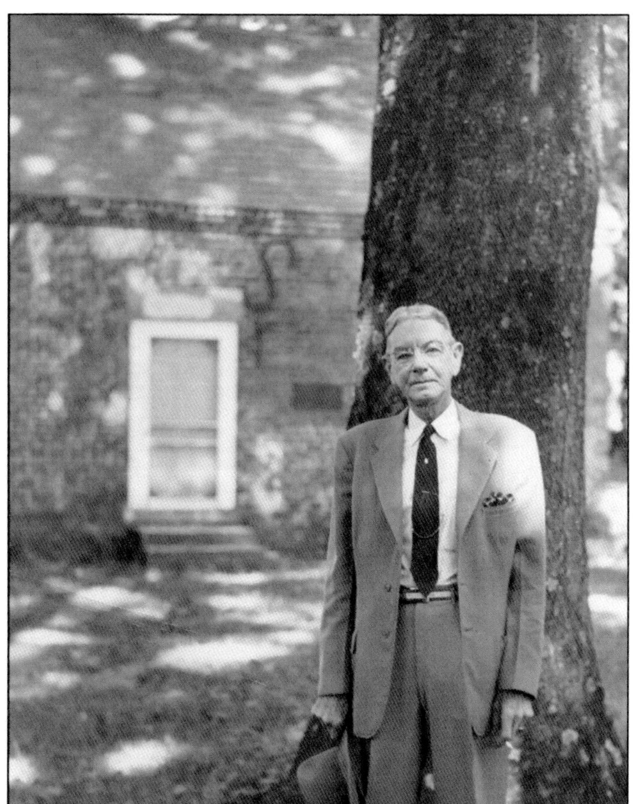

Gordon C. Berryman served as Surry County commissioner of the revenue from 1928 until 1976, the year he died. He is standing in front of the old clerk's office on the courthouse grounds. (Courtesy of Norma Roach.)

In the early 1900s, this serious-looking baseball team represented Dendron in league play against surrounding counties. (Courtesy of the Dendron Historical Society.)

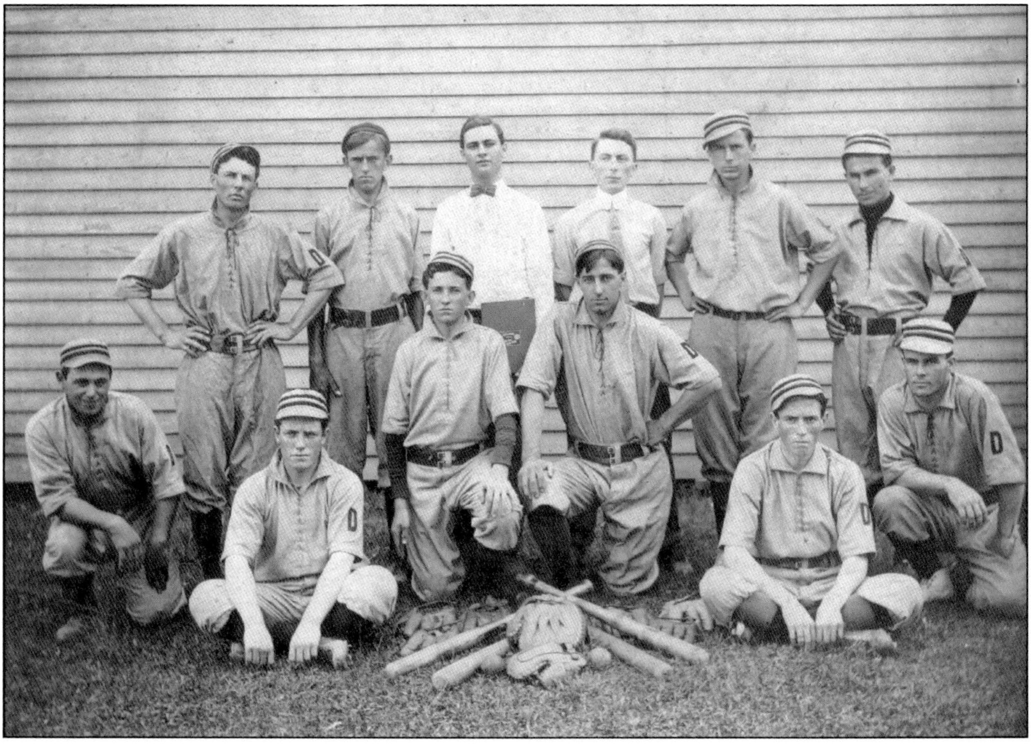

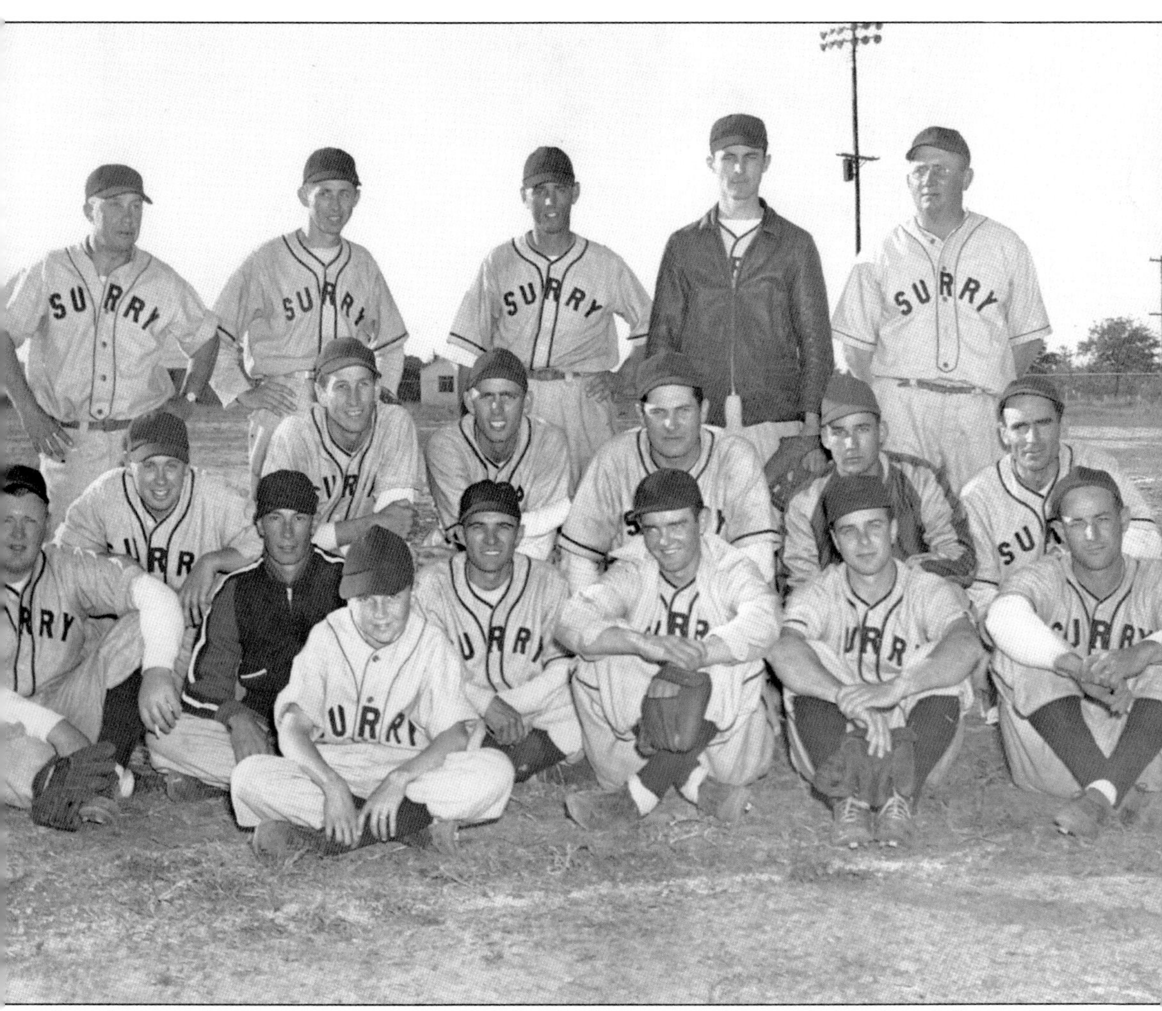

This photograph of Surry community adult baseball team members includes, from left to right, (first row, seated) Pete Goodrich, William Jones, Hunter Cox, Dick Pittman, Billy Warren, Melvin Cox, and William Berryman; (second row, kneeling) James Jones, Lloyd Price, H.B. Johnson Jr., Howard Jones, Ray Butts, and Pete Roach; (third row, standing) Jack Savedge, Pete Edwards, James Johnson, Albert Laine, and William Bruce Holleman. (Courtesy of Donna Slade.)

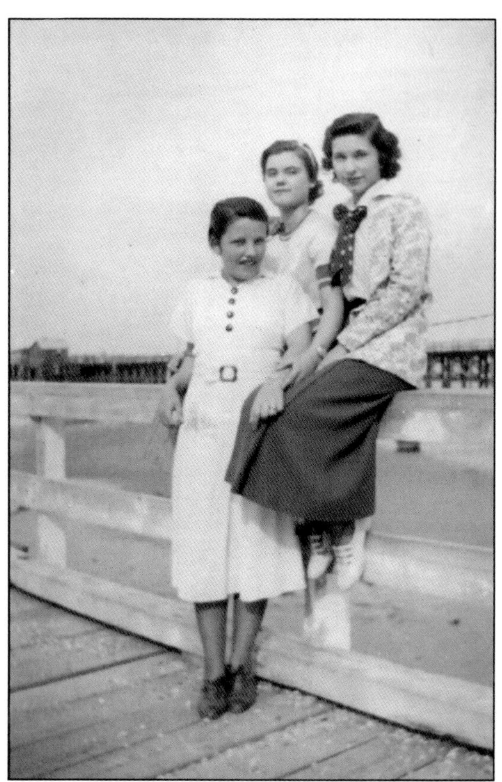

Pictured in this mid- to late-1930s photograph are, from left to right, Dorothy Grubbs, Edith Grubbs, and Armistead Ingram. They are on the Surry, Sussex & Southampton Railway pier at Scotland. (Courtesy of Donna Slade.)

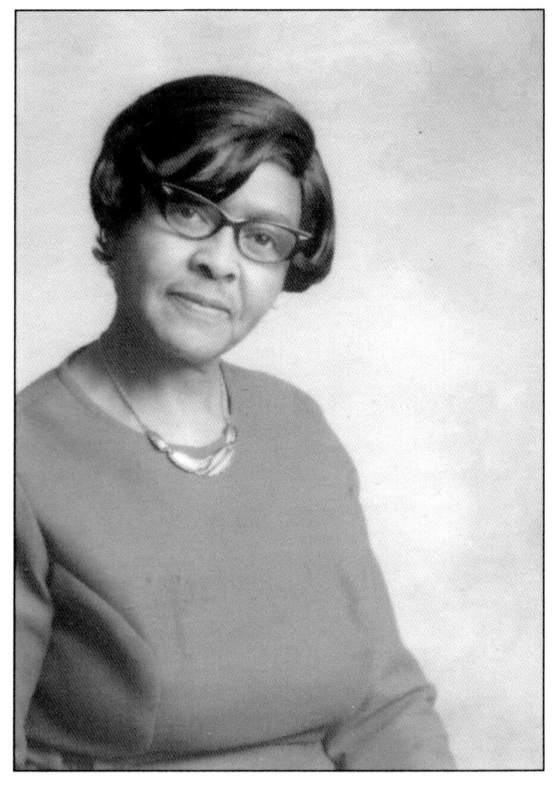

Juliana Green Johnson served as midwife to Surry County residents for over 37 years and delivered at least 341 babies. Johnson followed in her grandmother's footsteps when she became a midwife in the late 1930s. Her formal training amounted to one week of study at Virginia State College. At the college, she learned the birthing process, how to care for the mother during labor, and how to bathe the newborn child. Johnson's informal training was mostly observing her grandmother and advice from Dr. B.H. Knight, who consulted if a birth became too difficult or if medications were needed. (Courtesy of Faye Grandison.)

Pat Leary taught pre-algebra and algebra I at Surry County High School from the late 1970s through the early 1980s. She also served as the cheerleading coach. (Courtesy of Surry County Public Schools.)

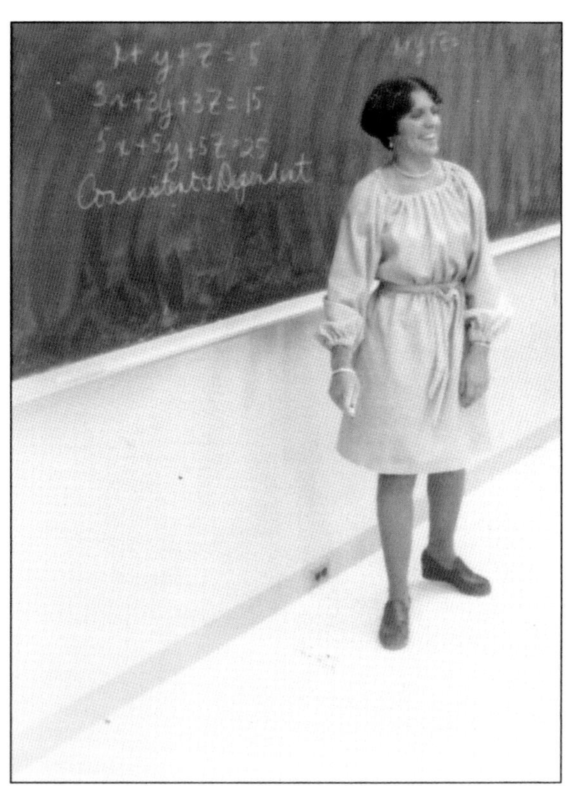

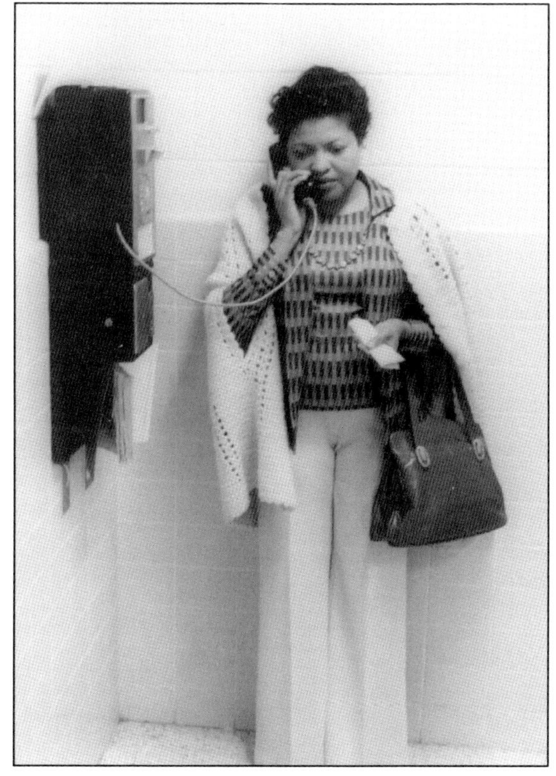

Cecilia Bacon Mickens taught piano, chorus, and music appreciation at L.P. Jackson and Surry County High Schools for over 20 years. She sponsored and developed numerous award-winning choirs, show choirs, and individual musicians. She inspired a generation of students to appreciate all types of music. (Courtesy of Surry County Public Schools.)

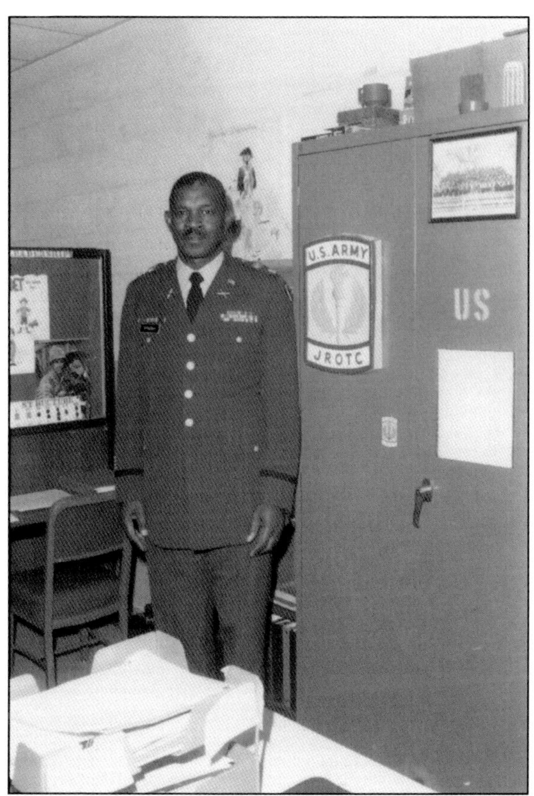

Col. Willie J. McFadden Sr. was the first officer to head the JROTC program at Surry County High School in the mid-1980s. (Courtesy of Surry County Public Schools.)

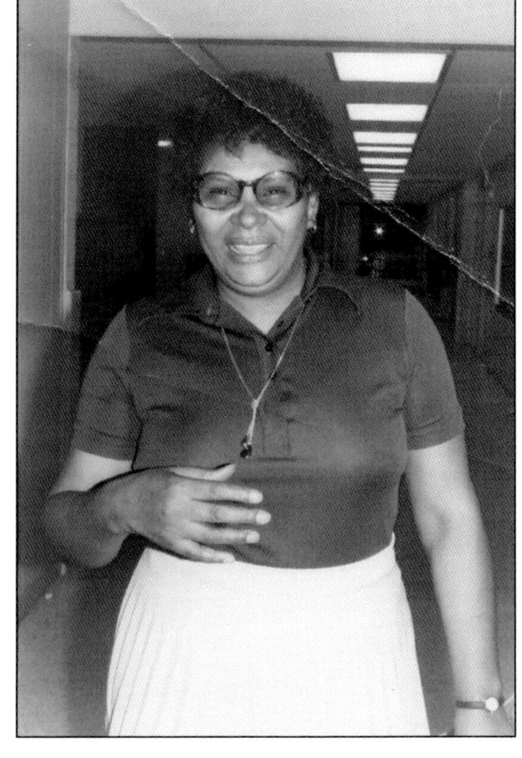

Doris Clayton Overby taught upper-level English classes at L.P. Jackson and Surry County High Schools for over 30 years. She was known to be a strict teacher and captured student's interest by mesmerizing them with her interpretations of various Shakespearean characters. (Courtesy of Surry County Public Schools.)

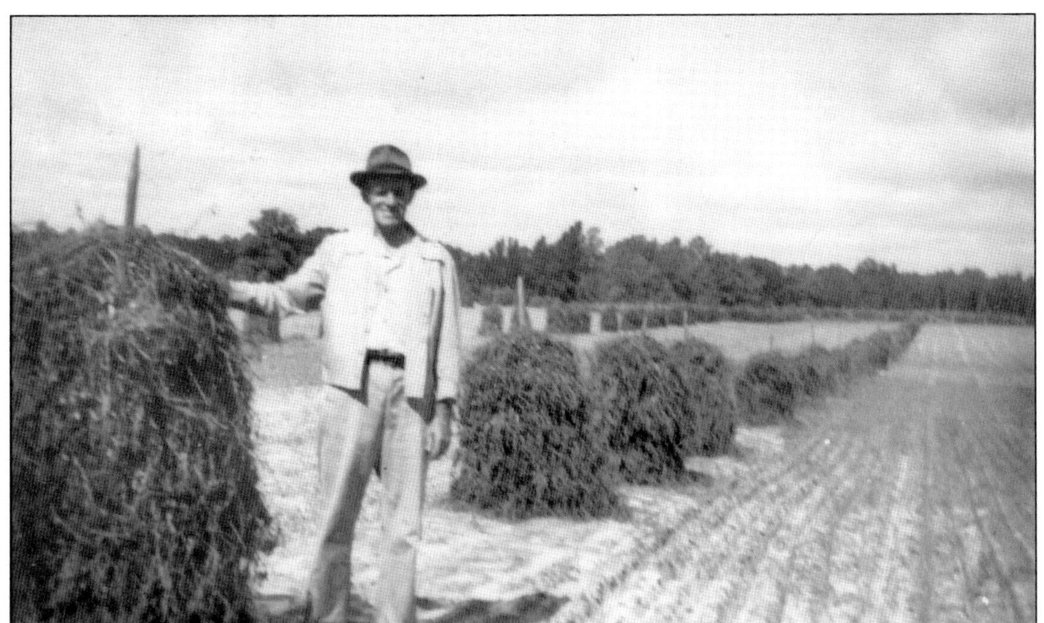

Shipyard engineer C. Lawrence Bartlett stands in his peanut field at Marl Spring Farm near Dendron in the fall of 1947. Bartlett married Sidney Johnson's daughter Bertha in 1920. After Sidney's death in 1942, Lawrence and Bertha bought the farm and enjoyed it as their summer home until the 1980s. A native of Maine, Bartlett had dreamed of being a farmer for all of his life. (Bertha Johnson Bartlett photograph, courtesy of Robert L. Bartlett.)

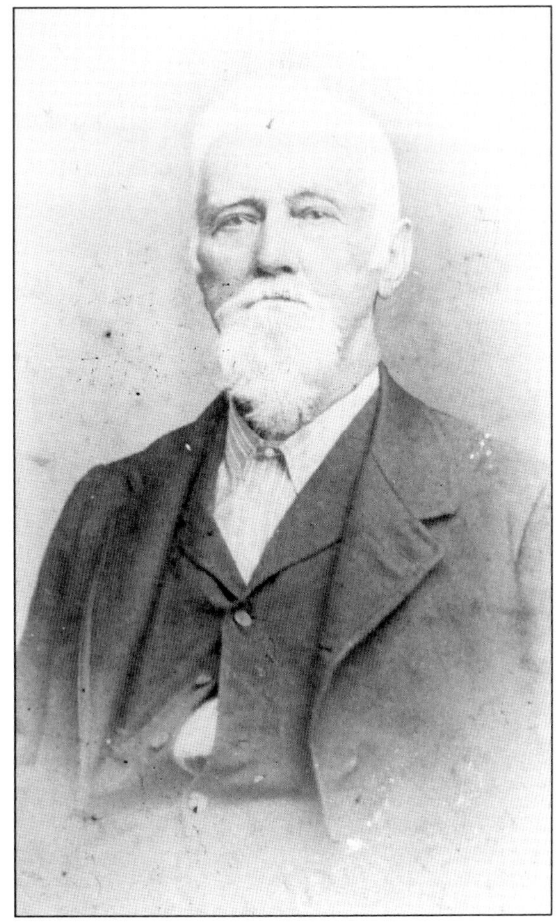

William Thomas Rogers was born to William R. and Harriet Davis Rogers in 1829 and was orphaned in 1832. He was apprenticed to blacksmith Thomas Bage until he was 21. Rogers married Julia Goodrich in 1851 and served in Company F, 59th Regiment of the Virginia Artillery during the Civil War. He and his wife lived in an old house on Route 614 near Route 615; it was owned by the Goodrich family and later became known as the Goodrich-Rogers House. William and Julia had nine children before she died in 1877. He then married Elizabeth Andrews in 1879, and they had 10 more. When he died in 1920 at age 91, he was the oldest man in Surry County. (Courtesy of William A. Fox.)

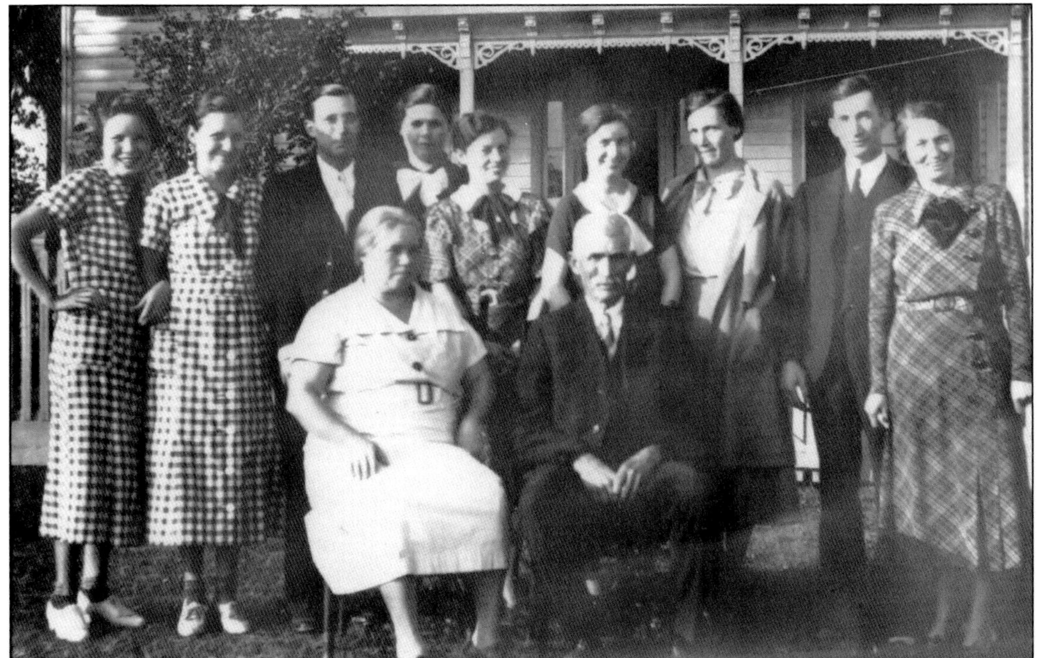

Members of the Sidney Thomas Johnson family, of Marl Spring Farm, are pictured around 1935. Ruth Rogers Johnson and Sidney are seated. Standing from left to right are Katherine, Edna, Hugh, Pauline, Myrtie, Bertha, Myra, Albert, and Ruth. (C. Lawrence Bartlett photograph, courtesy of Robert L. Bartlett.)

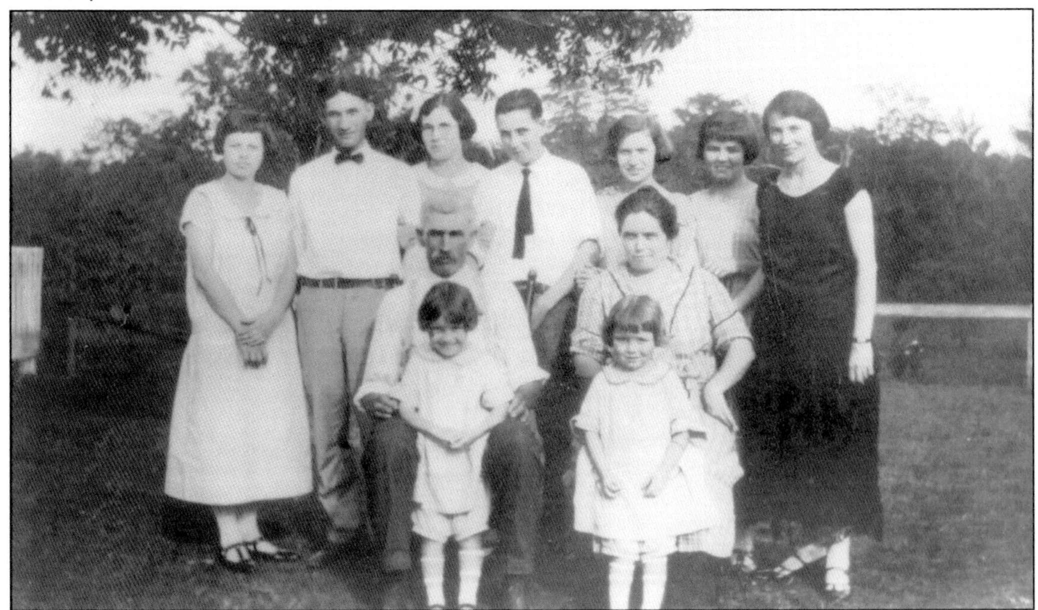

Members of the Sidney Thomas Johnson family, of Marl Spring Farm, are pictured around 1925. Sidney and Ruth Rogers Johnson are seated with Edna (left) and Katherine (right) in front. Standing from left to right are Myrtie, Albert, Myra, Hugh, Bertha, Pauline, and Ruth. Sidney and Ruth married in 1911 and had the three youngest children. Mary Etta Cotton, Sidney's first wife and mother of the six older children, died in 1909. (Courtesy of Katherine Johnson Fox.)

This close-up of the Marl Spring farmhouse was taken in 1947. Sidney Johnson built it himself after he married Mary Etta Cotton in 1892. Their first child, Ruth, was born in an old cabin there in 1893 before the house was completed. The other eight children were born in the house and occupied the nursery (on the second floor, over the front door) during their infancy. (C. Lawrence Bartlett photograph, courtesy of Robert L. Bartlett.)

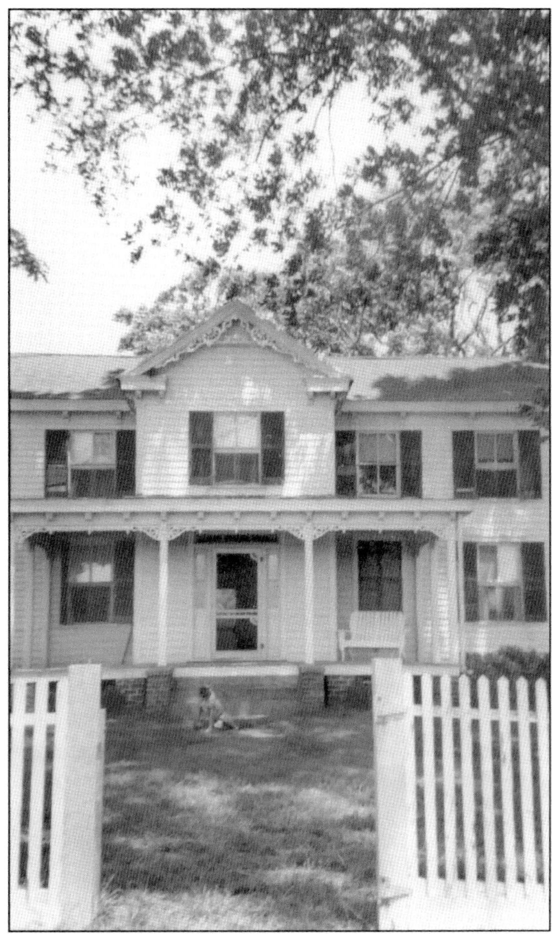

Sidney Johnson built the Marl Spring farmhouse in 1892 on the ruins of the old manor house of his first wife's uncle Dr. Cary Cotton. It is said that the bricks in the chimney came from the old house. Sidney was very industrious, and he built a forge to make nails and other hardware for the new house. He later became a justice of the peace and used the small building on the left as his office. The house, which had been intermittently occupied since 1942, was sold to Mack and Stephanie Headley in 1986. The Headleys lovingly restored it, adding indoor plumbing and modern systems and making it a beautiful home again. (C. Lawrence Bartlett photograph, courtesy of Robert L. Bartlett.)

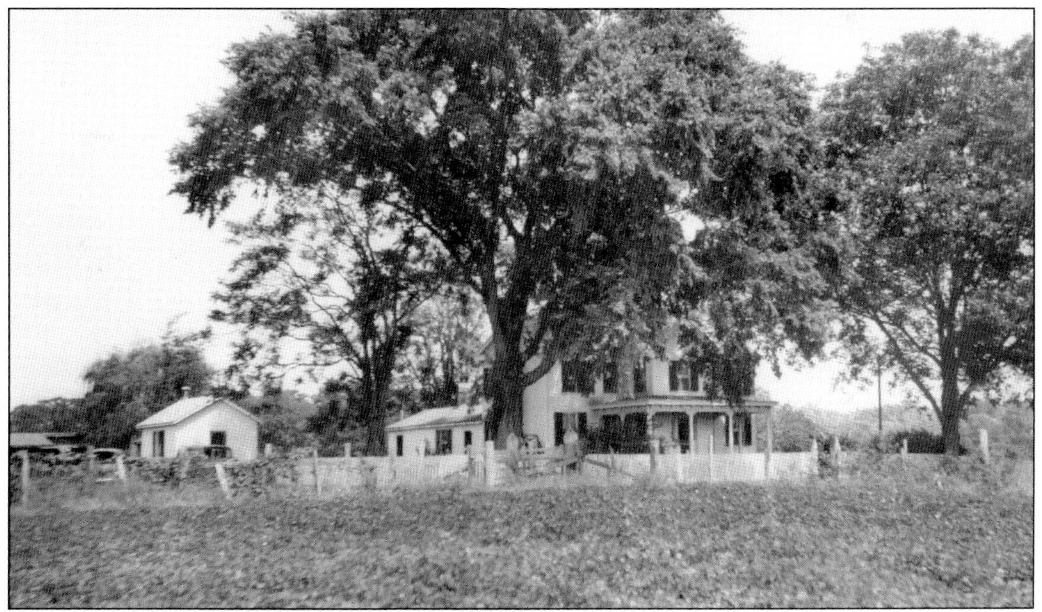

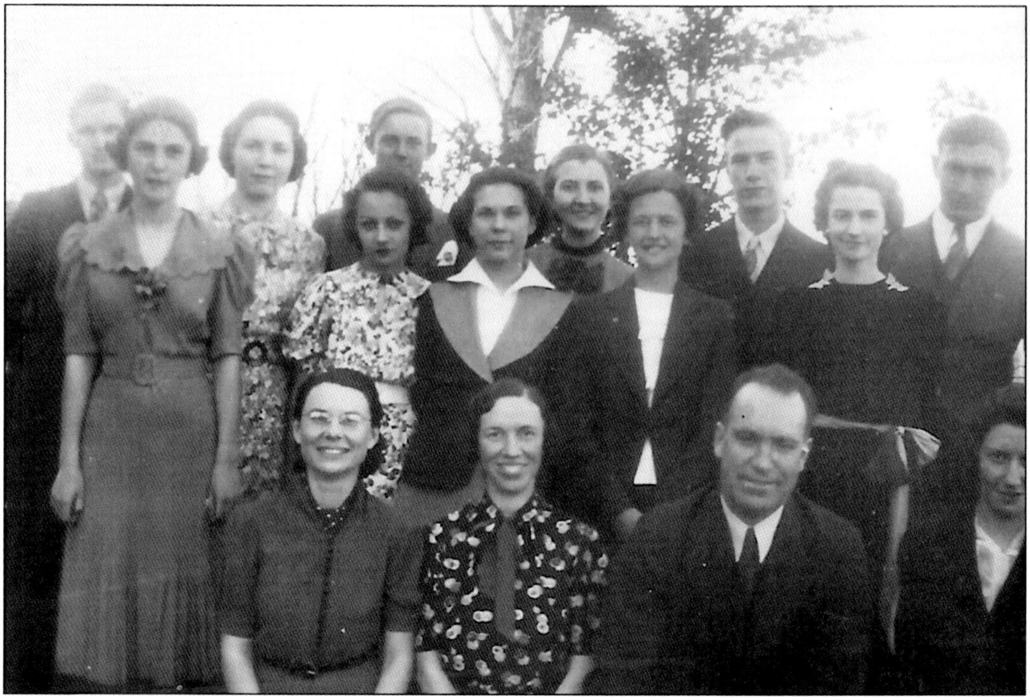

In 1937, Dendron High School graduated 11 seniors. From left to right are (first row) teachers Sarah Rowell, Hazel Joyner, Mr. Farrer, and Miss Davis; (second row) students Marion Hart, Emma Eure, Arlene Ingram, Frances Goodrich, and Lois Hargrave; (third row) students Willard Emery, Katherine Johnson, Clarence Clark, Marjorie Gardner, Bill Atkinson, and Robert Slade. (Courtesy of Katherine Johnson Fox.)

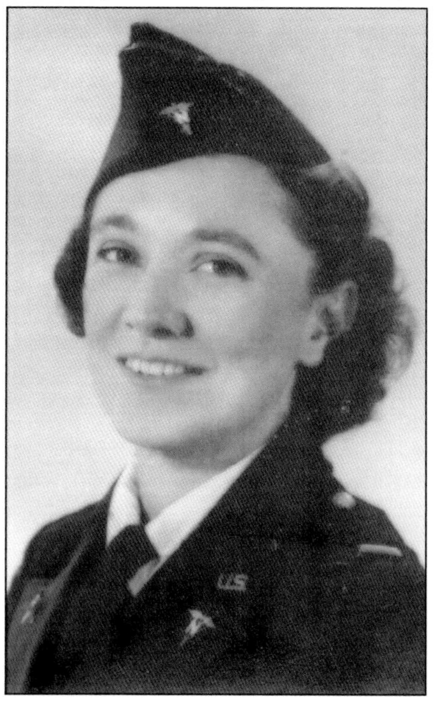

Affectionately known as "Tib," Col. Carrie Elizabeth Barrett was born in 1911 to Waverly S. and Mae H. Barrett, of Dendron. She graduated from Dendron High School in 1928, Shenandoah College in 1930, and Stuart Circle Hospital School of Nursing in 1933. She took special courses in operating room technique before enlisting in the Army Nurse Corps as a lieutenant in 1933. When the first five spaces were opened to the rank of full colonel for women in the Army, Barrett was among the chosen. Colonel Barrett was stationed at Scofield Barracks in Hawaii and witnessed the bombing of Pearl Harbor. She was head nurse at several of her stations, including Fort Story, Virginia; Camp Grant, Illinois; and Fort G.G. Meade, Maryland. During one of her tours of duty at Walter Reed Army Hospital, she had noteworthy patients, such as Dwight Eisenhower and Douglas McArthur. Colonel Barrett ended her 30-year career as head nurse of Walter Reed Army Hospital in 1966. She moved back to Dendron and enjoyed country life for a number of years. She passed away in 2003. (Courtesy of the Dendron Historical Society.)

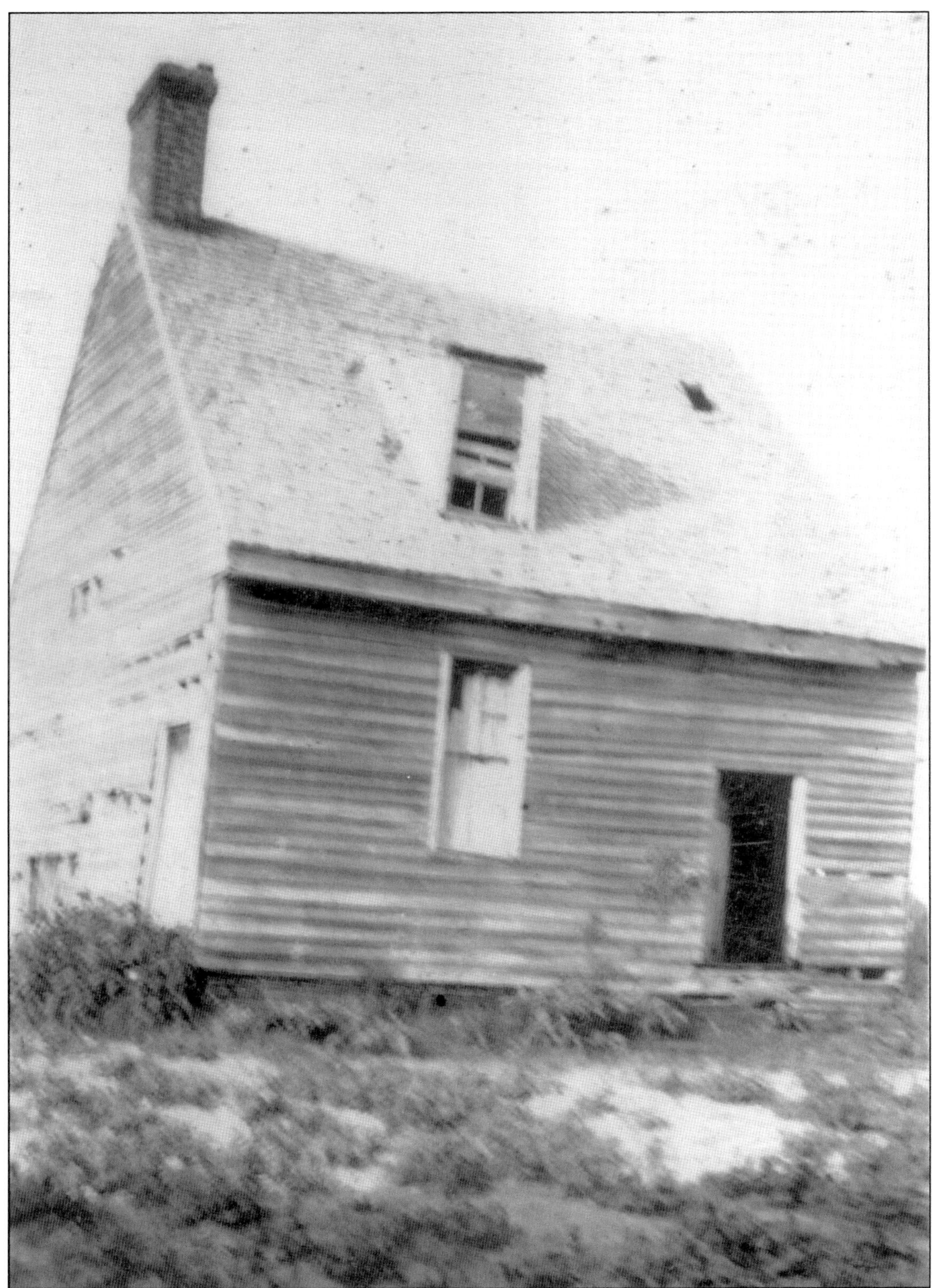

This is the last survivor of the houses in the town of Cobham at the mouth of Gray's Creek. The photograph was taken in 1928, and the house was torn down in 1929. The town was laid out in lots in 1738. During the 18th century, it became a considerable town and an important port. The house was probably standing when Cornwallis's army camped at Cobham in 1783.

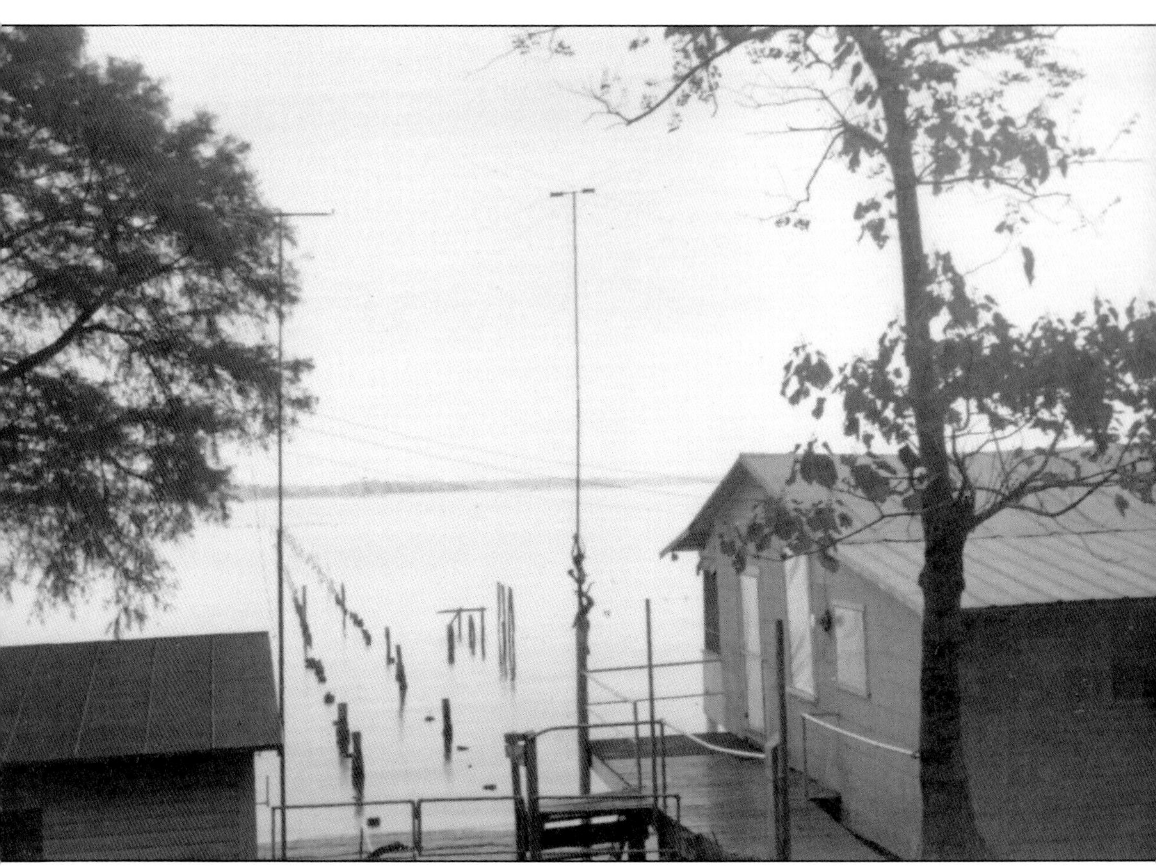

By the 1960s, rather than a thriving depot, Cobham Wharf was mostly a summer vacation area with cabins on and near the James River.

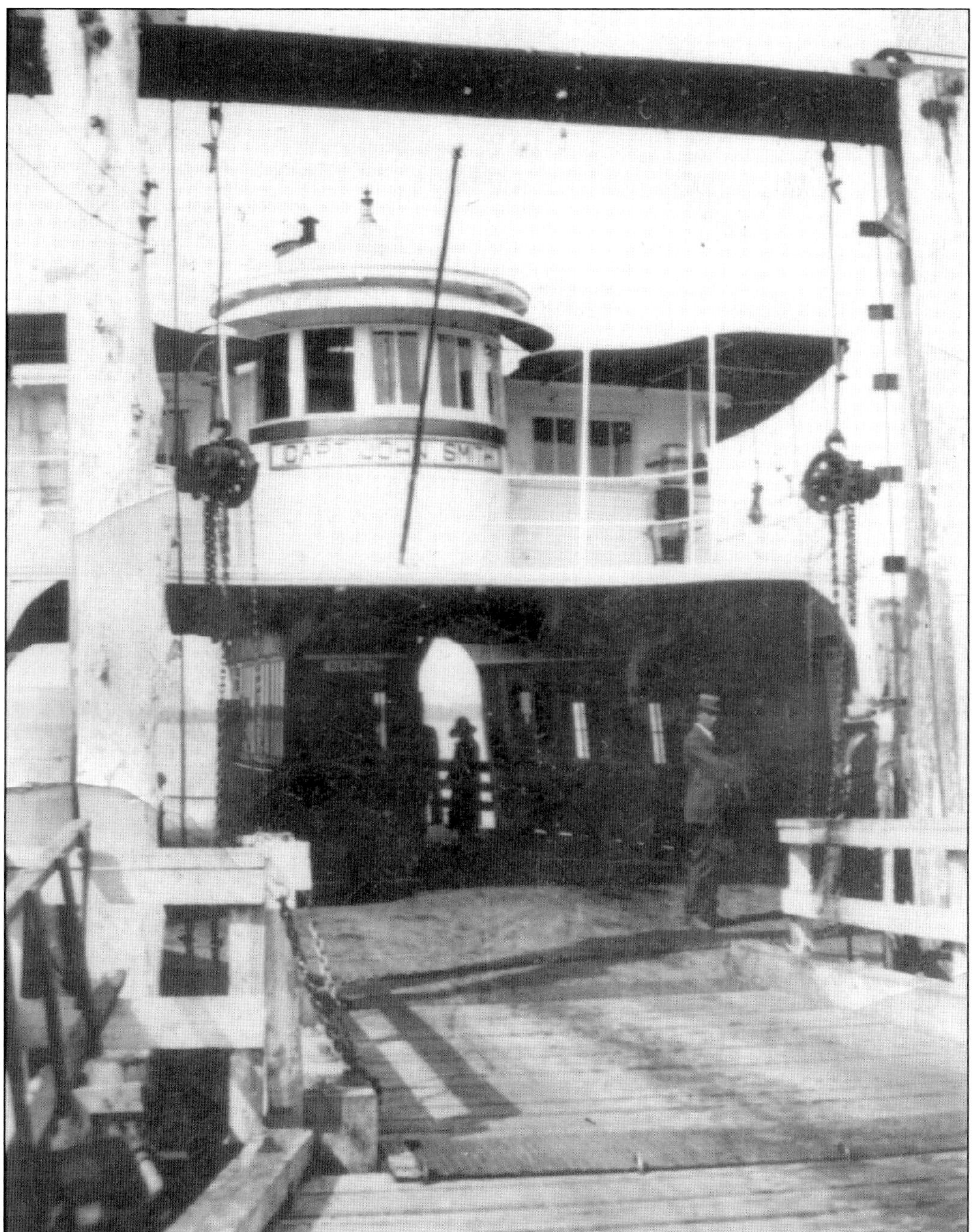

The ferry *Captain John Smith* made the first automobile crossing of the James River on February 26, 1925. The privately owned business, which connected Jamestown Island and Surry County, was founded by Capt. Albert F. Jester. The Commonwealth of Virginia acquired the Jamestown-Scotland Ferry Service in 1945. The upper deckhouse of the *Captain John Smith* did not get destroyed but was used as a waterside cottage in the Elizabeth River near Portsmouth for about 50 years. In 2003, the deckhouse was recovered and eventually donated to the Surry County Historical Society. The society is currently restoring this important piece of history. (Courtesy of Donna Slade.)

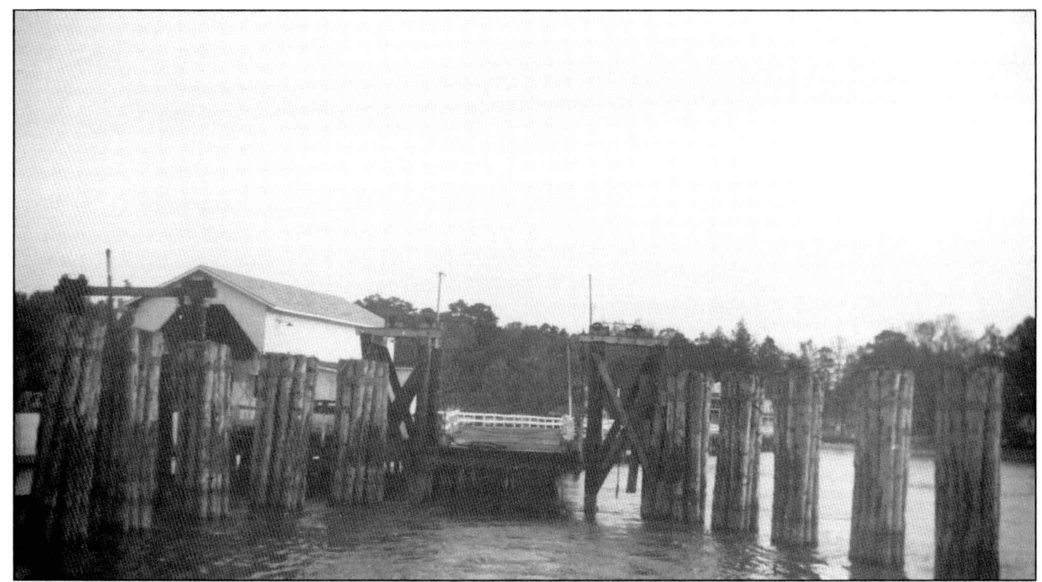

This is a 1950s view of a ferry landing dock on the Surry County side, or south side, of the James River. Since the 1950s, the Virginia Department of Transportation has expanded the fleet of ferries to four modern vessels: *Virginia*, *Surry*, *Williamsburg*, and *Pocahontas*. The ferries can safely carry from 20 to 70 cars each. (Courtesy of Mary Alma Savedge.)

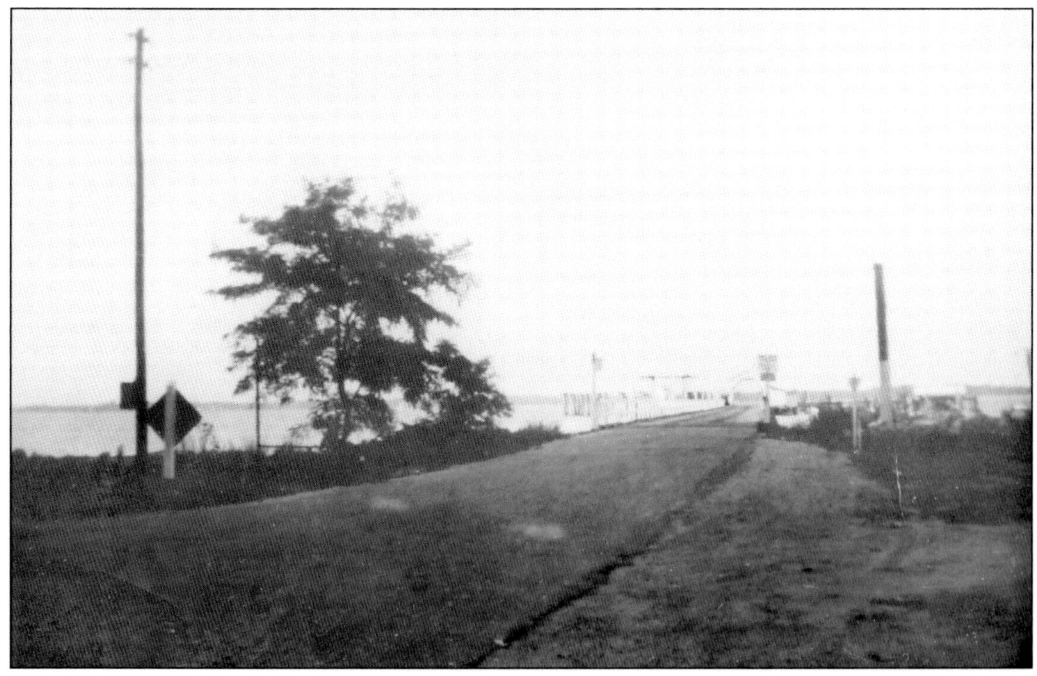

This is a very early view of the entrance to the Jamestown-Scotland Ferry Service. The suggestion to build a bridge at the ferry location has not won great support. The major concerns have been the substantial cost of building a bridge over a navigable waterway and the impact a bridge would have on such a historic area of the country.

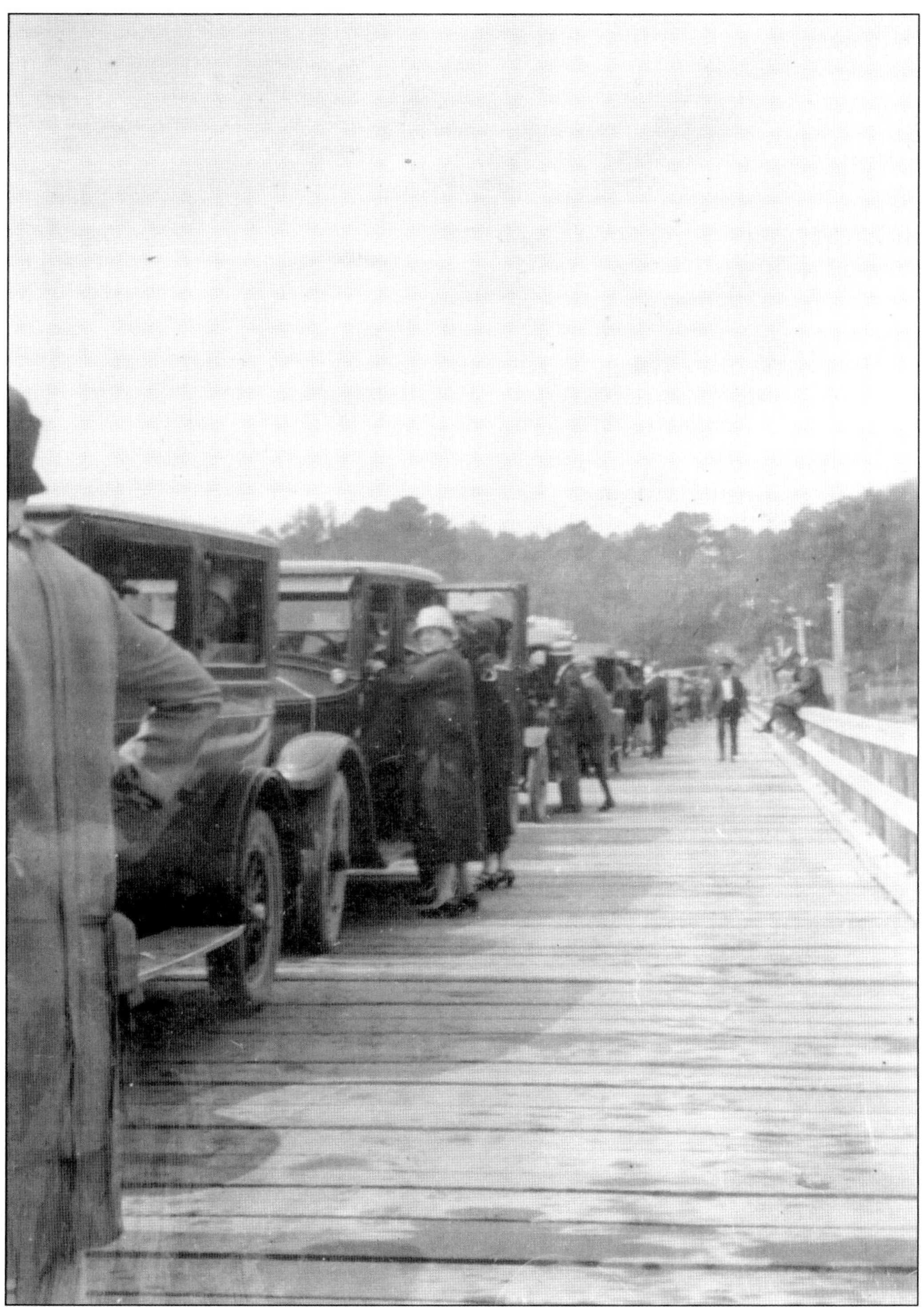

Passengers wait to board the Jamestown-Scotland ferry in the 1920s. The crossing by ferry to Jamestown and Williamsburg continues to be a popular and necessary mode of transportation to recreation, shopping, and employment for Surry citizens.

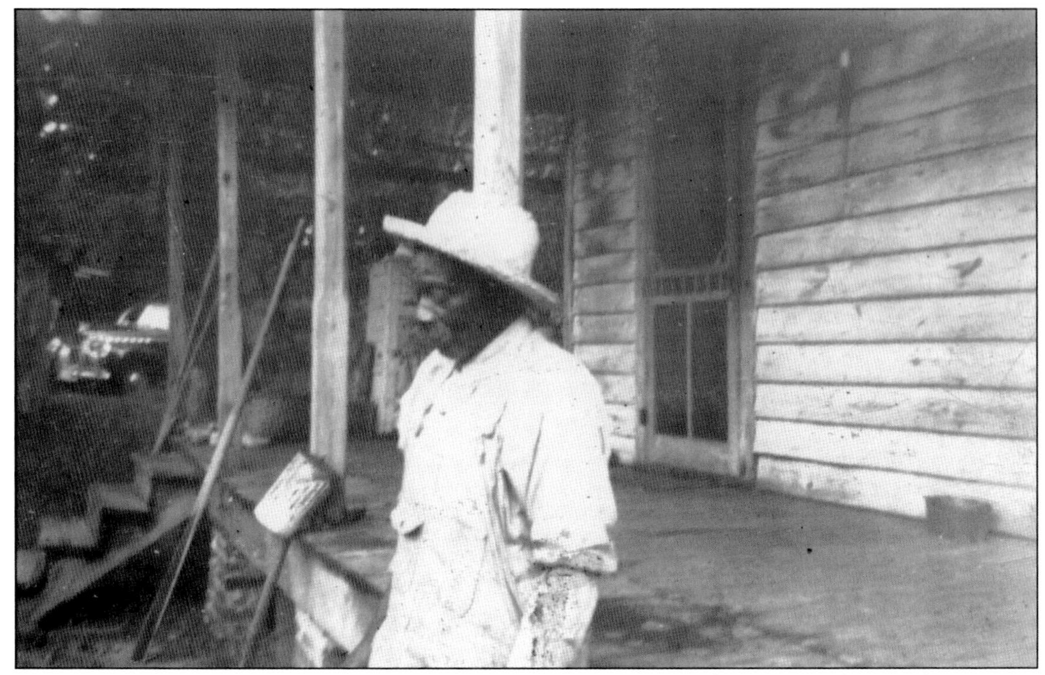

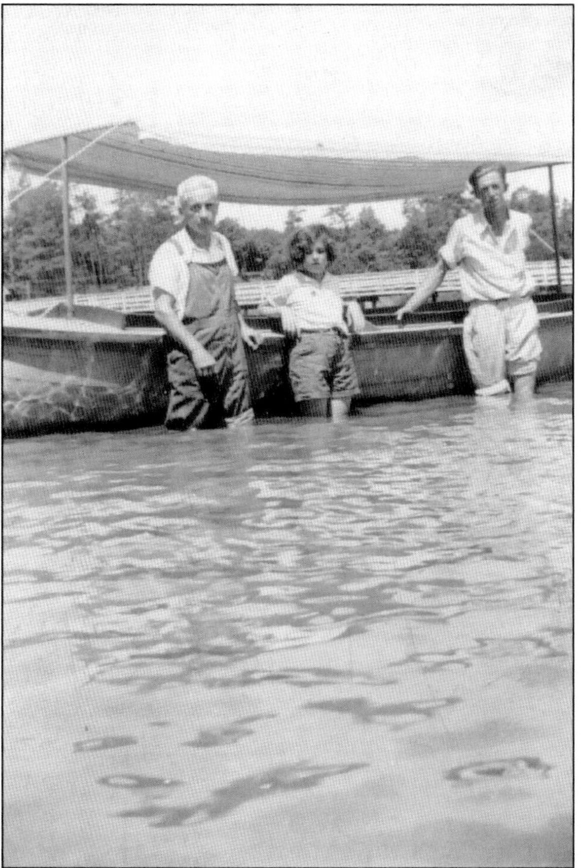

Moses Johnson stands outside his cottage at Scotland where he rented rowboats and took groups out on fishing trips. Older Surry residents remember him because of his hospitality when local churches would baptize congregants in the James River. He would allow male church members to change clothes in his home. (Courtesy of Mary Alma Savedge.)

Pictured with the rowboat are, from left to right, Leslie Franck, Mary Franck, and Lloyd Glass. The Franck family was from Colonial Height, Virginia and would visit Surry during summer vacations. They were frequent customers of Moses Johnson. (Courtesy of Mary Alma Savedge.)

Early telephones were given a special place in homes, as shown in the Bohannan house. The one featured here is a candlestick telephone that was common from the late 1890s to the 1930s. It was widely used by independent phone companies. (Courtesy of Gordon "Bo" Bohannan.)

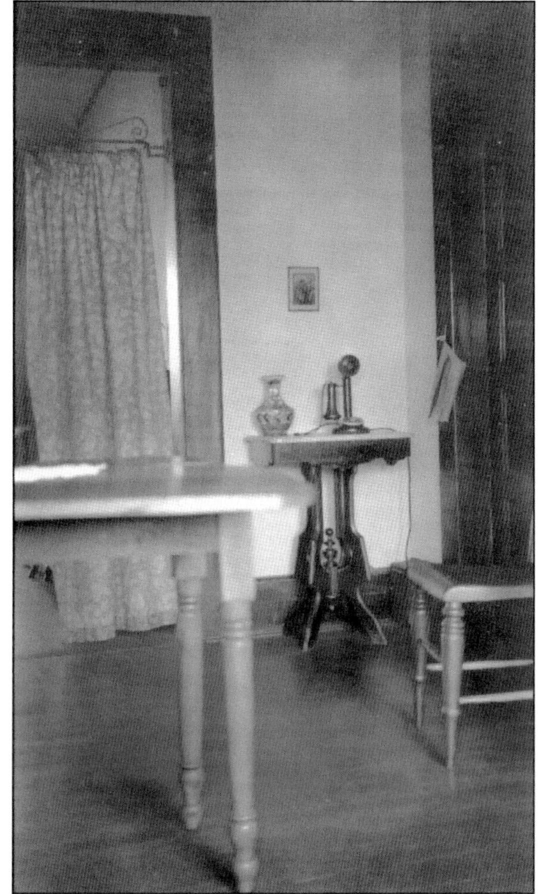

This postcard shows the old clerk's office in Surry, Virginia. This brick building in the northeast corner of the courthouse yard was erected in 1825–1826 and used as a clerk's office for 70 years. It now houses the A.W. Bohannon Memorial Museum. (Courtesy of A. Tynes, Elberon, Virginia.)

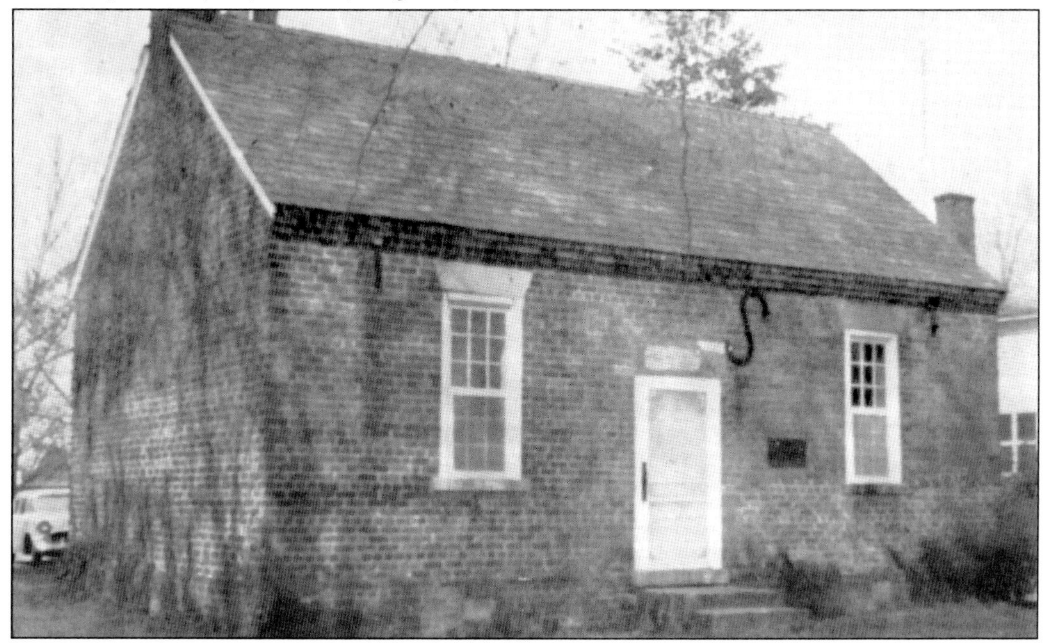

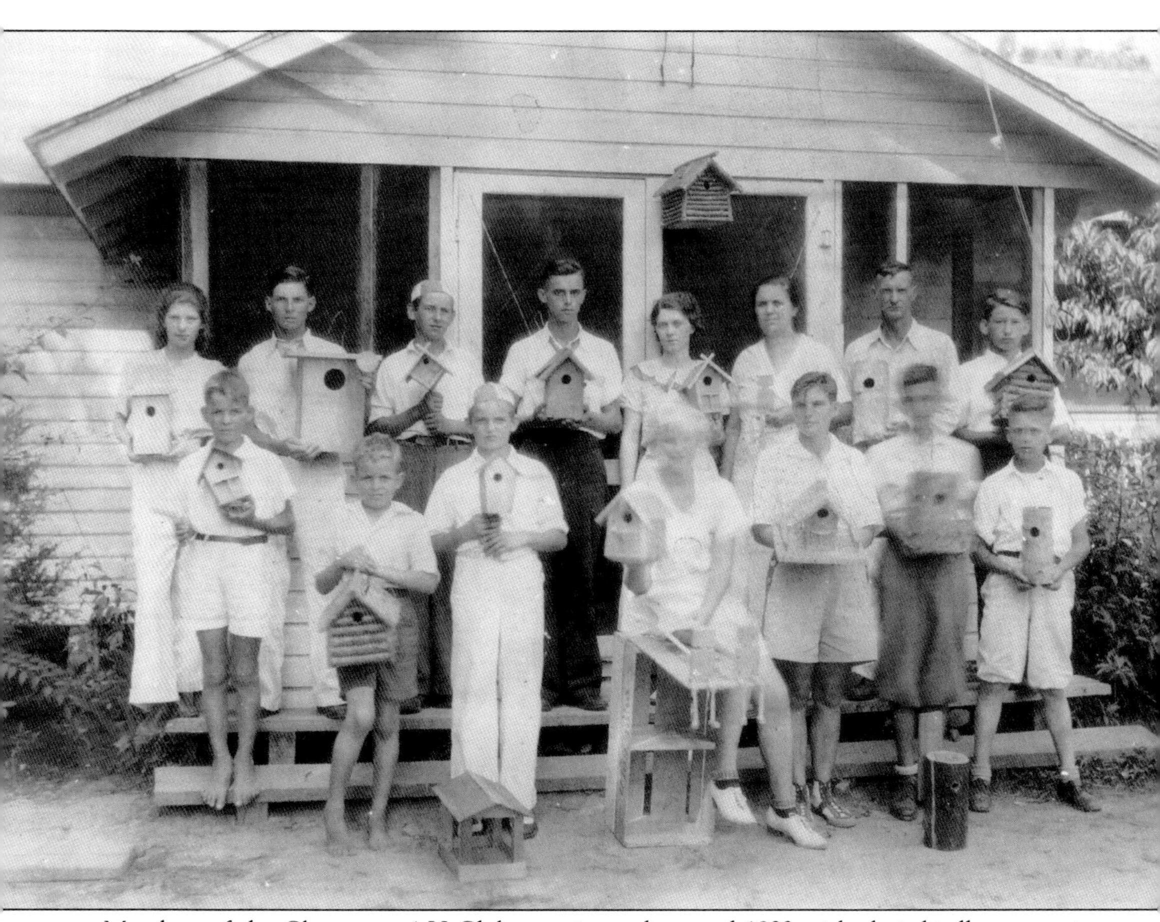

Members of the Claremont 4-H Club are pictured around 1933 with their birdhouse projects, completed at the summer camp held at the Jamestown 4-H Educational Center.

Sgt. Melvin G. Harrison (1929–1980) served in the US Army during the Korean War. He was the ninth child born to William B. and Parthenia Harrison. The family lived at Floods near Eastover, and they later moved closer to the town of Surry. Pictured below is Sergeant Harrison's oldest son, Maj. Gen. Michael T. Harrison Sr., who graduated from Surry County High School in 1976 and Howard University in 1980. At graduation, he was commissioned as a second lieutenant in the Army, and he reached the rank of major general in 2009. He is one of the first major generals to hail from Surry County, Virginia. While stationed at Schofield Barracks in Hawaii, Major General Harrison discovered that his father had also been stationed in Hawaii. The clue to the discovery was the patch on Sergeant Harrison's left arm. The leaf with a lightning bolt is the patch worn by members of the 25th Infantry Division, nicknamed "Tropic Lightning." The father and son served in the same division but in different battalions. Pictured with Major General Harrison is his wife, Alissa, and son Jesse. (Both, courtesy of James Harrison.)

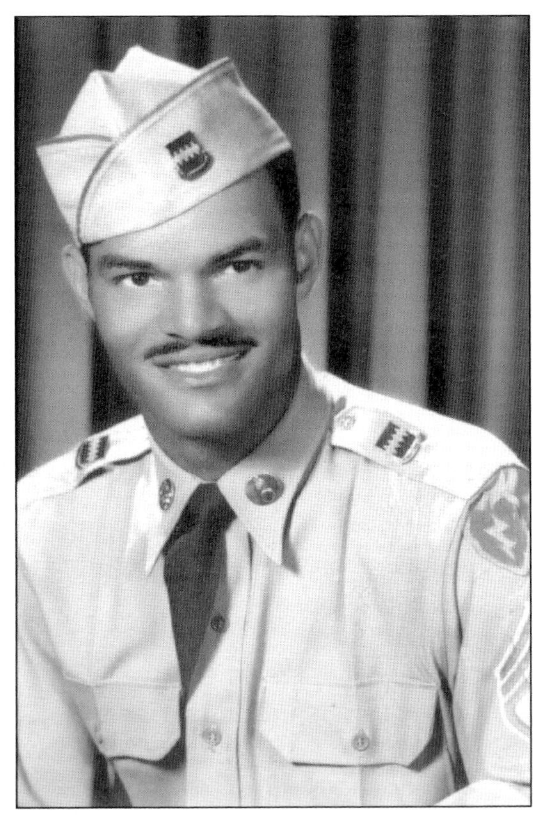

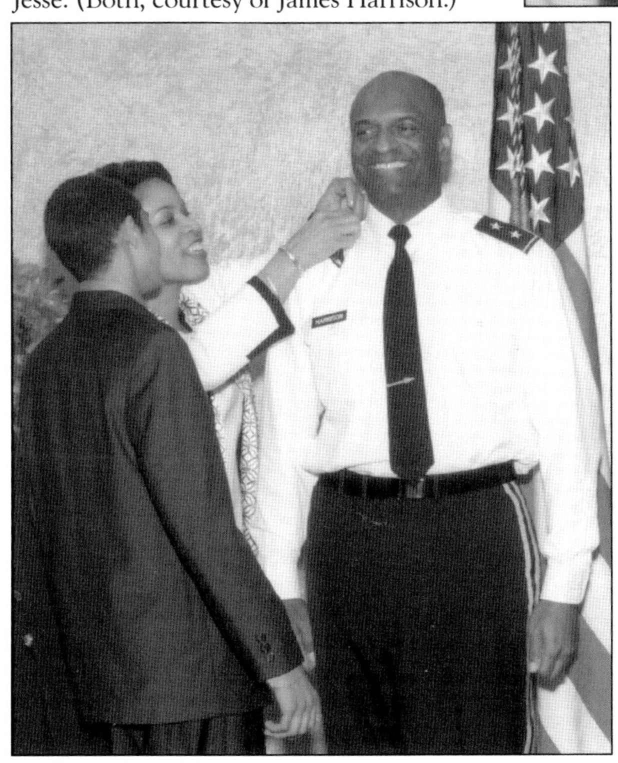

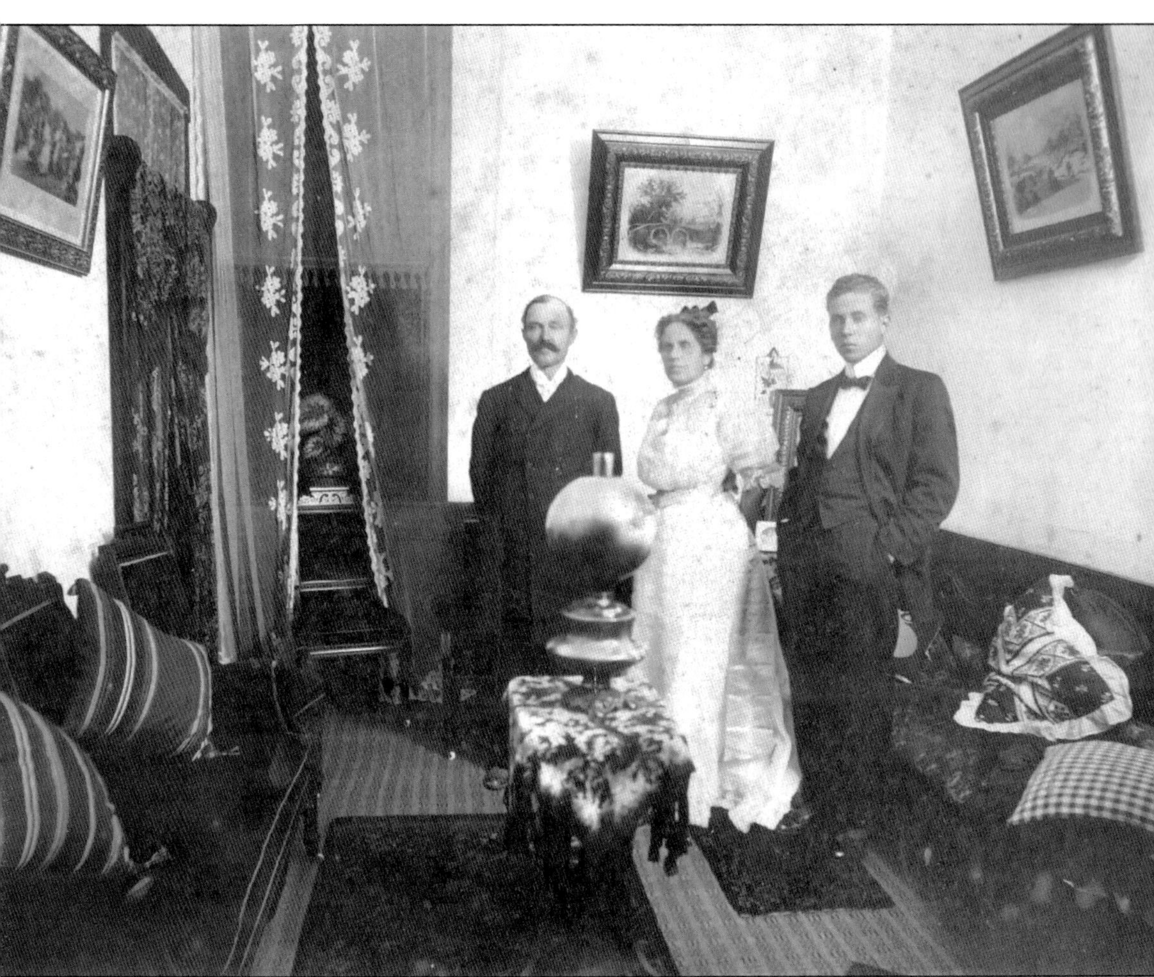

In this 1910 photograph taken in Surry, the Astrop family stands in their parlor. From left to right are Dr. Charles Wesley Astrop, Clara Collins Astrop, and Robert Astrop. Dr. Astrop was a medical doctor who practiced in Surry in the late 1890s. His son Robert was a well-known psychology professor at the University of Richmond in the 1920s.

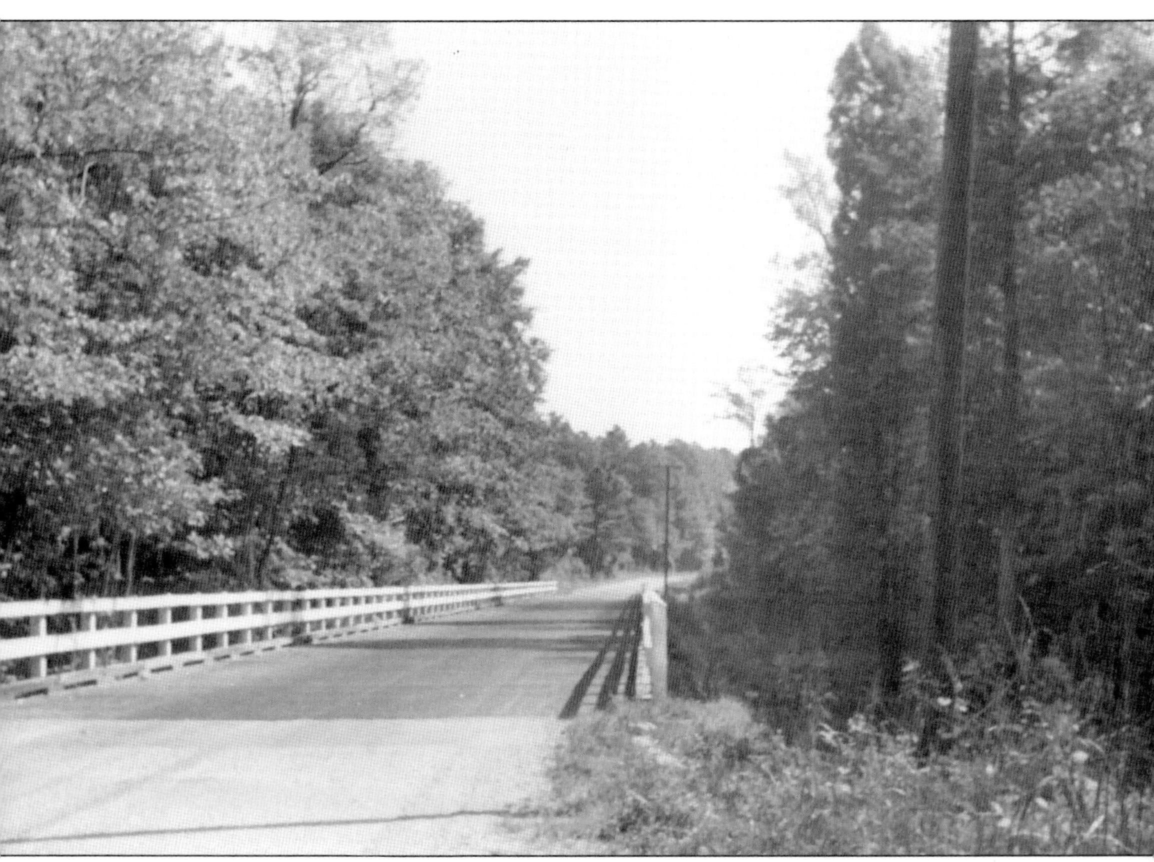

This photograph of Wall's Bridge in Surry County was taken in October 1967. At one time, there was a town center located near the bridge.

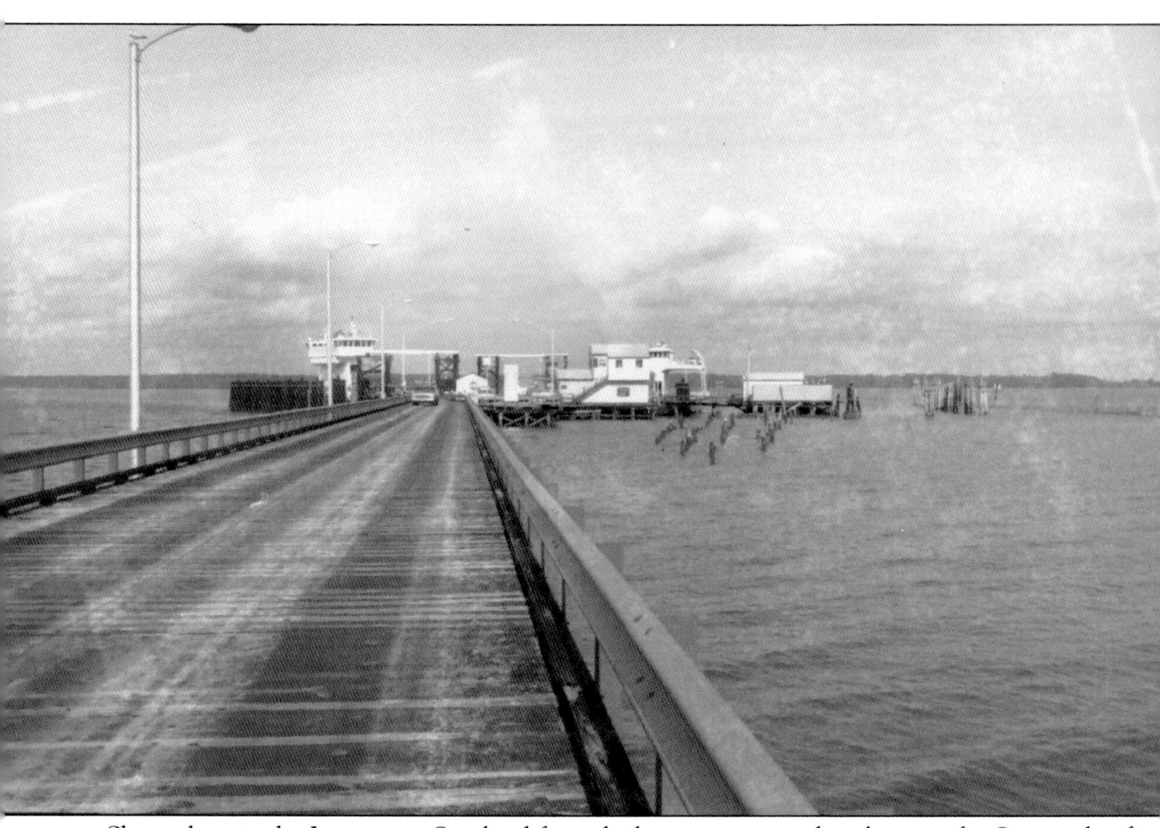

Shown here is the Jamestown-Scotland ferry dock as it appears when leaving the Surry side of the James River heading to Jamestown, Williamsburg, and points north.

Bibliography

Baird, Marion Sims, Jr. *Claremont on the James: Its Beginnings and Early Years Circa 1880–1920.* Zuni, VA: Pearl Line Press, 2002.

Burke, Lynn. "Cougars Were Extraordinary." *Daily Press.* February 14, 1999.

Crittenden, H. Temple. *The Comp'ny: The Story of the Surry, Sussex & Southampton Railway and the Surry Lumber Company.* Parsons, WV: McClain Printing Company, 1967.

Crockford, Hamilton. "Dendron Proud of One-Room School." *Richmond Times-Dispatch.* October 27, 1952.

Drew, Mary E.C. *Divine Will, Restless Heart: The Life and Works of Dr. John Jefferson Smallwood 1863–1912.* Bloomington, IN: Xlibris Corporation, 2010.

Kornwolf, James D. *Guide to the Buildings of Surry and the American Revolution.* Surry, VA: Committee, 1976.

Malveaux, Judith. "You Can't Erase the Memories: School Gone, Spirit Remains." *Daily Press.* February 14, 1999.

Stephenson, Mary A. *Old Homes in Surry & Sussex.* Richmond, VA: Dietz Press, 1942.

Taylor, Phillip. "Praising a Midwife: Service Draws Worshipers Across Region, Many of Whom She Delivered." *Daily Press,* April 9, 2000.

Toloken, Steve. "Hard Lessons from the Past." *Daily Press.* August 1, 1994.

Ward, Courtney. "Informal Give-and-Take Discussions Feature Tobacco Company's Employees' Seminar." *The Richmond News Leader.* March 17, 1960.

Whitehead, Bobbie. "A Hundred Years of Service." *Daily Press.* July 28, 2005.